China's Approach to Central Asia

This book examines, comprehensively, the Shanghai Cooperation Organisation, the regional organisation which consists of China, Russia and most of the Central Asian countries. It charts the development of the Organisation from the establishment of its precursor, the Shanghai Five, in 1996, through its own foundation in 2001 to the present. It considers the foreign policy of China and of the other member states, showing how the interests and power of the member states determine the Organisation's institutions, functional development and relations with non-members. It explores the Organisation's activities in the fields of politics and security cooperation, economic and energy cooperation, and in culture and education, and concludes with a discussion of how the Organisation is likely to develop in the future. Throughout, the book sets the Shanghai Cooperation Organisation in the context of China's overall strategy towards Central Asia.

Weiqing Song is Associate Professor in the Department of Government and Public Administration at the University of Macau, China.

Routledge Contemporary China Series

For a full list of titles in this series, please visit www.routledge.com.

China's Approach to Central Asia

The Shanghai Cooperation Organisation

Weiqing Song

Routledge
Taylor & Francis Group

LONDON AND NEW YORK

First published 2016
by Routledge
2 Park Square, Milton Park, Abingdon, Oxon OX14 4RN

and by Routledge
711 Third Avenue, New York, NY 10017

Routledge is an imprint of the Taylor & Francis Group, an informa business

© 2016 Weiqing Song

British Library Cataloguing in Publication Data
A catalogue record for this book is available from the British Library

Library of Congress Cataloging in Publication Data
A catalog record for this book has been requested

ISBN: 978-1-138-78078-1 (hbk)
ISBN: 978-1-315-77048-2 (ebk)

Typeset in Times New Roman
by Taylor & Francis Books

MIX
Paper from
responsible sources
FSC
www.fsc.org FSC® C013604

Printed and bound by CPI Group (UK) Ltd, Croydon, CR0 4YY

Contents

Illustrations

Figures

Tables

Abbreviations

ASEAN	Association of Southeast Asian Nations
APEC	Asia Pacific Economic Cooperation
BRICS forum	Brazil, Russia, India, China, and South Africa Forum
CAEC	Central Asian Economic Community
CDB	China Development Bank
CISCO	China Institute for SCO International Exchange and Judicial Cooperation
CSTO	CIS Collective Security Treaty Organisation
CHG	Council of Heads of Government
CHS	Council of Heads of State
CNC	Council of National Coordinators
CCP	Chinese Communist Party
RDF	Collective Rapid Deployment Force
CICA	Conference on Interaction and Confidence Building Measures in Asia
CNPC	Chinese National Petroleum Corporation
EAEC	Eurasian Economic Community
EAEU	Eurasian Economic Union
IBC	Inter-Bank Consortium
IMF	International Monetary Fund
GDP	Gross Domestic Products
GNI	Gross National Income
NATO	North Atlantic Treaty Organization
OBOR	One Belt One Road
OSCE	Organization for Security and Cooperation in Europe
PLA	People's Liberation Army
RATS/RCTS	Regional Anti-terrorist Structure/Regional Counter-terrorist Structure
SCO	Shanghai Cooperation Organisation
UN	United Nations

Preface

As a native of Shanghai, I have a clear memory of the first 'Shanghai Five' summit in 1996 and the inaugural summit of the Shanghai Cooperation Organisation (SCO) in 2001. Even when I was a layman of international relations as an academic field, I was curious about this international event that attracted leaders and diplomats from Russia and several Central Asian countries. Although these countries are geographically close to China, they are unfamiliar to ordinary Chinese people due to longstanding political separation. Nevertheless, the Chinese people are proud of this first and only international organisation named after a Chinese city, particularly as the SCO has become more visible internationally as it has developed.

After I embarked on my academic career as a professional international relations specialist, my interest in the SCO became more scholarly. The SCO is the first inter-governmental organisation largely initiated and driven by China. In this respect it is quite unusual, considering China's age-old doctrine of bilateralism and suspicion of Western-dominated multilateral cooperation. From the perspective of foreign policy analysis, this change alone deserves special attention. The SCO also refreshes Chinese analysts' memories of the historical links between China and Central Asia associated with the legendary Silk Road. Most Chinese learn about the Silk Road in school history classes and it seems that people today only think of it as part of history. Nevertheless, the Silk Road story is central to Chinese people's feelings about the glorious past of their country and civilisation. Through this difficult yet enduring route people living far apart were able to exchange goods, ideas and cultures until the Silk Road finally became obsolete in the Cold War era.

After the end of the Cold War and the sudden and shocking collapse of the Soviet Union, the geopolitics of Central Asia began to undergo a dramatic change. Since then, there has been an increase in public discussion in China about the almost forgotten Silk Road. The change in the international political system has opened a door between China and its Central Asian neighbours.

In fact, China's Xinjiang Uyghur Autonomous Region is geographically part of Central Asia and has significant ethnic and cultural ties with countries in the region. Furthermore, China's rediscovered interest in Central Asia is due to several factors, including its frontier stability, national security, economic expansion and search for new sources of energy. Recognition of the importance of the region has culminated in the recent Chinese grand strategy of 'One Belt, One Road', which highlights Central Asia as the essential link in China's planned New Silk Road strategy. In this regard, the SCO has a crucial role in China's 'Go West' strategy.

This book mainly focuses on China's foreign strategy and policy towards Central Asia via the SCO. It discusses the power and interests of the SCO member states and their influence on the formation and evolution of the organisation, concentrating on China's leading role in this process, and covering a range of issues related to the SCO's organisational development. This discussion covers the broad context of China's neighbourhood policy, a coherent framework of analyses of interests and power relations, the internal aspects of the SCO institutionalisation and external aspects of its international interactions, and finally the SCO's emphasis on cooperation in the three major areas of politics and security, economy and energy, and culture and education. The book will be of great interest to academics, practitioners and students. Others with an interest in Chinese foreign policy, Central Asia and international relations in general may also find this book useful.

I wish to thank the University of Macau for its financial support through a research grant, and my former and current graduate students of the same university, who provided helpful research assistance.

Figure 0.1
Source: https://en.wikipedia.org/wiki/Shanghai_Cooperation_Organisation, accessed online 10 October, 2015.

Introduction
The Silk Road rediscovered

The return of Central Asia

Corresponding to its peripheral status in the perceptions of people from other parts of the world, the region of Central Asia does not rank highly in Chinese public discourse or the Chinese people's imagination. Little public attention has been paid to the region by the media or the populace and ordinary Chinese people have very little personal experience of the region. However, when prompted, it will almost immediately occur to most Chinese people that Central Asia is an important region, closely associated with Chinese history and national glory. Indeed, Central Asia features in the Chinese collective memory of the renowned Silk Road, which connotes Chinese military, political and commercial expansion and influence well beyond the western frontier of China over the past two millennia. China's first 'discovery' of Central Asia can be traced back to the second century BC, when the legendary Zhang Qian, an ancient Chinese envoy authorised by Emperor Wudi of the Han Dynasty, embarked on his courageous expedition to the Xiyu region (or West Land, largely referring to today's Central Asia). Superficially, this historic event opened up a commercial trade route. More deeply, it linked China to regions as far away as Europe and Africa and led to an exchange of civilisations lasting for the next two thousand years. There is evidence that although the close links between China and Central Asia ebbed and flowed, they remained for a very long time. In fact, until the Russian occupation about two hundred years ago, parts of Central Asia were still territories of China's Qing Dynasty. The ancient link between China and Central Asia was practically suspended during the time of the Russian Tsarist Empire, and later when the Soviet Union ruled the region.

This suspension of contact between China and Central Asia was suddenly disrupted in 1991 when the Soviet empire imploded at the end of the Cold War. A group of former Soviet republics became independent, some of them reluctantly and most of them unprepared. This transformation brought the region back to the world stage. Observers became increasingly aware of the strategic significance of Central Asia in terms of geopolitics, economics and regional development. Geopolitically, the return of the region reminds onlookers of

Sir Halford Mackinder's famous 'Heartland Theory' which defines Central Asia as part of the pivotal heartland area of the World Island. For historians the situation is also reminiscent of the 'Great Game' of the nineteenth century during which the Russian and British empires launched strategic rivalries for supremacy in the region. Given its heartland position in Eurasia – connecting Asia, the Middle East, the Caucasus and Europe – the geopolitical importance of Central Asia still holds. Its significance accounts for the widespread predictions that the region would resume its position as a battlefield for the great games of the major powers when the Soviet Union collapsed in the early 1990s. Central Asia is rich in oil and natural gas and boasts other natural resources.[1] Kazakhstan has an estimated oil reserve of 30 billion barrels and natural gas reserves of 2.407 trillion cubic metres, ranking twelfth and fifteenth in the world, respectively. It is now one of the top ten oil exporters in the world and a major gas exporter. Turkmenistan, a relatively small country, has estimated natural gas reserves of 17.5 trillion cubic metres, ranking fourth in the world, and it is now the world's eighth largest exporter of natural gas. Uzbekistan is also a major exporter of natural gas and has large reserves. Besides oil and gas, Kazakhstan is also the world's largest producer of uranium. This abundance of energy and other natural resources appeals to the rest of the world, which is thirsty for ever more scarce resources. The geographical position of the region also makes it a hugely promising transit route for commercial products and people. In terms of regional development, the newly independent republics have undertaken a political, economic and social transformation. The transition is truly an enormous project, which has had varying degrees of success and has led to both convergent and divergent trends across countries in the region. The consequences of this upheaval are directly borne by the individuals and social groups of the new nations but the transformation has also attracted much attention from the outside world. Numerous activists and organisations observe, and sometimes participate in, the processes of transition, focusing on such issues as democratisation, human rights, anti-corruption and good governance.

As a close neighbour and an emerging global power, China cannot afford to neglect this newly open region, with which it has a long and significant history and a potentially huge stake in the present. It is imperative for China to re-establish working relationships with the new nations to solve urgent matters including the demarcation of common borders, the emergence of organised crime, and, more seriously, religiously motivated terrorism. Moreover, China sees an opportunity to pursue its more profound national interests in the region. China has geopolitical interests in Central Asia for many reasons. The primary motivation for expanding its influence in the region is securing its own border. A strong connection with the region could also provide a more effective counterweight against external powers in its close neighbourhood, and prevent encirclement around its borders. Almost equally important, China is attracted to the rich energy reserves, sizeable export market and potential transit role of the region. China relies on sea lanes for the foreign supply of more than half the oil it consumes and feels insecure because most of the maritime shipping routes are out of its control and some pass through unstable regions. This leaves the country in a vulnerable position, especially as demand for imported energy and other natural resources is steadily increasing. Central Asia provides a valuable alternative, in this regard. For the first time, China could import energy resources more conveniently from neighbouring countries. Meanwhile, countries in Central Asia could be a valuable market for China's manufacturing industries. The region has a population of more than 50 million. For historical reasons, the Central Asian countries have not developed sufficient industrial capability to provide many consumer or industrial products for their own markets. Geographic proximity is another advantage for China, particularly in its western provinces such as Xinjiang. In addition, China desires to expand its cultural, educational and other 'soft' influences in the region.

The strategic value of Central Asia is well understood in China. The veteran Chinese analyst Wang Jisi (2012) has proposed a 'Go West' strategy, which advocates an assertive approach to China's western frontier. Ancient China always set its strategic focus on its interior, with further expansion along its western frontier, as exemplified by the Silk Road which served as the key land bridge and facilitated commercial and cultural exchanges between the East and the West. In more recent times, China was forced to adopt an 'open door' policy, as a result of gunboat diplomacy by Western powers, and maritime routes have become the key channel connecting China with the outside world. Coastal areas in China's southeast have had the advantages of external exchange and overall development but the northwest regions have lagged far behind. Wang argues that it is time to make a strategic shift towards the northwest, given the constraints and competition in the southeast and the new opportunities in Central Asia and beyond.

Central Asia in China's foreign strategy

It seems that by highlighting the strategic importance and opportunities of China's northwest frontier, Wang is prescribing a new strategy for the Chinese government. In fact, Chinese policymakers took the opportunity to engage with the region almost immediately after the former Soviet republics became independent in the early 1990s. Since then, China has made continued efforts to manage relations with Central Asian states and pursue its interests and influence in the region. What makes China's effort in the region different now is its practice of largely experimental multilateral diplomacy. This practice is centred on the Shanghai Cooperation Organization (SCO), an international organisation that brings together China, four Central Asian states and Russia. This Chinese experiment fits perfectly with China's official priorities for foreign strategy. At a practical level, the current Chinese government has defined 'four major dimensions' to its comprehensive foreign policy for the new century: great powers as the key, neighbouring countries as the priority, developing countries as the basis, and multilateralism as the important venue. The four dimensions are further elaborated in President Hu Jintao's report to the 18th National Congress of the Chinese Communist Party in November 2012.[2]

Through this comprehensive approach, China has begun to implement more active policies towards selected states, regions, issues and venues. The SCO is extremely important to China because it represents all four prioritised dimensions of China's foreign strategy. First, great power diplomacy targets countries with the most powerful status, predominantly in the Western developed world, of which the US is the most important. Chinese policymakers also identify other major powers, including Russia, Japan and some other traditional and emerging great powers. Given their status and influence, relations with these great powers are crucial to Chinese national interests. However, Chinese leaders admit that difficulties exist in developing relations with most Western powers, due to various differences and divergences. Therefore, they will improve and grow relations with great power states by expanding areas of cooperation and properly addressing differences. Recently, China has defined the concept of a 'new type of great power relations', mainly with reference to the United States. This concept stresses the need to base workable relations on equality and mutual respect for long-term stability and development. Within the SCO, China can manage its great power relations with Russia and very soon India, considering the probable admission of India in the near future. The SCO could provide China with a venue to coordinate its relations with great powers in a multilateral and institutionalised framework.

Neighbourhood diplomacy, in which geographically near countries are targeted, is another key dimension of China's overall foreign policy. The Chinese leadership is determined to construct a favourable environment in its immediate neighbourhood. The Chinese top leadership has made a commitment that China will continue to promote friendship and partnership with its neighbours, consolidate friendly relations and deepen mutually beneficial cooperation to ensure that China's own development will bring more benefits to its neighbours. China has, however, suffered major setbacks in the smooth implementation of this policy, mainly due to territorial disputes with several neighbouring countries, particularly India, Japan, the Philippines and Vietnam. Tensions have intensified in recent years and analysts have no reason to be optimistic about the possibility of solving these disputes in the foreseeable future. China's neighbourhood diplomacy is therefore to some extent structurally weakened. Fortunately, China has successfully solved border disputes on its northwest frontier through peaceful negotiations with its neighbours, including Russia and the three Central Asian states of Kazakhstan, Kyrgyzstan and Tajikistan, and created a favourable environment for further engagement with these northwestern neighbours.

Since Mao's time in the Cold War, China has made continuous efforts to strengthen relations with the wider developing world, formerly better known as the Third World. However, after the adoption of the reform and opening policy in the late 1970s, the developing world was gradually marginalised in the minds of Chinese policymakers and attention was focused on industrialised countries in the West for opportunities of trade, investment and technology. Only in recent years, with the 'Go Global' strategy for the expansion of its economic and overall power, has China realised the importance of the developing world as a valuable source of energy and raw materials, a target for markets and investments, and a venue for global influence. For this reason, the Chinese leadership has promised that China will remain a reliable friend and sincere partner of developing countries. It will increase unity and cooperation with these countries, and work with them to uphold their legitimate rights and interests, including their representation and voice in international affairs. However, China's approach has undergone a fundamental shift. In the past, driven by ideological thinking, China took a more 'selfless' attitude towards the Third World. Despite its own poverty, the Chinese government managed to contribute large-scale aid to developing countries, mostly in Asia and Africa. In more recent years, China has adopted a pragmatic approach, focusing on countries that are of strategic significance to its national interests. These include emerging regional powers and regional blocs in Africa, Latin America and Southeast Asia. In this arena, China finds it much more useful to exercise its economic statecraft, for example, by providing preferential loans and constructing basic infrastructure in return for market, energy and other natural resources. In Central Asia, China is faced with a group of newly independent countries that are rich in energy but desperately in need of investment for infrastructure. There is therefore a good match between the two parties.

Multilateral diplomacy is a new focus of China's foreign strategy. China is more used to traditional bilateral diplomacy and has long been suspicious of multilateral organisations, which were perceived as a Western conspiracy to collectively control world affairs. Through more interactions with the outside world, the Chinese government has gradually come to realise that its national interests are increasingly intertwined with the outside world in complex interdependencies. First, a stable and amenable external environment is crucial to China's national development. Second, protection of China's ever-growing overseas interests requires direct participation in external cooperation. Multilateralism is generally effective for a wide variety of common demands and challenges. China's determination in strategic shift towards multilateralism is typically illustrated by its joining the World Trade Organization in 2001, which meant enormous opportunities for its domestic economic sectors, but also a daunting overhaul of its economic structures. The report of the Chinese Communist Party's 18th Plenary Committee explicitly states that such multilateral venues as the United Nations, the G20, the SCO and BRICS (Brazil, Russia, India, China and South Africa) are prioritised in China's endeavour to 'make the international order and system more just and equitable'. The importance of the SCO for China is self-evident. It is a Chinese experiment in international leadership in multilateral diplomacy. Never before has China tried to play a leading role in a multilateral organisation. In this context, Central Asia provides an opportunity for China's exercise of multilateral leadership.

It is no exaggeration to say that Central Asia is a region where China can apply all four prioritised aspects of its foreign strategy. This book assesses China's approach to Central Asia through the SCO. It traces the evolution of the SCO, from its predecessor to its most recent development, focusing on how China interacts with other member states in the organisation. The book has two major themes: Chinese foreign policy towards Central Asia and the internal dynamics of the SCO. The former theme is discussed in relation to the Chinese grand strategy and its neighbourhood policy. The latter concerns the international politics of China, other SCO members and other countries with substantial stakes in the region, such as the United States. More specifically the book has several objectives:

- to identify China's motivations, opportunities, and strategies towards Central Asia, in relation to its overall foreign strategy;
- to trace the evolution of the SCO from its very beginning;
- to describe and explain the development of the SCO in terms of institutionalisation and functional cooperation;
- to describe and explain the interactions between China and other SCO member states, namely, Russia and four Central Asian countries; and
- to describe and explain the interactions between the SCO and some non-member states, particularly the United States.

Structure of the book

This book is intended to be a comprehensive study of the context, evolution and scope of the SCO that provides the reader with a detailed and well-rounded analysis from a Chinese perspective. The first part of the book introduces the general context of China's interests and motivations for engaging with its neighbours, in particular, its strategies towards Central Asia through the SCO framework. The first chapter traces the trajectory of China's foreign strategy in the post-Cold War era as it relates to the country's grand development plan. Within this broad context, China has adopted and implemented a neighbourhood policy towards Central Asia. This chapter describes the general context of China's relations with Central Asian countries, its interactions with Russia in the region and the role of Chinese leadership in the origin and evolution of the SCO. Chapter Two establishes a framework for empirically analysing the SCO process, with special reference to China's role. It identifies the various interests, motivations and power statuses of SCO members and argues that they have individual, albeit occasionally mutual, interests and priorities. An initial asymmetry of interests is observed – the principal reason the SCO's strategic situation is largely a suasion game between China and the other members – with China demonstrating a greater interest in the SCO. The power asymmetry between China and the Central Asian members and the power equality between China and Russia further complicates the situation. China attempted to exercise leadership by creating and running a regional organisation for the first time. However, SCO members' interests in promoting the organisation's further development have converged in recent years. China and Russia now have more common ground on which to cooperate with the Central Asian states in this regional initiative.

Part two of the book addresses the internal and external dimensions of the SCO, focusing on the organisation's institutionalisation process and the interactions between the SCO and its member states and other actors, including observers and great powers with substantial stakes and influence in the region. Chapter Three focuses on the SCO's regional institutionalisation process. It traces the evolution of the SCO from its origin as a border settlement mechanism to the informal coordination process of the 'Shanghai Five' and eventually to its current formalised incarnation. This chapter also discusses the consolidation of the SCO's organisational structure and functional divisions. Chapter Four touches upon factors external to the SCO, including the foreign policy orientations of the SCO member states, international responses to the SCO and interactions between SCO members and others, particularly China and interested non-member states. Many analysts argue that the SCO is essentially an inward-looking organisation that concentrates on managing internal relations and developing cooperation between its member states. However, factors external to the SCO cannot be neglected. Since the organisation's inception, its implications have extended beyond Central Asia and increasingly it has developed links with other states and organisations to promote its international visibility and participation. This chapter addresses the SCO's relations not only with the observer and dialogue states, including Afghanistan, India, Iran, Mongolia and Pakistan, but also with countries with strong stakes and interests in the region, including the United States, Japan, Turkey and EU countries. It also considers the SCO's participation in major international organisations such as the UN and contact with other international organisations such as the Commonwealth of Independent States (CIS) and Association of Southeast Asian Nations (ASEAN).

Part three of the book provides detailed information on and analysis of the SCO's substantive cooperation in three major areas: political and security spheres, economic and functional areas, and cultural and educational matters. Chapter Five examines the SCO's security and political cooperation. Beyond formalisation and institutionalisation, SCO member states have expanded the scope of security cooperation from issues of border settlement, military confidence building and regional stability to international terrorism, trafficking, weapons proliferation and political and foreign strategic cooperation. The SCO's cooperation involves various military, public security, judicial and political actors and departments. Development of member states' cooperation in this area is described using major variables previously discussed, particularly, configuration of power relations and convergence and divergence of national interests. When the interests of member states, particularly the most powerful China and Russia, converge, the SCO can more easily promote political and security cooperation and take collective action. Chapter Six examines another major aspect of SCO collaboration, namely, cooperation in functional economic areas including trade, investment, energy, transport, telecommunications, technology and agriculture. Encouraged by progress in the institutional setting and cooperation on security, some SCO member states, particularly China, have made efforts to promote economic cooperation in the SCO framework. This chapter describes the development of member states' cooperation in these areas, with major variables discussed within the analytical framework defined in Chapter Two. It argues that given members' divergent interests, developing the SCO is challenging, despite some moderate progress. Member states that are keen to promote economic and functional cooperation, such as China, have to resort to bilateral options to push their agendas forward. Chapter Seven covers cooperation within the SCO in the fields collectively known as *renwen* (the Chinese term for the humanities or culture). The humanities represent an interesting but often neglected area of member states' cooperation. In this chapter, the major components of the SCO's cultural cooperation are described, and the motivations of individual member states are analysed using the framework defined in Chapter Two. Culture, education and related issues are relatively new and undeveloped areas of focus for studies of the SCO. However, China and other members of the SCO have become increasingly motivated to increase their 'soft' power by pursuing cultural and educational advancement through channels such as public diplomacy. In recent years, the SCO has made some progress in its cultural cooperation. However, this cooperation is significantly impeded by member states' lack of resources and motivation, as well as cultural and religious differences across the SCO. Of the many SCO member states, China has the greatest motivation and capacity to contribute to the SCO's cultural cooperation.

Notes

1 Information on energy and other natural resources of the Central Asian states is drawn from the Central Intelligence Agency (CIA) *World Factbook*, https://www.cia.gov/library/publications/the-world-factbook, accessed 9 July 2015.
2 Report of Hu Jintao to the 18th CPC National Congress, 8 November 2012, http://www.china.org.cn/china/18th_cpc_congress/2012-11/16/content_27137540.htm, accessed 10 July 2015.

References

Wang, Jisi (2012) 'Go West: China's Rebalancing in Geopolitical Strategy', *Global Times*, 17 October 2012, http://opinion.huanqiu.com/opinion_world/2012-10/3193760.html, accessed 8 July 2015.

1 Anatomy of China's neighbourhood policy

This chapter traces the trajectory of China's neighbourhood strategy in the post-Cold War era as it relates to the country's grand development plan. Within this broad context, China has adopted and implemented a neighbourhood policy towards Central Asia. Thus, this chapter describes the general context for China's relations with Central Asian countries, its interactions with Russia in the region and the role of Chinese leadership in the origin and evolution of the Shanghai Cooperation Organisation (SCO).

Introduction: a close neighbour is dearer than a distant relative[1]

At the Conference on the Diplomatic Work on Neighboring Countries in October 2013, Chinese President Xi Jinping gave an elaborate speech about China's foreign policy towards neighbouring countries. President Xi has given several talks at a number of conferences organised by the Chinese Communist Party (CCP) since assuming his position in the new Chinese leadership. Through these talks, the new Chinese leadership, which took over from the previous Hu-Wen government, has tried to set keynotes, proclaim strategies and identify directions in several key areas including the economy, rural development, legal work and propaganda.[2] President Xi delivered his talk about neighbourhood policy within this context. He emphasised the importance of China's foreign policy towards neighbouring countries and realising the 'centenary goals' set out by the 18th CCP National Congress in November 2012.[3] These goals relate mainly to China's socioeconomic development. All seven of the members of the Politburo Standing Committee of the CCP attended the conference, demonstrating the importance that top Chinese leadership attached to the issue of China's neighbourhood. Why is China's neighbourhood policy a high priority? Why is it connected to the objective of China's domestic development? These questions delve into the core of China's neighbourhood policy, including its motivations, environments and strategies. They must be answered to clarify China's neighbourhood policy and foreign strategy and policy at large.

Before addressing these key issues, it is necessary to define Chinese neighbourhood policy. Neighbourhood policy refers to how an international actor (usually a state) defines, formulates and implements its foreign policies towards the other states in geographical proximity. In a time of globalisation, new technological advancements have accelerated the communication speed, density and mobility of people residing in the 'global village'. Terms like 'de-territorialisation' and 'instantaneity' have been coined to describe the on-going de-emphasis of the importance of distance (McGrew, 2008: 18–19). However, distance still matters, as '[p]hysical proximity increases the opportunity for neighboring states to interact, although the results of this interaction can be either conflict or cooperation' (Chan, 2013: 376). Few people can deny that the individuals and communities within close proximity to one another have a far greater chance of interacting. Indeed, whether it is a blessing or a curse, proximity is important.

In the context of international relations, geopolitical factors are also important. Geopolitical theory posits that every state in the world follows a 'geopolitical code' that indicates how it orientates itself in relation to the world. This is why states usually pay special attention to nearby 'politically relevant' countries. Some states even adopt well-defined foreign strategies and policies in relation to their neighbourhoods.[4] A neighbourhood policy is generally defined as a foreign policy instrument that a country uses to target nearby countries with the aim of achieving certain policy objectives important to its interests.

China has pursued a neighbourhood policy towards the countries surrounding its territories. According to the report of the 16th CCP National Congress in 2002, the neighbourhood policy was put in place to consolidate friendly relations with neighbouring countries by 'demonstrating good intentions, seeking partnerships, and enhancing regional cooperation'. Well-known rhetoric portrays China's neighbourhood policy as a 'good neighbour policy' (or *Mulin Youhao Zhengce* in its Chinese origin) (Chung, 2010: 13). Some scholars have preferred to label the policy as China's 'periphery policy' (i.e., Zhao, 1999; Shi, 2000). However, most scholars use the Chinese term '*Zhoubian Waijiao*' (meaning 'policy and diplomacy towards surrounding areas') (i.e., Su, 2004; Zhong and Zhang, 2011). All of these different terms refer to the same domain of policies and practices China implements to deal with its neighbouring countries.

This book adopts the term 'neighbourhood policy' for several reasons. First, the term is relatively neutral compared with the official Chinese term of 'good neighbour policy', which infers a type of propaganda. Moreover, the term is more comprehensive than 'peripheral policy', which refers narrowly to the areas linked to China's remote areas. Furthermore, 'neighbourhood policy' is more internationally standardised due to its wide adoption by other actors, most notably the European Union (EU), in policy areas of similar scope and nature.

There are different views of the origin and history of China's neighbourhood policy. Shi (2000) argues that China's neighbourhood policy has a long history that began immediately after the CCP took power in 1949. Although China has long implemented concrete policies towards most of its neighbouring countries, its neighbourhood policy was formalised as a foreign strategy only very recently. Throughout most of the Cold War era, China faced severe hostility in its neighbouring environment, imposed by the United States and later the Soviet Union. These circumstances were quite exceptional, as most of the other states were aligned with either of the two superpowers. As such, China made it an urgent priority to break the 'strategic siege' and find a way out. This largely explained Mao's formulation of the well-known 'third worlds theory' and China's corresponding adoption of its grand strategy to unite with the third world, cooperate with the second world and counter the first world.[5] Chinese leadership placed little emphasis on the country's neighbourhood in terms of its strategic thinking because China had little chance of exercising its influence over the nearby regions. For a time, China was able to develop its good neighbour policy only towards a small number of its neighbours such as North Korea, North Vietnam and Pakistan.

Since its rapprochement with the United States and other Western countries in the early 1970s, China has been able to develop its substantial neighbourhood policy, starting with Japan and the Association of Southeast Asian (ASEAN) countries. The end of the Cold War further boosted the process. Many of China's neighbours were less constrained after the end of the bipolar system, offering China more room to operate. More specifically, the implosion of the Soviet Union created a number of new neighbours for China, a trend that has continued ever since. As China's global reach has increased, its neighbourhood policy has become a focal point of its grand strategy. The following sections focus on three major issues. They define China's motivations as the driving forces of its neighbourhood policy, discuss China's various possibilities in pursuing its interests in the neighbouring regions and identify its main strategies for implementing its neighbourhood policy.

Multifaceted motivations

The Chinese grand foreign strategy is known as '*Sige Buju*' or the 'four layouts' strategy as summarised by former Chinese President Hu Jingtao.[6] The *Sige Buju* strategy covers the four main dimensions and focuses of China's foreign policy agenda. It defines 'major powers as the key; neighbourhood as the priority; developing countries as the basis; and multilateralism as an important platform'. This strategic plan complements long-term Chinese foreign policy objectives including sovereignty and territorial integrity, economic development and international respect and status (Medeiros, 2009: 13). Although the three objectives are on different levels of the national strategic hierarchy, they are all important to national interests. The Chinese government defines four main venues for achieving these policy priorities. Of these, Chinese policymakers prioritise the establishment of great power relations and the neighbourhood policy.

In terms of strategic planning, China's neighbourhood policy is an essential part of its grand foreign strategy, which is in turn formulated and implemented according to the overall national development strategy. Its high profile demonstrates the importance of the neighbourhood to Chinese foreign policymakers, as the success of the neighbourhood policy is key to realising all three of the major foreign policy objectives. Because China has a vast area and borders a dozen neighbouring countries both on land and overseas, its relations with its neighbours have direct effects on its major foreign policy objectives: sovereignty, economic development and international status. China engages in territorial disputes with its neighbours, and huge economic interests drive its relations with its neighbourhood. Its ambition to become a major power of global influence naturally begins with its neighbourhood. Thus, the Chinese government emphasises its neighbourhood policy for many reasons related to peripheral stability, national security, economic development and international status. Although some of these motivations are immediate, others are more long term.

Peripheral stability

The most immediate consideration behind China's neighbourhood policy is the Chinese leadership's concern for the peripheral stability of the borderlands. A big state's borderlands usually present a problem for the central authority due to their unique characteristics compared with the mainland. This uniqueness is reflected in several main processes, which are involved in relative separation from the rest of a state and make it difficult to accommodate groups of other states (Flint, 2011: 146–147). This usually poses challenges to the national unity of a state and gives leeway to foreign intervention. Borderlands are therefore weak spots in a state's national security construction.

Considering the importance of Chinese borderlands, Hao and Chou (2010: 3–6) identify several major relevant issues for China's foreign relations and domestic affairs. The borderlands have profound implications for China's sovereignty due to their high exposure to external influences. In fact, the Chinese borderlands are the direct frontline, and comprise areas where China continues to struggle with a number of countries over territorial disputes. Furthermore, China's borderlands are crucial to its national unity and territorial integrity due to the strong presence of ethnic minorities in these areas.

China is home to many ethnic groups. The government has recognised 55 ethnic minorities in the country in addition to the dominant Han ethnic group. Most of the minority groups live in China's remote areas, and its borderlands are mostly inhabited by ethnic minorities. For centuries, the central government struggled to bind the peripheral areas together (Yu and Xu, 2009). The Chinese Communist regime inherited this thorny issue. Since its entry into power in 1949, the CCP has relentlessly attempted to cope with the challenges presented by the peripheral areas. The most important policy implemented by the CCP is known as the '*Minzhu Quyu Zizhi*' ('regional autonomy by ethnic minorities') policy.[7] Under this policy, regional autonomous governments are established in areas populated by dense collections of ethnic minorities who may not necessarily dominate the regional population. The regional autonomous government is supposed to have the autonomy to administer regional affairs. There are regional autonomous governments at different levels, including the provincial, prefectural and county levels. Within the country, five autonomous regions have been established at the provincial levels and they are all located in the Chinese borderlands.[8] These regions are crucial to China's efforts to ensure ethnic, social and territorial integrity.

The most acute problems currently occur in the two autonomous regions of Tibet and Xinjiang (Mackerras, 2010). In both cases, ethnic problems have brought about sharp and sometimes violent conflict with the Han-dominated areas or the Chinese state and had far-reaching implications for China's international relations. This tension is most typified by the July 5 incident in 2009, when a riot by some Uyghur rebels in Urumqi, the capital of Xinjiang Uyghur Autonomous Region, resulted in the deaths of about 200 and injuries to more than 2,000 people (Hao and Liu, 2012: 205). The causes of inter-ethnic tension in the Chinese peripheries are deep-rooted and both historical and contemporary in nature. Other factors such as the issue of transnationalism or trans-boundary ethnic groups across state borders further complicate the situation (Ma and Ma, 2010). The Chinese central government fully realises that domestic policy alone cannot solve the problem. Rather, foreign policy and particularly the neighbourhood policy must be made essential parts of the overall measure to cope with the acute problems in the borderlands.

National security

According to geopolitical theory, boundaries and borders are an integral component of a state's geopolitical code. A regime's legitimacy and tenure largely depend on its ability to maintain boundaries against external threats (Flint, 2011: 153). China's emphasis on planning its neighbourhood policy is equally motivated by its concern for national security in a world its leaders perceive as largely harsh and hostile. An effective neighbourhood policy is helpful for creating and maintaining a favourable external environment for China both near and abroad, ensuring its domestic stability and state security.

In fact, there are a number of key geographical variables that have significant effects on China's national security considerations and its international relations (Chan, 2013). China's large physical size, measured by its territories and population, give the country strategic depth and resilience. However, it makes it difficult to govern a wide array of outlying frontiers and ethnic minorities and to cope with territorial disputes. To quote Chinese strategists, China has one of the most difficult geopolitical environments (Yang, 2012; Yang, 2013), one that threatens its national unity and territorial integrity. In fact, China shares a border with about 11 states on land and has many other neighbours overseas. The Chinese government has struggled to solve the issue of territorial disputes with neighbouring countries. Despite some controversy both at home and abroad, China has reached agreements on border demarcations and solved land disputes through peaceful negotiations with Russia, Mongolia, Kazakhstan,

Kyrgyzstan, Tajikistan, Afghanistan, Pakistan, Myanmar and Vietnam. However, China remains engaged in territorial disputes with India over land; with Japan over the East China Sea; and with Vietnam, the Philippines and a number of other Southeast Asian countries over islands, reefs, and territorial waters in the South China Sea. Furthermore, it has not determined whether the renegade province of Taiwan will one day be unified with the mainland.

This difficult situation is further exacerbated by external powers and particularly the United States. Since the end of the Cold War, China has been cautious about the American presence and influence in the region. The United States has several important security allies in Japan, South Korea, Australia and the Philippines. Most of these countries are located within China's vicinity. Furthermore, the United States stepped into Central Asia after the war in Afghanistan in 2001. Since the late 1990s, it has continually improved and strengthened its relations with India, China's big neighbour and long-time competitor. China is particularly concerned about the Obama Administration's recent adoption of its high-profile 'rebalancing of Asia' strategy, which China interprets as the United States' effort to penetrate into and play a leading role in Asian affairs. For China, this has been the most important American strategic shift since the end of the Cold War (Chen, 2012: 65). Indeed, China must find effective measures to counter the perceived American strategy, break the American encirclement and protect its national interests. Chinese strategists have proposed building a regional cooperation structure centred around China (Zhong and Zhang, 2011: 60). This proposed strategy argues that in line with its rise, China has the capability and responsibility to shape the regional orders around its neighbourhood. Given China's central role in the region, no other big power, including Russia, Japan, India, or even the United States, can take its place. Analysts suggest that China should play a leading role by formulating and implementing a grand strategy that promotes a mutual interest in the central issues of sovereignty, development and security between China and its neighbouring countries. If necessary, China should also contribute to providing common goods. China's neighbourhood policy is thus significantly linked to the protection of its national security.

Economic development: energy, market

In geo-economic terms, China's neighbourhood regions are also important to its economic development. Its prioritisation of economic development drives its interest in securing a favourable external environment. Problems in its neighbourhood would surely divert its concentration and resources away from domestic development. In addition, China has big economic stakes in its neighbourhood. It has strong socioeconomic ties to its neighbouring countries due to their geographic proximity. Six of China's top 10 trading partners are close neighbours and include the two special Chinese regions of Hong Kong and Taiwan, Japan, South Korea, Malaysia and Russia.[9] As illustrated in Table 1.1, China and most of its neighbours are currently substantial economic partners.

Table 1.1 China's economic links with neighbouring countries and territories (Unit: USD1 million)

Region	Trade		Investment	
	China's exports	*China's imports*	*FDI inflow to China*	*China's outflow FDI*
Afghanistan	464.05	5.19	1.63	17.61
Bhutan	15.6	0.01	0	0
Brunei	1252.44	373.1	151.09	0.99
Cambodia	2708.11	215.32	16.6	559.66
Myanmar	5673.71	1298.23	3.84	748.96
Korea DPR	3532.4	2503.76	1.55	109.46
India	47677.51	18795.82	44.06	276.81
Indonesia	34283.38	31950.7	63.78	1361.29
Japan	151621.83	177833.95	7351.56	210.65
Laos	934.14	786.63	2	808.82
Malaysia	36525.28	58306.77	317.51	199.04
Mongolia	2653.5	3947.7	0.25	904.03
Nepal	1968.16	29.52	0.03	7.65
Pakistan	9275.39	3138.25	1.83	88.93
Philippines	16731.33	19644.13	132.21	74.9
Singapore	40741.87	28530.78	6305.08	1518.75
Korea Rep.	87677.68	168737.62	3038	942.4
Thailand	31196.2	38554.66	77.72	478.6
Vietnam	34208.11	16231.29	3.16	349.43
Taiwan, China	36777.43	132203.64	2847.07	112.88
Kazakhstan	11000.73	14680.84	5.55	2995.99
Kirghizia	5073.37	88.95	0.27	161.4
Tajikistan	1747.87	108.83	0.11	234.11
Uzbekistan	1783.34	1091.85	1.55	-26.79
Russia	44055.96	44155.04	29.92	784.62
Total of Neighbors	609579.39	763212.58	20396.37	12920.19
ASEAN	204254.58	195891.61	7072.99	6100.44
Hong Kong	323430.62	17880.37	65561.19	51238.44
Total sum	2048714.42	1818405	111716.14	87803.53

Sources: Statistical Bulletin of China's Outward Foreign Direct Investment (2012); *China Trade and External Economic Statistical Yearbook* (2013).

Their economic ties cover a range of areas including trade, investment, finance and development aid.

In recent years, China's neighbourhood has been important for its economic development. Incumbent Chinese Foreign Minister Wang Yi expressed his view in an essay years ago that China's neighbouring countries were essential partners given their historically high economic interdependence (Wang, 2003: 19). China's development lends opportunity to its neighbouring countries. The neighbouring regions have become key parts in China's implementation of its 'go global' strategy, which aims to promote China's economic expansion into the outside world. China has traditionally been a recipient state of foreign investment, technology and managerial skills. With the increase of the country's economic power in recent years, the Chinese government has been more confident in encouraging Chinese enterprises to 'go abroad' in expanding their economic strength. In this context, the close neighbourhood is a convenient target for China's ambition of economic expansion. China is especially interested in its neighbourhood as an export market for its manufactured products and an opportunity to increase its foreign direct investment outflow.

China also seeks to promote its international prestige and status through its neighbourhood policy. In fact, the Chinese government has focused on its international status and image since its takeover of the nationalist regime in 1949. During the Mao era, China worked hard to act as a respectable socialist state that appealed to third world countries. To this end, it devoted its valuable resources by providing aid and assistance to the developing world with the aim of removing itself from isolation and gaining acceptance from the international community. This emphasis has resumed in recent years and been expanded to the developed world and multilateral organisations. In contrast, China's concern for its international status is now more motivated by realistic considerations and a drive to exercise an international influence with the support of its ever-growing power. Scholarly discussion of a state's international prestige has been conceptualised according to the framework of soft power, which refers to the 'ability to get what one wants through attraction, not coercion or payment'. China has invested in areas such as public diplomacy to promote its soft power. It has sufficient reasons to increase its soft power in its close neighbourhood.

Opportunities amidst obstacles

At the Working Conference on Neighbourhood Diplomacy in October 2013, President Xi stated that China's diplomacy with neighbouring countries had the strategic goal of national rejuvenation. To this end, China must make the best use of its current strategic opportunities.[10] Chinese policymakers have well examined the changes in the international system and tried to seek out opportunity in a complex and uncertain environment.

China is encountering both opportunities and obstacles in implementing its neighbourhood strategy. The structure of the international system has undergone fundamental shifts, most important among them a reconfiguration of the power relations and increasing trends of economic and social inter-dependence. Within this context, China's steady rise provides the country with more opportunities, such as the opportunity to exercise its economic statecraft and attract more partners over to its side. A more powerful China is more assertive when exercising its capabilities and pursuing its national interests within its neighbourhood.

Changes in the international environment

The Chinese leadership has claimed that the first 20 years of the twenty-first century will comprise a historic period of strategic opportunity and that China should make good use of the time to ensure peaceful development.[11] A 'period of strategic opportunity' is a relatively long period characterised by several essential conditions that are favourable to the realisation of a state's overall goals or most important priorities (Yang, 2003: 61–62). The Chinese government has reiterated this claim in several important documents such as the reports of the 17th and 18th CCP Plenary Meetings in 2008 and 2013, respectively.

Which conditions and environments does the Chinese leadership consider favourable to its overall objective of peaceful development? The Chinese leadership plans to peacefully assume the status of a major global power without repeating the historical mistakes of other emerging powers such as Germany and Japan in the last century. The Chinese government has officially declared that peaceful development is the only way to modernise China and that the country should make its own contributions to world peace and development.[12] The conditions and environments involved are largely external. Several China analysts (Gong and Sun, 2011; Qin, 2009; Yang, 2003) argue that contemporary international relations have undergone several fundamental changes that offer more opportunities for China to concentrate on its development into a global power. The systemic shifts that have occurred worldwide since the Cold War have had significant consequences. Most importantly, a global rebalance of power has taken effect. The relative decline of the American superpower has been complemented by the existence of second-tier Western great powers and the emergence of several other powers in the developing world. China is not alone. Among the BRICS group of the most representative emerging powers of the contemporary world, Russia, India and China hail from the same region. It would not be an exaggeration to say that the focus of the world economy and politics has shifted from the Atlantic to the Asia Pacific region.

In addition, sovereign states are becoming increasingly interconnected and interdependent. They are drawn together by different driving forces that comprise not only the market force of economic globalisation but also many issues that demand a global effort of effective governance. These issues include non-traditional security issues such as transnational terrorism, climate change, energy and resource depletion, public health, humanitarian assistance and development aid. Achieving solutions to this wide array of issues and problems is beyond the efforts of any single powerful state. As such, emerging powers are becoming more assertive in global and regional affairs. This trend is most vividly reflected by the G20's replacement of the G7/8 in the coordination of global policies. Several Chinese strategists (e.g., Qin, 2009) agree that the most recent financial crisis originating in the West in 2008 provided China with an opportunity to play a more active role in global and particularly regional affairs.

Nevertheless, China continues to face the traditional challenges of power politics. As a strategic readjustment, the United States government recently adopted the 'pivot to Asia' strategy, which it soon redubbed the 'rebalancing of Asia' strategy. This articulation suggests that the United States government is paying more attention to China's neighbourhood while attempting to avoid suspicion. Beyond the rhetorical level, the United States government has taken concrete measures in response to the rise of China. It has restated the importance of military and security cooperation with its traditional allies in the region, including Japan, South Korea, the Philippines and Australia. In addition, it has tried to make progress on security cooperation with ASEAN countries such as Vietnam and greatly improved its relations with India.

Apart from traditional security measures, the United States government has used economic instruments to strengthen its power status in the region. The Trans-Pacific Partnership Agreement (TPP) represents a concrete step. The United States aims to use the TPP as a major multilateral platform to handle its economic and trade relations in the region. This has put pressure on China, which perceives the TPP as an American conspiracy to consolidate its economic domination and an effort to surpass other regional trade agreements such as the Asia Pacific Economic Cooperation (APEC) and ASEAN + 3. China is worried that it will be excluded from this United States-led economic grouping and thus marginalised from regional economic cooperation. After all, the rebalancing strategy represents a struggle for conceptual leadership in the Asia Pacific region that includes winning support from countries on the issue of true leadership (Chen, 2012). These developments undoubtedly pose new obstacles to the rise of China.

Increased power

The rise of China is widely recognised as one of the most important international relations issues of the twenty-first century. In fact, China has become one of the largest economies in the world in terms of aggregated GDP, second only to the United States. Even more astonishing is the speed at which the country is developing. In 2010, China surpassed Japan to become the world's second largest economy, and in 2013 its overall GDP was twice that of Japan. To put things in perspective, in 2013, China's economy was as big as the neighbouring economies of Japan, Russia and India combined in both nominal and purchasing power parity terms.[13] Compared with other great powers and its neighbours, China has exhibited comprehensive strength in the economic, political and military spheres.

Table 1.2 The relative strength between China and its main neighbours (Unit: USD1 million; sq km)

Country	GDP1 (2014)	GDP2 (2014)	Population (July 2015)	Geography (July 2014)	Military expenditures (2014)
China	17,630,000	10,380,000	1,367,485,388	9,596,960	217980 (2.1%)
Japan	4,807,000	4,616,000	126,919,659	377,915	46160 (1.0%)
Russia	3,568,000	1,857,000	142,423,773	17,098,242	83565 (4.5%)
India	7,277,000	2,050,000	1,251,695,584	3,287,263	49200 (2.4%)
Korea Rep.	1,786,000	1,410,000	49,115,196	99,720	36660 (2.6%)
Pakistan	884,200	250,100	199,085,847	796,095	8503.4 (3.4%)
Vietnam	509,500	186,000	94,348,835	331,210	4278 (2.3%)
Korea DPRK	40,000 (2013)	28,000 (2013)	24,983,205	120,538	Not available

Sources: *The World Factbook of Central Intelligence Agency* and The World Bank: World Development Indicators; https://www.cia.gov/library/publications/the-world-factbook; http://data.worldbank.org/indicator/MS.MIL.XPND.GD.ZS/countries?display=default.

1. GDP1 represents one country's GDP at purchasing power parity and GDP2 represents one country's GDP at official exchange rate
2. The percentage following the Military Expenditure is its percentage of GDP1.
3. The latest data of military expenditure comes from the data base of the World Bank.

However, problems persist for China both domestically and externally. Within the country, the government is troubled by various problems such as rampant government official corruption, developmental gaps between the countryside and cities and between the coastal and interior regions, a lack of social and economic welfare in the huge migratory population, ethnic separation forces in some frontier regions, and further economic restructuring. Due to the unique nature of its increasing power and internal problems, China has been described as a 'fragile superpower' (Shirk, 2008). China's situation is no less difficult from an external perspective. It faces territorial disputes with several of its neighbouring countries, trade disputes with a number of important economic partners, collaborations between its ethnic separation forces and external terrorist groups, and some Western governments' perceived suspicion of its development model and foreign policy. In turn, China is particularly suspicious of the United States government's response to its economic improvement. Indeed, Chinese analysts frequently observe that the United States has adopted an encirclement policy to stop China's rise.

Facing both domestic and external challenges, China must find appropriate ways to use its rising power. Domestic debate over appropriate foreign strategies has increased in recent years, driven by China's status as a 'deeply conflicted rising power with a series of competing international identities' (Shambaugh, 2011: 7). For example, China is struggling between the opposing ideologies of nationalism and liberalism. At the policy level, China is hesitant to take action and participate in global governance activities such as the provision of public goods. However, it is clear that the Chinese government has become more confident in implementing a strategy of 'hiding its ambition while contributing if necessary'.[14] In other words, China has realised the necessity of actively participating in global affairs while still adopting a Hobbesian mentality of cautiously guarding its state interests whenever possible.

This gradual strategic shift has affected China's foreign policy behaviour. Given its increased power, China is in a transitional period on the world stage. Although the country was once passive in international participation, it has had and been expected to have an increasing influence on various global and regional venues. The changing international environment has posed challenges to the Chinese leadership. However, Chinese policymakers see new opportunities in the global power transformation. Most importantly, Chinese policymakers and analysts have described Sino-American relations as '*dou er bu po*', or a struggle that does not lead to conflict. Chinese leaders are careful and confident in their ability to manage stable bilateral relations with the United States. However, the states diverge in important ways. China is flexible in its use of resources and capabilities through various means of economic statecraft such as foreign aid, development policy and public diplomacy. It is the largest trade partner of a number of neighbouring countries. Moreover, a number of its neighbouring countries enjoy trade surpluses in their trade relations with the country. Indeed, China sees opportunities to develop its neighbourhood policy based on its economic and other influences.

Looking for partners

The calculation of a geopolitical code relates to a state's strategic understanding of its current and potential allies and enemies and accordingly its options for maintaining or countering the corresponding relations (Flint, 2011: 44). China adopted a non-alliance policy following its breakaway from the Soviet Union in the early 1960s. This policy has given China more flexibility in its international affairs. However, it has also presented a problem, as China has very few reliable allies and can only find itself in isolation. Furthermore, East Asia is one of the most complicated regions in the world in terms of power relations and geopolitics. In fact, the region has several hotspots that may break out into violent conflict. According to geopolitical code theory, this complicated situation has made it difficult for the Chinese government to find reliable partners. However, the change in international environment and the rise of its state power may allow China to find more trustworthy partners in its neighbourhood.

In recent decades, China's bilateral relationship with Russia has greatly improved Sino-Russo relations. Although both China and Russia deny that the Sino-Russo Strategic Partnership established in 1996 aims to develop into an alliance, the two states have strengthened their overall military, economic and political cooperation since the turn of the century. China values its good relations with Russia, particularly in terms of their mutual support for important domestic concerns that are targets of international criticism and their general consensus on major issues related to contemporary international affairs (Wishnick, 2010: 65–69). China is also interested in cooperating with Russia to share in its military technologies and energy resources. Although the two countries remain slightly distrustful of each other, they recognise the convenience of cooperating for mutual benefit.

Economic links have enhanced China's relations with its neighbouring countries. In northeast Asia, South Korea and Japan are big economic partners of China. The two countries have enjoyed noticeable trade surpluses with and benefited from direct investment in China. Despite being an ally of the United States, South Korea has generally taken a balanced approach in handling its relations with the United States and China. Although bilateral political relations between Japan and China have worsened due to issues such as their territorial disputes over Diaoyu Island, their substantial economic relations have stabilised the situation, as they restrain both countries from taking more dangerous actions. The regional block of ASEAN countries is more divisive in terms of foreign policy choices than it appears. For example, some ASEAN countries are keen to invite the American presence as a counterbalance against the rising Chinese power in the region, and others are happy to see more Chinese participation in regional affairs. Nevertheless, every country realises the importance of China. China's substantial economic relations with all of the ASEAN countries led to the conclusion of the China-ASEAN Free Trade Agreement. In addition, China has good political relations with most of the ASEAN states. On its southwest front, China has maintained its traditional quasi-alliance relations with Pakistan and striven to improve its relations with India in recent years. On its northwest front, China has greatly developed its relations with its relatively new neighbours in Central Asia. It has established roots in the region by engaging in partnerships with all of the Central Asian countries. Of China's surrounding regions, the northwest front offers the greatest opportunity for China to adopt a more assertive neighbourhood policy, as it provides a big pool of potential partners and less competition.

Strategic approaches

One veteran China analyst argues that China has systematically implemented a series of strategies to promote its regional rise since the turn of the new century (Shambaugh, 2004: 72–89). These strategies include engaging its neighbours in regional organisation, creating strategic partnerships and improving bilateral relations, expanding regional economic ties and decreasing its neighbours' distrust and anxiety in the security sphere. These are largely accurate observations of China's policy practice. Furthermore, the various strategies are used in an integrated way. Depending on the circumstances, China makes selective use of multilateral and bilateral diplomacy in handling its relations with its neighbours. Economic statecraft has become a frequent diplomatic weapon to influence other countries through pressure or inducement. China is also interested in promoting its soft power, which is its ability to influence others through attraction. This more subtle aspect of national power is often promoted by public diplomacy targeted at the general publics of other countries.

Tactical use of multilateral and bilateral diplomacy

Chinese policymakers are typically more comfortable with bilateral diplomacy towards individual states. For a long time, they were suspicious of multilateral institutions, which they considered part of a Western conspiracy to control less-powerful states in the developing world. However, China has become increasingly confident in participating in multilateral games in recent years. It has participated more actively in various multilateral organisations, institutions and formal and informal forums. In terms of its neighbourhood, China has participated in major regional groupings such as the APEC, the ASEAN Regional Forum, the SCO, ASEAN + 3/China and the Six-Party Talks on North Korean's nuclear programme. In all of these settings, China has become accustomed to multilateral diplomacy. In fact, it has had some important effects on the nature and direction of these regional groupings. It has also attempted to initiate and lead in multilateral cooperation on several occasions (Chung, 2010).

This change in attitude and practice was caused by the increase of China's capabilities and motivations in carrying out multilateral diplomacy. Its rise has made China better equipped with necessary resources and international participation skills. Furthermore, China has dramatically expanded its international outreach geographically and across sectors. This has required more active involvement on the part of China to protect its national interests in both its neighbourhood and the broad international arena.

However, China's newfound interest in multilateral diplomacy has not hindered its traditional approach to bilateral diplomacy. Rather, China has become more adept in its tactical use of both multilateral and bilateral approaches in its foreign relations. Since the mid-1990s, China has established various strategic partnership relations with countries around the world. Many of its neighbouring countries are now its strategic partners, including Afghanistan, India, Mongolia, Pakistan, Russia, South Korea, several ASEAN states and some Central Asian states. China uses its bilateral and multilateral approaches selectively depending on the circumstances. For example, it is interested in promoting economic cooperation with the ASEAN countries as a group while firmly stressing the bilateral nature of territorial disputes over the South China Sea with individual countries. Although China finds it difficult to enhance economic cooperation within the multilateral framework of the SCO, it has tactically reached bilateral agreements with some of the organisation's partners. China is more accustomed to bilateral diplomacy and uses multilateral diplomacy to develop its foreign relations.

Economic statecraft: China takes advantage of its increasing economic strength

Economic statecraft is a foreign strategy used by a state government to achieve its foreign policy objectives. States have two general approaches to the political use of their economic capabilities: economic payments and sanctions. The former is a positive option in which the donor state provides economic benefits in return for attaining its policy objectives. The latter is a negative option in which the state economically punishes a target state to change its policy and behaviour. State governments use both methods frequently. With the continued growth of its economic power, China has begun to show ambition by practising its economic statecraft in recent years. It typically adopts the positive method of economic payment, as the negative approach makes it much more difficult to achieve its intended goals. Given its tremendous manufacturing capabilities, China has become a major participant in the international trade of manufactured goods, technology and equipment. Its huge foreign reserves have made it able to invest abroad.

In the context of its neighbourhood policy, China has partially realised its economic advantage over its neighbours. It recognises opportunities and the importance of promoting its national interests through economic statecraft in the surrounding regions (Song, 2013). As such, China has adopted some new initiatives. In its economic cooperation with the ASEAN countries, China made a sole contribution to the establishment of the China-ASEAN Investment Cooperation Fund in 2010, providing total funding of USD 10 billion in support of large infrastructure projects. In this context, China has established several other cooperation schemes with the ASEAN countries, including the China-ASEAN Cooperation Fund, China-ASEAN Public Health Cooperation Fund and China-ASEAN Oceanic Cooperation Fund.[15]

Most recently, the Chinese government officially introduced the 'One Belt, One Road' (OBOR) initiative in reference to the 'New Silk Road Economic Belt' and '21st Century Maritime Silk Road'. The former will link China with Europe through Central and Western Asia, and the latter will connect China with Southeast Asian countries, Africa and Europe. The Chinese government stressed that by adopting this strategy it was working towards an 'interest community' of mutual benefit and a 'community of common destiny' of joint development and co-prosperity. On behalf of the Chinese government, President Xi proposed the two project ideas on two international occasions in September and October 2013, respectively. On 7 September 2013, he expressed the initiative of the 'New Silk Road Economic Belt' in a speech he delivered in Kazakhstan while visiting the Central Asian country for the SCO Summit. He suggested that China and its neighbouring countries could take a gradual and piecemeal approach to the joint construction of the economic belt and thereby strengthen economic cooperation between the partner countries. One month later, on 3 October 2013, President Xi delivered another speech at the Indonesian Parliament and introduced the plan of the 'Silk Road on the Sea'. During the speech, he expressed China's interest in strengthening its economic and oceanic cooperation with the ASEAN countries.

The OBOR initiative was an important step taken by China to achieve its national development and foreign policy objectives. According to one senior Chinese official, the strategy was adopted based on both domestic and foreign considerations (Huchen, 2014). There are development gaps between China's more prosperous coastal regions in the east and less-developed regions in the west. China adopted the 'One Belt, One Road' strategy to strengthen its economic links with its neighbouring countries and stimulate the economic development of its interior and less-prosperous western regions, particularly those bordering neighbouring countries. China's foreign objectives are not negligible, as the country is also attempting to use its economic capabilities to strengthen its links with neighbouring countries in Southeast and Central Asia.

Public diplomacy

Although implemented by a state government, public diplomacy is targeted at the general publics of foreign countries with the hope of influencing public opinion and ultimately the governmental policy of the target state. Compared with Western countries, China has a short history of implementing public diplomacy. The Office of Public Diplomacy was not established within the Chinese Ministry of Foreign Affairs until 2004. Since then, the Ministry has routinely published a public diplomacy section in its annual white paper related to Chinese foreign policy (Qu, 2010: 7). In fact, public diplomacy has been defined as a new and increasingly important dimension of Chinese diplomacy because it follows the trend of a globalised world (Yang, 2011: 12). China's public diplomacy has the clear goal of serving national interests, mitigating misperceptions, winning over foreign public opinion, improving China's national image, struggling for dominant discourses, strengthening the country's soft power and paving the way for hard power expansion (Qiu, 2010: 2). Thus far, China's public diplomacy efforts have focused on several areas such as using high-level Chinese leader visits to communicate with foreign publics; engaging in activities at big international events held within the country; and participating in cultural and educational exchange activities put on by foreign-oriented media.

At the Work Conference on Neighbourhood Diplomacy in October 2013, President Xi suggested that public diplomacy should be used to focus on strengthening the long-term social basis of the public opinions of neighbouring countries. According to President Xi, public diplomacy provides China with the opportunity to introduce its national situation, state policy and ideals for better regional cooperation. China's public diplomacy towards its neighbourhood has been implemented as part of its overall public diplomacy strategy rather than neighbourhood policy. However, the country has intensively engaged in public diplomacy towards many of its neighbouring countries due to its substantial stakes in and links with those countries. Indeed, China has traditional links with most of its neighbours and has a substantial cultural influence on some of them.

As a major part of its public diplomacy, China has ardently promoted the Confucius Institute project across the world. The project follows the practice of some Western states such as the British Council of the United Kingdom, the Goethe Institute of Germany and Alliance Française of France. It aims to introduce Chinese language and cultures and ultimately promote China's soft power. By the end of 2013, China had established 440 Confucius Institutes and 646 Confucius classrooms in 120 states and regions. Among these, 93 Confucius Institutes had been established in 32 Asian countries.[16] In fact, the first institute was established in Seoul, South Korea in 2004. Some neighbouring countries including Japan, South Korea, Thailand and Indonesia currently host more than 10 Confucius Institutes. Compared with activities in Western countries, the Confucius Institute project has been better received in China's neighbouring countries, particularly those under the influence of traditional Chinese culture.

Conclusion: jumping off the 'Great Wall'

The Chinese leadership has faced daunting challenges in governing the world's most populated countries. It must strike many complex balances at the same time, including balances between its international projection of economic, military and political power and the primary domestic goals of economic growth and social stability (Hu and Chan, 2012: 674). China analysts almost unanimously agree that China's first priority is its domestic affairs and particularly regime stability. This first objective can only be achieved if the country is prosperous and stable. To that end, it is crucial to ensure a stable external environment in the neighbourhood.

In this context, one can better understand the importance the new Chinese leadership attaches to its neighbourhood policy. According to President Xi, China is striving for a sound neighbouring environment to ensure its own development and seeks common development with its neighbouring countries. In his talk at the Conference on neighbourhood policy, President Xi stressed the necessity of good diplomatic work in neighbouring countries to realise the 'centenary goals' set forth by the 18th CPC National Congress in November 2012. According to Chinese policymakers, China's international environment and particularly its neighbourhood have become increasingly challenging since 2008. This is typified by the on-going territorial disputes between China and some of its neighbouring countries in the South and East China Seas. These regional disputes are exacerbated by the interference of external powers and particularly the United States, which has forcibly implemented its 'rebalancing of Asia' strategy.

Meanwhile, China aspires to expand its influence beyond its borders. In this context, the 'go west' strategy has been proposed, arguing that China should use its increasing power to create a more favourable regional environment and if possible its own sphere of influence (Wang and Ji, 2012). The most probable direction for such an expansion lies beyond China's western frontiers. Following this line of argument, China adopted the 'One Belt, One Road' strategy with the hope of strengthening its economic links and influence in its neighbouring regions and beyond. The strategy involves linking China's competitive industries with the geographical features and development needs of many of its neighbouring countries by building the 'belt' and the 'road'. Different from the ancient Silk Road, which mainly focused on trade, the 'One Belt, One Road' strategy may include the flow of financial elements, information, technology and personnel. The Chinese policymakers predict that the 'One Belt, One Road' strategy could be sound given that China and almost all of its neighbouring countries consider economic development their foremost goal in their policy agendas. Based on this common interest, related countries could shelve or even discard their political and security disputes to cooperate with one another in their pursuit of economic development. Therefore, this project is conducive to building mutual trust and solving security problems in Asia.

Notes

1 This is a Chinese idiom.
2 Hu Jintao and Wen Jiabao respectively served as the president and premier in the previous Chinese government between 2002 and 2012.
3 'Xi Jinping: China to further friendly relations with neighboring countries', http://news.xinhuanet.com/english/china/2013-10/26/c_125601680.htm, accessed 21 January 2014. The 'centenary goals' refer to the objectives of developing China into a moderately prosperous society by 2021 and a prosperous, strong, democratic, culturally advanced, harmonious, and modern socialist country by 2049.

4 Of the major international actors, the European Union has pursued an explicitly claimed, well-defined and consistent neighbourhood policy, according to which it 'works with its southern and eastern neighbours to achieve the closest possible political association and the greatest possible degree of economic integration' (http://eeas.europa.eu/enp, accessed 22 January 2014).

5 'Three worlds theory' was developed by the later Chinese CCP leader Mao Zedong, who argued that the world systems comprised three different economic and political worlds. The first world consisted of the two super powers, the second world consisted of other developed states, and the third world consisted of all of the developing states.

6 Hu Jingtao's speech at the 10th Working Conference for Ambassadors in Beijing in 2004.

7 The idea was originally borrowed from Lenin's theory and practice in the Soviet Union and adapted to China by the CCP leadership in the 1950s.

8 The five autonomous regions with provincial status are Guangxi, Inner Mongolia, Ningxia, Xinjiang and Tibet.

9 According to official statistics, China's top 10 trading partners by total trade volume in 2013 were the United States (USD 521 billion); Hong Kong SAR, China (USD 401 billion); Japan (USD 312.55 billion); South Korea (USD 274.24 billion); Taiwan, China (USD 197.28 billion); Germany (USD 161.56 billion); Australia (USD 136.37 billion); Malaysia (USD 106.07 billion); Brazil (USD 90.27 billion); and Russia (USD 89.21 billion) (http://www.chinadaily.com.cn/bizchina/2014-02/19/content_17290565.htm, accessed 30 September 2014).

10 http://news.xinhuanet.com/english/china/2013-10/26/c_125601680.htm, accessed 23 September 2014.

11 It was first officially mentioned in the CCP report at the 16th Plenary Meeting in 2002.

12 *China's Road to Peaceful Development*, white paper published by the Press Office of the State Council of the Chinese Government, 22 December 2005.

13 In 2013, China's GDP was USD 9,330 billion (USD 13,390 in purchasing power parity terms), followed by Japan at USD 5,007 billion (USD 4,729 billion), Russia at USD 2,113 billion (USD 2,553) and India at USD 1,670 billion (USD 4,990 billion). The World Factbook of Central Intelligence Agency, https://www.cia.gov/library/publications/the-world-factbook, accessed 27 September 2014.

14 Part of the '24 character strategy' developed by Chinese leader Deng Xiaoping.

15 http://www.china-asean-fund.com/sc/about-caf.php, accessed 22 September 2014.

16 http://www.hanban.edu.cn/confuciousinstitutes/node_10961.htm, accessed 6 October 2014.

References

Chan, Steve (2013) 'Geography and International Relations Theorizing: Their Implications for China', *Eurasian Geography and Economics*, 54(4): 363–385.

Chen, Yali (2012) 'Meiguo de Zaipingheng Zhanlue: Xianshi Pinggu he Zhongguo de Yingdui' [The America's Rebalancing Strategy: Practical Appraisal and China's Response], *Shijie Jingji yu Zhengshi (World Economy and Politics)*, 11: 64–82.

China Trade and External Economic Statistical Yearbook 2013 (2013) China Statistics Press.

Chung, Chien-peng (2010) *China's Multilateral Cooperation in Asia and the Pacific: Institutionalizing Beijing's 'Good Neighbour Policy'*, Abingdon, UK: Routledge.

Eichengreen, Barry (2006) 'China, Asia, and the World Economy: The Implications of an Emerging Asian Core and Periphery', *China & World Economy*, 14(3): 1–18.

Flint, Colin (2011) *Introduction to Geopolitics*, 2nd ed., New York: Routledge.

Gong, Li and Dongfang Sun (2011) 'Zhanlue Jiyuqi yu Zhongguo de Heping Fazhan' [Period of Strategic Opportunities and China's Peaceful Development], *Guoji Guanxi Xueyuan Xuebao (Journal of University of International Relations)*, 3: 25–29.

Hao, Yufan and Bill K. P. Chou (2010) 'China's Borderlands and their International Implications: An Overview'. In Yufan Hao ad Bill K. P. Chou (Eds.), *China's Policies on its Borderlands and the International Implications*, pp. 1–17. Singapore: World Scientific.

Hao, Yufan and Weihua Liu (2012): 'Xinjiang: Increasing Pain in the Heart of China's Borderland', *Journal of Contemporary China*, 21(74): 205–225.

Hu, Richard W. and Steve Chan (2012) 'China's New Generation of Leaders and Regional Challenges in East Asia', *Eurasian Geography and Economics*, 53(6): 674–687.

Huchen, Gao, Minister of Commerce, 'Shenhua Yingmao Hezuo, Gongchuang Xin de Huihuang' [Furthering Economic and Trade Cooperation, Jointly Creating the New Glories], *People's Daily*, 2 July 2014, http://opinion.people.com.cn/n/2014/0702/c1003-25226196.html, accessed 27 September 2014.

Lu, Guangsheng (2011) *Diyuan Zhengzhi Shiye xia de Xinan Zhoubian Anquan yu Quyu Hezuo Yanjiu* [Studies on Regional Security and Cooperation in China's Southwest Borderlands from a Geopolitical Perspective], Beijing: People's Press.

Ma, Manli and Lei Ma (2010) 'Lun Kuaguo Zuti Wenti de Fazhan jiqi dui Zhongguo Bianjiang Anquan de Weixie yu Duize' [A Discussion on the Issue of Trans-boundary Ethnic Groups, its Threat to China's Frontier Security and Policy Solutions], *Zhongnan Minzu Daxue Xuebao (Journal of South-Central University for Nationalities)*, 30(1): 1–4.

Mackerras, Colin (2010) 'The Disturbances in the Tibetan Areas and Ürümqi 2008–2009: Implications for China's International Relations'. In Yufan Hao and Bill K. P. Chou (Eds.), *China's Policies on its Borderlands and the International Implications*, pp. 19–45. Singapore: World Scientific.

McGrew, Anthony (2008) 'Globalization and Global Politics'. In John Baylis, Steve Smith, and Patricia Owen (Eds.), *The Globalization of World Politics: An Introduction to International Relations (4th ed.)*, pp. 14–33. Oxford and New York: Oxford University Press.

Medeiros, Evan S. (2009) *China's International Behavior: Activism, Opportunism, and Diversification*. Santa Monica, CA: Rand Corporation.

Qin, Yaqing (2009) 'Guoji Tix Zhuanxin yiji Zhongguo Zhanlue Jiyuqi de Yanxu' [Transformation of the International System and Extension of China's Historical Period of Strategic Opportunities], *Xiandai Guoji Guanxi (Contemporary International Relations)*, 4: 35–37.

Qiu, Yuanping (2010) 'Zhongguo de Heping Fazhan yu Gonggong Waijiao' [China's Peaceful Development and its Public Diplomacy], *Guoji Wenti Yanjiu (Studies of International Affairs)*, 6: 1–3.

Qu, Xing (2010) 'Gonggong Waijiao de Jingdian Hanyi yu Zhongguo Tese' [The Classic Meaning of Public Diplomacy and the Chinese Characteristics], *Guoji Wenti Yanjiu (Studies of International Affairs)*, 6: 4–9.

Shambaugh, David (2004) 'China Engages Asia: Reshaping the Regional Order', *International Security*, 29(3): 64–99.

Shambaugh, David (2011) 'Coping with a Conflicted China', *Washington Quarterly*, 34(1): 7–27.

Shi, Yuanhua (2000) 'Lun Xinzhongguo Zhoubian Waijiao Zhengce de Lishi Yanbain' [The Historical *Evolution* of the New China's Foreign Policy Towards its Periphery], *Dangdai Zhongguoshi Yanjiu (Contemporary China History Studies)*, 7(5): 38–50.

Shirk, Susan L. (2008) *China: Fragile Superpower*, New York: Oxford University Press.

Song, Guoyou (2013) 'Zhongguo yu Zhoubian Guojia Jingji Guanxi ji Zhengce Xuanze' [China's Economic Relations with Neighbouring Countries and Policy Choices], *Guoji Wenti Yanjiu (Studies of International Affairs)*, 1: 33–43.

Statistical Bulletin of China's Outward Foreign Direct Investment (2012) Ministry of Commerce of People's Republic of China, Series: Statistical Bulletin of China's Outward Foreign Direct Investment.

Su, Changhe (2004) 'Zhoubian Zhidu yu Zhoubian Zhuyi: Dongya Quyu Zhili zhong de Zhongguo Lujin' [Zhoubian Institutions and Zhoubianism: China's Approach to Governance in East Asia], *Shijie Jingji yu Zhengzhi (World Economy and Politics)*, 20(1): 7–14.

Wang, Jisi and Xi Ji (2012) 'Zhongguo Diyuan Zhanlue de Zai Pingheng' [Go West: Rebalancing of China's Geopolitical Strategy], *Global Time*, 17 October 2012, http://opinion.huanqiu.com/opinion_world/2012-10/3193760.html, accessed 5 October 2014.

Wang, Yi (2003) 'Yu Ling Wei Shan, Yi Ling Wei Ban (To Deal with Neighbours with Good Will and Partnership Mentality)', *Qiushi (Seeking Truth)*, 4: 19–22.

Wishnick, Elizabeth (2010) 'Why a "Strategic Partnership"?' In James Bellacqua (Ed.), *The Future of China-Russia Relations*, pp. 56–80. Lexington, KT: University Press of Kentucky.

Yang, Jiechi (2011) 'Nuli Katuo Zhongguo Tese Gonggong Waijiao Xinjumian' [Striving to Open a New Dimension of Public Diplomacy with Chinese Characteristics], *Qiushi (Seeking Truth)*, 4: 12–14.

Yang, Jiemian (2003) 'Zhongyao Zhanlue Jiyuqi yu Zhongguo Waijiao de Lishi Renwu' [Important Historical Period of Strategic Opportunities and Historic Tasks of China's Diplomatic Work], *Mao Zedong & Deng Xiaoping Lilun Yanjiu* (Studies of Mao Zedong and Dengxiaoping's Theories), 44: 60–67.

Yang, Yi (2012) 'Zhoubian Anquan Xuyao Quanfangwei Zhanlei' [Neighborhood Security Demanding a Comprehensive Strategy], *Global Time*, 26 October 2012.

Yu, Xiaofeng and Lili Xu (2009) 'Biananxue Chuyi' [An Opinion on the Development of Frontier Security Studies], *Journal of Zhejiang University*, 39(5): 5–18.

Zhao, Suisheng (1999) 'China's Periphery Policy and its Asian Neighbours', *Security Dialogue*, 30(3): 335–346.

Zheng, Yongnian (2013) Zhongguo de Ludi Diyuan Zhengzhi jiqi Tiaozhan' [China's Geopolitics on Land and its Challenges], *Lianhe Zaobao* (Singapore: Lianhe Daily), 24 December 2013.

Zheng, Zemin (2010) *Nanhai Wenti zhong de Daguo Yinsu: Mei Ri Yin E yu Nanhai Wenti* [Great Power Factors in South China Sea Issue: the United States, Japan, India, Russia and South China Sea Issue]. Beijing: World Knowledge Press.

Zhong, Feiteng and Jie Zhang (2011) 'Yanxin Anquan Moshi yu Zhongguo Zhoubian Waijiao de Zhanlue Xuanze' [Flying Geese Security Model and China's Strategic Choice in Neighbour Diplomacy], *Shijie Jingji yu Zhengzhi (World Economy and Politics)*, 25(8): 47–64.

2 China's international leadership in SCO

This chapter establishes a framework for empirically analysing the SCO process, with special reference to China's role.[1] It discerns the various interests, motivations and power statuses of SCO members and argues that they have individual, albeit occasionally mutual, interests and priorities. An initial asymmetry of interests is observed – the principal reason the SCO's strategic situation is largely a suasion game between China and the other members – with China demonstrating a greater interest in the SCO. The power asymmetry between China and the Central Asian members and the relative power equality between China and Russia further complicates the situation. China has attempted to exercise its leadership practice by creating and running a regional organisation for the first time in the history of its foreign relations. However, SCO members' interests in promoting the organisation's further development have converged more in recent years. Therefore, China and Russia have more common ground on which to cooperate with the Central Asian states in this regional initiative.

Various interpretations of the SCO

At the summit meeting held in Shanghai, China in June 2001, top leaders from China, Russia and the Central Asian states of Kazakhstan, Kyrgyzstan, Uzbekistan and Tajikistan formally announced the establishment of the SCO as the successor to the informal 'Shanghai Five' group, which included all of the founding SCO members except Uzbekistan. The official founding declaration asserted that the organisation's primary objective was to combat what are called the three evil forces of international terrorism, ethnic separatism and religious extremism. The SCO is therefore officially defined as a regional organisation for non-traditional security.

Nevertheless, the organisation has been interpreted in a variety of ways since its inception. One view holds that the SCO constitutes a joint effort by a group of authoritarian states to defend against regime changes in the face of regional or global democratic trends. This view is most popular among some Western analysts and is best personified by Ambrosio's argument (2008). According to Ambrosio, the SCO is a multilateral vehicle used by member governments to undermine democratisation trends in Central Asia. It uses a set of conservative norms known collectively as the 'Shanghai Spirit' as a weapon to preserve the autocratic regimes in the region. The 'critical states' of China and Russia play key roles in the process of promoting the principles of 'sovereignty' and 'non-interference' and in emphasising the values of 'stability' and 'diversity'.

The prism of geopolitics and interstate strategic interaction provides another view of the SCO. From an internal perspective, some analysts suggest that China is attempting to enter its neighbouring region via a multilateral approach (Chung, 2006: 10) and that Russia intends to check up on the increasing Chinese influence in the region from within the organisation (Kazantsev, 2008: 1080). Others suggest that the Central Asian states are trying to use the organisation to mutually constrain Russia and China. From an external perspective, some analysts claim that the organisation may constitute a multilateral approach adopted by member states, particularly China and Russia, as a counterweight to the American influence in the region (e.g., Gill, 2001; Chung, 2004).

Meanwhile, some analysts agree with the view held by the governments of the SCO member states that the organisation is primarily focused on internal security problems in the region. For example, Aris (2009: 462) argues that the SCO was created and developed as a result of common interests among the member states' elites and 'its ability to contribute to the main security concerns as they perceive them: internal challenges to their regime security'. Most Chinese analysts consistently express the view that the SCO is a regional organisation of non-traditional security aimed at combating religiously motivated terrorist groups seeking national separation.

The preceding interpretations are generally plausible because each can be justified by the various motivations that the SCO members derive from their respective national interests. In reality, the SCO is an organisation that addresses many factors such as regional stability, anti-radicalism, energy security and anti-foreign influence (Kerr and Swinton, 2008: 113). It is therefore natural that observers with different attentions and focuses have interpreted its role in different ways.

Despite the differences in understanding, most analysts, including Chinese analysts, agree that this regional organisation is largely a Chinese initiative and that China plays a 'leading role' in its process (Chung, 2006; Pan, 2008/ 2009; Yuan, 2010). China is clearly more motivated to promote the SCO than its other members. The benefits from this regional cooperation seem to be distributed unevenly, with China expected to gain more. Indeed, China has been a pivotal power behind the SCO from its origin to the current stage.

The game of the SCO

Why do states cooperate by establishing or joining an international regime or an organisation? Rationalist international relations (IR) theories hold that institutions are created by states to solve strategic interaction dilemmas

(Martin, 1992: 766). Furthermore, state actors face different strategic situations due to their varied power and interest configurations. One such situation is defined as a suasion game. Martin argues that there must be interest and power asymmetries between the state actors in a suasion game. When one hegemon that exceeds others in terms of power and wealth prefers multilateral cooperation, it is unilaterally willing to supply public goods (p. 777). This definition emphasises power asymmetry but is unclear about the role of interests. Another definition refers to a suasion game as a situation in which 'one actor receives her most preferred outcome, while the other does less well' (Hasenclever, 1997: 57). The second definition clearly stresses interest asymmetry as its defining characteristic. The two perspectives may be better applied in complementarity. Interest asymmetry is a necessary condition providing the state actor, which has more at stake, with the motivation to persuade or threaten other partners into cooperation. Power asymmetry is another necessary condition that provides an actor with the ability to lead a cooperative effort. Therefore, multilateral arrangements in a suasion game can usually be led by a hegemon that possesses the sufficient and necessary condition of both motivation and ability.

When one actor has both the motivation and ability to initiate multilateral cooperation, it must determine how to persuade or coerce others into cooperating. Issue linkage is usually the favoured method. The hegemon may tactically link issues in the form of either threats or promises (or side payments). This strategic interaction is a difficult game by nature because the state actor must persuade others to cooperate using 'carrots' or 'sticks' and avoid the free-riding actions of others. Other actors may also exploit the situation for their own benefit whenever an opportunity presents itself. In such a strategic game, it is predicted that a formal multilateral organisation that may facilitate a hegemon's attempt to link issues is created to maintain the *appearance* of international multilateralism and therefore have little effect on actual international multilateralism-based decisions (Martin, 1992: 767, 779–780). The strategic nature of the suasion game makes it difficult for the hegemon to accomplish its task.

Ever since its adoption of the reform and opening-up policy in the late 1970s, China has resolved internal disputes over its future direction by emphasising development as its first priority. It is with this grand strategy in mind that Chinese policymakers formulate foreign policy guidelines, giving preference to the neighbourhood (*zhoubian*) on their agenda. Chinese leaders realise the importance of the country's regional neighbours to their overall development strategy. In political terms, the neighbourhood is the primary setting in which China can defend its sovereignty and exert an international influence. In economic terms, it provides an effective context for China to implement its opening-up policy and cooperate with partners. In security terms, it serves as the immediate external environment in which China can stabilise its frontiers and harmonise its relations with different ethnic groups.[2] In fact, the term 'neighbourhood diplomacy' (*zhoubian waijiao*) was formally written into the resolution of the 16th Chinese Communist Party Congress in November 2002. In its adoption of the slogan 'good neighbour, good friend, good partner', China has forcibly implemented more proactive policies towards its neighbours. China's 'go west' strategy should be taken in the context of the country's overall neighbourhood policy, pointing to its northwest neighbourhood as its preferred direction.

Since the late 1990s, there has been a paradigmatic shift in the general orientation of Chinese foreign policymaking. Although they are more accustomed to traditional bilateral diplomacy, Chinese foreign policy elites are becoming increasingly interested in the multilateral approach to international affairs (Wang, 2005: 159–200). A great deal of evidence has confirmed this fundamental change. First, China has become more interested in international organisations. Second, China is becoming a more active participant in international activities. Third, China is trying to engage in regional cooperation (Kavalski, 2009), particularly with its neighbours (Breslin, 2009). The trend of Chinese involvement in multilateral diplomacy is indicated nowhere more obviously than by China's role in the SCO. Due to its importance to China's core national interests, Chinese leaders have made substantial and consistent investments in the SCO project, bringing together a group of states in its northwest neighbourhood that are different in many aspects. Moreover, official relations between China and its Central Asian neighbours were almost suspended for decades or longer, just as they were under Tsarist Russia and later the Soviet Union for more than 200 years. Chinese people could recall their close contacts only in the history of the ancient 'Silk Road'.

Consequently, China's opportunity to influence its northwest neighbourhood came relatively later than its opportunity to influence other boundaries. Its entry into the region became possible only after the dissolution of the Soviet Union and the relative decline of Russia. Nevertheless, its interests are both vital and manifold, and it has good reason to enter Central Asia (Swanström, 2005). As summarised by Zhao (2007a: 23), China's interests in Central Asia include border security, the anti-'East Turkestan Movement', geopolitical security and energy and economic interests. China shares a long border in its northwest with three Central Asian countries and Russia, and maintaining a secure border alone can be difficult. The Islamic separatist movement in China's Xinjiang Autonomous Region, which is believed to be part of the transnational network of the Islamic fundamentalist movement, is an annoyance to the Chinese central government. Meanwhile, the rapid growth of the Chinese economy has created an insatiable demand for energy. China has been a net importer of oil and natural gas since the 1990s and is eagerly seeking new energy sources. It is naturally turning to Central Asia, a region rich in oil and natural gas and located in its immediate neighbourhood. The region provides both economic opportunity in the form of potential consumer markets for Chinese manufactured goods and strategic significance. Chinese leaders perceive that the United States plans to surround China, a perception further strengthened by the formal establishment of American military bases in the region during the United States war in Afghanistan that began in 2001. In effect, Central Asia is the 'battleground' on which China must break this encirclement.

Hence, China has sufficient motivation to seek more effective engagement with the region.

Given Central Asia's historical legacy as a Russian sphere of influence and identity as a part of Tsarist Russia and the Soviet Union for two centuries, Russia has a tremendous stake in the region and therefore a strong motivation to implement an active engagement policy (Kazantsev, 2008: 1073). However, Russia has been able to manage its relations with countries in the region on a bilateral basis, and there are multilateral cooperative frameworks and substantial economic, cultural and ethnic links in place. Russia would be unwilling to see a new great power enter its traditional backyard. Furthermore, the attitudes of Russian elites towards cooperation with China are almost evenly divided. Although some perceive China to offer a major ally against the United States, others who are afraid of the ever-increasing power of China and the threat it poses to Russia's Far East even yearn for an alliance with the United States against China (Shlapentokh, 2007). This 'ambivalence' occasionally translates into hesitant and contradictory behaviour in Russia's cooperation with China.

Both the leaders and public of the newly independent states in Central Asia generally cherish their autonomy.[3] Although they possess close ties with Russia, the new states are fearful of the country's tremendous influence and welcome China's entry into the region to an extent due to the balance it offers.[4] The Central Asian states also consider China's arrival a new opportunity for their economic development. Indeed, these economically backward states are envious of China's phenomenal economic growth and therefore have high expectations of their cooperation with the country, such as the economic benefits they may derive. Furthermore, they are troubled by internal instability owing to various social and ethnic problems. Their political leaders suppose that multilateral cooperation with both China and Russia may help stabilise their authoritarian regimes, as they share a similar understanding of the principles and rules of social and political governance. Nevertheless, they remain wary of China's influence becoming too great.

China obviously has a strong motivation to engage with Central Asia, a region vital to its core interests in multiple ways. One of the most efficient approaches in IR involves engaging through multilateral institutions. A regional organisation that incorporated both China and Central Asian states thus offered a fitting solution to China's engagement plan. However, this plan became difficult to implement due to the power configurations in the region.

At the most abstract level, power in IR is conventionally defined as a state's ability to use material resources to get others to do what they would not do otherwise. Although the dominant state is the strongest in terms of power or capability, in a suasion game, the state has to make every effort to persuade or coerce others into cooperation. Although China's Central Asian neighbours consider it a regional 'hegemon', its hegemonic status is not well established because it must also face Russia, a fairly equal power. Although Russian power has declined significantly compared with that of China since the end of the Cold War (Lo, 2008: 86–89), it has retained the status of a major international power in large part due to its military might, energy reserves and diplomatic influence. It is true that there is an increasing power gap between the two countries, but the notion that Russia will become China's 'junior partner' in time currently seems farfetched.

The great power politics game in Central Asia is not played exclusively by China and Russia. Indeed, it features other players, particularly the United States. As the only superpower with global interests and projection capabilities, the United States has strong stakes in and the motivation to adopt a well-defined strategy for the region. The major objectives of its Central Asian strategy, which is part of its overall global strategy, include geopolitical considerations, the war on terrorism, democracy promotion and energy interests. Central Asia is geopolitically significant simply because it is the 'battleground' on which the United States directly confronts two of its potential competitors: Russia and China. Their interests in anti-terrorism, democracy promotion and energy control have motivated United States policymakers to pay special attention to a region that was 'forgotten' in the 1990s. This landlocked region has also attracted many other state and non-state players with different interests and types of involvement. The long list includes nearby countries such as India, Iran, Pakistan and Turkey; countries located farther away such as Japan and South Korea; and some of the EU member states. It seems that the 'great game' has restarted in the twenty-first century and is being played by many more actors in the same place.

The complicated relations between the Central Asian states exacerbate the complexity of the 'internal difficulties' associated with this regional cooperation framework (Yang, 2009). Problems and even disputes arise between the states. China may promote the SCO when the interests of the member states and particularly those of China and Russia converge. However, the SCO would hardly progress if the two hegemons were to diverge in their calculation of interests. In practice, the 'two cores' problem has annoyed Chinese policymakers throughout the SCO process (Liang, 2006) and the American factor is also a frequent concern. Thus, the game played in the SCO is difficult due to its complexity. Against this background, China has started exercising its leadership in multilateral cooperation.

China's international leadership

It is widely acknowledged that China was the 'major impetus' behind the formation of the SCO as a multilateral security cooperation in Central Asia (Lanteigne, 2006/2007: 607). Based on his observation that China has persistently taken 'a leading role' in the establishment and institutionalisation of the 'Shanghai Five' and SCO and desires to continue this trend, Chung (2006: 5) remarks that 'China's enthusiasm for helping to establish, develop and structure this regional multi-lateral organisation is obvious'. It is true that the SCO process marks the first time China has taken the active and leading role of initiating, constructing and consolidating a formal regional organisation that is not exclusively economic in nature. Chinese scholars and policy advisors have agreed on this observation (Jia, 2007; Pan, 2008/2009). In particular, Pan (2008/2009: 59–61) admits that China plays a driving role in the SCO in three main areas: formulating the theoretical guidelines, driving forward institutionalisation and providing direct support to major projects.

It is worth studying China's role in the SCO process in depth. Because the SCO was the first regional organisation initiated and promoted by China, a systematic study of this 'experiment' may help clarify the Chinese practice of diplomatic leadership. However, determining how to conceptualise diplomatic leadership is problematic. Most of the current research related to political leadership focuses on domestic politics and general governmental organisations. Few studies focus on international organisations and diplomacy. Jia (2007: 114) proposes that 'leadership is a process by which a person or an actor manages an organisation or influences others to take action'. He further suggests that effective leadership in international diplomacy entails 'vision, will, resources and skills'. His argument is based on his rich empirical studies of the leadership issue in international relations. It is useful, despite insufficiency of conceptual accuracy.

In fact, Young conducts the most systematic conceptualisation of diplomatic leadership in negotiations and specifically that leading to regime creation (Young, 1991). He argues that diplomatic leadership can be categorised into three types: 'structural leadership', 'entrepreneurial leadership' and 'intellectual leadership' (p. 288). According to the author, structural leadership involves 'devising effective ways to bring structural power (power based on material resources) to bear in the form of bargaining leverage over the issues at stake in specific interaction'; entrepreneurial leadership involves 'making use of negotiating skill to influence the manner in which issues are presented and to fashion mutually acceptable deals'; and intellectual leadership involves the 'power of ideas to shape the way in which participants understand the issues at stake and to orient thinking about options available' (p. 288).

Young suggests that structural and entrepreneurial leaderships apply to either collective actors such as states or individual diplomats. However, intellectual leadership is almost exclusively applicable to individuals. It can be argued that all three types of diplomatic leadership can be comfortably applied to collective actors. In particular, evidence suggests that the SCO has largely been achieved through an elite-driven model of regional cooperation (Aris, 2009: 471). Therefore, the process is largely driven by political elites including leaders and diplomats rather than social forces. Although political elites are individuals, they act in their capacities as state representatives. Thus, it is not essential to distinguish strictly between individuals and collective actors.

Exercise of structural leadership

The ability of an actor and very often a state to exercise its bargaining leverage usually derives from its structural power vis-à-vis the other participants or stakeholders in a negotiation process. In reality, this means that there are 'asymmetries' among participants (Young, 1991: 289). These asymmetries can relate to power, resources, or knowledge. In the China case, the steady rise of its overall state power has undoubtedly been conducive to its exercise of structural leadership in the international arena. This is reflected in its increased confidence in contributing its power and resources to a number of areas, for example, the UN peacekeeping missions, development aid to the less developed countries bilaterally and multilaterally, and its increasing role in existing global and regional institutions such as the IMF and the APEC. More noteworthy, China takes more active initiatives in attempting to construct policy and institutional settings in its favour, for example, its role in the BRICS and the OBOR initiative in most recent years.

Comparing the SCO partners, it is evident that China enjoys structural power vis-à-vis the Central Asian SCO members and to a lesser extent Russia. Table 2.1 lists the major statistics related to the SCO members' natural, economic and military capabilities.

China and Russia are obviously the two giants when compared with the other SCO members. Whether in terms of natural, economic, or military strength, there is a huge capability gap between the groups. In particular, Uzbekistan, Kyrgyzstan and Tajikistan have a tiny fraction of the area, population, economy and military power belonging to China and Russia. Indeed, the landlocked states of Central Asia encounter a variety of overlapping policy challenges (Maksutov, 2006: 1). They face serious problems associated with regressive economies, unemployment, social poverty and political instability. There is a clear asymmetry in the economic and military capabilities of the SCO member states.

Although there is a rough power symmetry between China and Russia, China has an advantage over Russia in terms of aggregated economic power. Russia may have a comparative advantage in terms of its possession of natural resources and military capabilities. However, China makes use of its manufacturing capabilities and tremendous foreign reserves in exchange for Russian natural resources. Although Russia may have more advanced weaponry due to its Soviet legacies, the military gap between the two countries has decreased rapidly in recent years. In fact, Russia relies partially on Chinese imports of its weapons and natural resources as a large part of its foreign reserves earnings. Following the current trend, the power gap between China and Russia should widen further in the coming years.

The end of the Cold War, the collapse of the USSR and improvement in Sino-Russian relations have made it possible for China to exercise its structural power in Central Asia (Sutter, 2008: 6; Karrar, 2009: 49–65). China understands the problems and challenges the Central Asian states face following their independence. These new states are in desperate need of help to protect their national security and achieve domestic and regional stability. Due to their suspicion of the Russian influence, they consider China a welcomed newcomer into the region. Furthermore, the Central Asian countries have other motivations

Table 2.1 Power and capabilities of the SCO member states

Index country	Area (km2)	Population (July 2015 est.)	GDP (PPP, billion, 2014 est.)	GDP per capita (PPP, 2014 est.)	Foreign reserves and gold, billion (31/12/ 2014 est.)	Military expenditure (% of GDP, 2014)
China	9,596,960	1,367,485,388	$17620	$12,900	$3899	2.1%
Russia	17,098,242	142,423,773	$3565	$24,800	$385.5	4.5%
Kazakhstan	2,724,900	18,157,122	$418.5	$24,000	$27.55	1.1%
Uzbekistan	447,400	29,199,942	$171.7	$5,600	$18	3.5% (2010)
Kyrgyzstan	199,951	5,664,939	$19.16	$3,400	$2.184	3.4%
Tajikistan	144,100	8,191,958	$22.32	$2,700	$0.6518	1.1%

Sources: The World Factbook of Central Intelligence Agency; The World Bank: World Development Indicators; and 'Uzbekistan Military Stats', NationMaster; https://www.cia.gov/library/publications/the-world-factbook; http://data.worldbank.org/indicator/MS.MIL.XPND.GD.ZS/countries?display=default; http://www.na tionmaster.com/country-info/profiles/Uzbekistan/Military#2010; accessed 12 October 2015.

for banding together. With more international involvement that includes membership in international organisations, the Central Asian leaders hope that their new states will gain more 'international attention and recognition' (Chung, 2006: 9). Indeed, before the United States war in Afghanistan in 2001, regional government leaders feared that their countries would be marginalised, as the region as a whole had almost been forgotten.

Actors with structural leadership are usually 'experts in translating the possession of material resources into bargaining leverage' (Young, 1991: 288). Furthermore, structural leadership refers partly to the actor's timing in deploying its power and ability to promote cooperation in ways that are both carefully crafted and credible (Young, 1991: 290). However, China is a green hand in multilateral diplomacy, particularly when it comes to initiating and leading an international organisation. In addition, China is not the only and most powerful hegemon in the region, a fact that largely constrains its structural power. Of the two options usually available for a hegemon in international negotiations, China takes the persuasion approach rather than the coercion approach. The coercion approach is unfeasible given the power of the United States and Russian. China can persuade the Central Asian states into multi-lateral cooperation only by offering side payments (also known as 'arm twisting' and 'bribery'). Because China has more to gain than others from the successful creation and operation of the SCO, it has both strong motivations and a noticeable ability to provide more immediate benefits to the Central Asian states. Due to its economic strength over the other five SCO member states, China has granted substantial direct assistance to the Central Asian states and major SCO projects. To exercise its structural leadership, China lends its support to the Central Asian states when deemed necessary.

Practice of entrepreneurial capability

Apart from structural power, diplomatic leadership is derived from an actor's ability to mobilise its partners to reach an agreement and take collective action. This is often achieved as a result of compromise. An actor with effective negotiating skills may serve as an agenda setter, a populariser, an inventor and a broker (Young, 1991: 294). Agenda setters shape the way issues are presented for consideration at the international level. Popularisers highlight the importance of the issues at stake. Inventors formulate innovative policy options to over-come bargaining impediments. Brokers strike deals and garner support for salient options. A state under entrepreneurial leadership should exhibit timely negotiating skills to seize the opportunity to put an issue on the agenda.

Traditionally, China was more awkward in exercising entrepreneurial leader-ship in international relations although it was active in developing relations with the third world countries in the Cold War time. It used to conduct bilateral diplomacy and often relied on donation of aid in order to buy friends in the developing world. In international organizations, it was more dogmatic, following the third world theory. Since the end of the 1970s, its foreign policy became more pragmatic. However, it lacks sufficient confidence and motivation to exercise entrepreneurial leadership and was more satisfied with the role of follower.

This began to change since the late 1990s when the Chinese leadership became more confident and aware of the importance of active leadership in international diplomacy. Increasingly, one may observe that China is playing the role of an agenda setter, a populariser, an inventor and a broker on different international occasions. In existing institutions and organisations, it tries to increase its influence, for example, in the UN and its affiliated units. In relations with the developing world, it initiated multilateral mechanisms such as the China ASEAN summit and China Africa summit. In newly created settings, China tries to influence agenda setting, for example, in the G20. China also plays some constructive role on issues of great security implications, for example, the six-party talks on the North Korean nuclear issue and the Iranian nuclear issue.

In an international organisation like the SCO, it is crucial for the hegemonic state to play these entrepreneurial roles when mobilising its partners to make deals. In a situation where two or more parties possess substantial yet not necessarily equal amounts of structural power, the prospects for success in institutional bargaining activate the ability of these parties to make use of bargaining leverage and foster agreement on the provision of mutually acceptable terms (Young, 1991: 290). China has played the role of inventor in the SCO process. Recognising its diversity and lack of knowledge in addition to those of other SCO members, China has initiated cultural cooperation among the SCO partners. In June 2001, China proposed that the cultural ministers of the SCO member states should engage in regular meetings. Chinese leaders such as then President Hu Jintao stressed the need for cooperation in the fields of education, culture, sports and tourism through the SCO framework. Then Premier Wen Jiabao called for promoting more enhanced cooperation in the cultural, educational, scientific, tourism and sports fields. China has tried to strengthen cultural exchanges through elements of the SCO framework such as cultural ministerial meetings and the SCO Secretariat. It set up the Chinese Cultural Centre in Kazakhstan and Uzbekistan and has organised cultural days and festivals and sponsored performances and exhibitions. It also introduced educational cooperation to the SCO framework. Since 2005, China has offered scholarships to college students in SCO member states (largely from Central Asia) to study at Chinese universities. However, cooperation in these areas has met with some difficulty. For example, activities are largely dominated by governments without much participation from the civil society. Central Asian states lack sufficient financial means to support cultural and educational exchanges. Cultural diversity and differences present other challenges for China to take the initiative to cooperate further in these areas.

China works hard as a broker to solve deadlocks in the SCO process. For example, it has stressed the role of trade development as an essential component of its Central Asian policy, in terms of both energy supplies and other goods

(Lanteigne, 2006/2007: 619). However, the Chinese initiative of achieving economic and trade cooperation through the SCO process did not receive much feedback from the SCO partners. Russia did not like the increase of Chinese economic influence in the region, believing that it undermined the traditional status and encouraged the Central Asian states to turn to China for help and decrease their reliance on Russia. However, the Central Asian states were afraid of the possible dumping of Chinese goods on their market if a closer cooperation agreement on trade and economic issues such as a free trade agreement were reached. Given the huge asymmetry between China and the Central Asian states, the latter were reluctant to accept China's call for economic cooperation. In fact, Kazakhstan proposed that the Central Asian states be economically self-reliant and establish closer regional economic cooperation among themselves. Young (1991: 293) suggests that a state with entrepreneurial leadership should have the ability to reap joint gains by coordinating their behaviour in a mutually agreeable fashion. The difficulty that China faces in expanding the SCO into the economic field indicates that it continues to lack sufficient abilities and resources. Without substantial progress in the multilateral SCO framework, China instead tries to promote trade and economic relations, particularly, energy cooperation on a bilateral basis.

A state actor that negotiates leadership relies on the skill of framing issues in ways that foster integrative bargaining and put deals together (Young, 1991: 293). China chose the energy sector as its starting point because it matched its concerns. China was in need of energy after its economic take-off, and Kazakhstan and Uzbekistan were both eager to find foreign markets for their oil and gas. The energy cooperation between China and the two member states seemed a promising area for the SCO. At a meeting on 23 September 2003, then Chinese Premier Wen Jiabao proposed the long-term establishment of an SCO-wide free trade area designed to improve the flow of goods in the region by easing trade restrictions such as tariffs. China also heavily emphasised energy projects, including the exploration of new hydrocarbon reserves, joint use of hydropower resources and the development of water works (Cohen, 2006: 53). The two smallest members, Kyrgyzstan and Tajikistan, were poor states that generally lacked important energy resources such as oil and gas. Although they had potential hydropower energy, they were unable to develop it due to a lack of capital and technology. China offered to lend a hand if the countries could reach economic and trade agreements in these areas.

Practice of intellectual innovations

An actor with diplomatic leadership may also be productive in terms of 'intellectual capital' or 'generative systems of thought'. The perspectives of participants in a negotiation process may be shaped or at least strongly influenced by the 'intellectual capital' or 'systems of thought' produced (Young, 1991: 298). Ideas matter when they can engender persuasive power to participants in the processes of international negotiation and appeals to outsiders.

China is strikingly unique on aspects of its traditional civilisation, political system and developmental model. Particularly, China is a civilisational state of mighty size and tradition, different from the currently dominant Western civilisation. This puts China in a more difficult position to extract intellectual resources and sell them to the international audience. In the SCO process, China spares no effort in generating and promoting ideas and concepts. China has indeed played the leading role in 'formulating the theoretical guidelines' of the SCO (Pan, 2008/2009: 59). In the SCO process, China has been intellectually innovative in creating and promoting a number of concepts, such as 'the Shanghai Spirit', 'New Outlook on Security', and 'Harmonious World'. The three institutional norms derive respectively from three major sources: modified from existing international norms, inspired by scholarly work, and adapted from domestic norms. The primary or original purpose of China's efforts in norm promotion was mainly to encourage solidarity among SCO members through the provision of institutional guidelines and values.

According to Pan's (2008/2009: 59) summary of China's contributions to the SCO, China formulates theoretical guidelines, collectively known as the 'Shanghai Spirit', that include 'mutual trust, mutual benefit, equality, consultation, respect to different civilizations and common prosperity'. At the SCO Shanghai summit in June 2006, then Chinese President Hu Jintao proposed that the region should be built into a perpetually peaceful and co-prosperous area. To that end, China applies the concepts of new security and regional cooperation to Central Asia based on the 'Shanghai Spirit' (Zhao, 2007a: 20). It is clear that China acts as an intellectual leader by providing new concepts that serve as guiding principles for the new regional organisation. It has a greater ability in this area than its SCO partners, and promotes norms in the process of building international institutions.

It is obvious that the 'Shanghai Spirit' philosophy espoused by China is akin to the traditional principles of mutual respect between different sovereignty states. In fact, the 'Shanghai Spirit' reminds one of the age-old 'Five Principles of Peaceful Co-existence' of which China was an initiator in the early 1950s.[5] However, China has shown an ability to frame old principles in innovative ways. Although it is considered 'old wine in a new bottle', the concept of the 'Shanghai Spirit' is generally well applied to its purpose, at least from a rhetorical standpoint, and SCO partners share the underlying philosophy. Furthermore, there is consensus among the leadership of the member states that 'the Shanghai Spirit sets out a map of cooperation based on a set of ideas and principles of how relations should be conducted within and outside the SCO' (Aris, 2009: 479). In particular, the 'Shanghai Spirit' stresses the principle of non-interference in the internal affairs of SCO partners and thereby reassures the leaderships of the smaller Central Asian member states that their SCO membership not only protects but also strengthens their authority. Furthermore, with the stronger powers of China and Russia as their partners, they are better able to withstand external and internal pressures and threats that challenge their rules.

Nevertheless, the West has interpreted the Chinese promotion of various concepts such as the 'Shanghai Spirit' as a joint deliberate effort of SCO members to promote authoritarian norms and therefore impede the democratisation process (Ambrosio, 2008). Authoritarian regimes established and consolidated the SCO to protect their own governments from regime change through consultation and coordination. The SCO members and China in particular make instrumental use of the SCO to promote norms that cannot be refuted easily by Western countries. Policies that reflect support for regime changes in other countries may be perceived as illegitimate because they violate the principles of non-interference in state sovereignty. In this sense, China is a critical state in the process of authoritarian norm promotion. It serves as the engine for the SCO's regional organisation and helps shape its values and principles, including its most basic definitions of state sovereignty, non-interference, diversity and stability. This was largely confirmed by the joint responses to the 'Colour Revolution' in Kyrgyzstan and the Andijan Incident in Uzbekistan in 2005.

China also initiated and currently promotes the 'New Outlook on Security' or 'comprehensive security', an overall and multilevel concept that covers a variety of issues (Wang and Xu, 2003). The concept draws inspiration from the Copenhagen School's concept of sectoral security and includes military, political, economic, society and environmental aspects. In terms of categorisation, it includes traditional security, which covers state sovereignty, territorial integrity, military capabilities, arms and arms control. It also includes non-traditional security, which covers economic, ecological, social, informational and cultural security. In practice, comprehensive security may be achieved through political, military, economic and diplomatic means to protect international actors from domestic and external threats.

The 'New Outlook on Security' concept was first proposed by China at the ASEAN regional forum in March 1997, and incorporated into the official Chinese Communist Party's Guidelines on Foreign Policy in the 16th plenary session of the CCP on 8 November 2002. The SCO has adopted the 'New Outlook on Security' at the initiative of China. It emphasises the principles of 'mutual trust', 'mutual benefit', 'equality', and 'cooperativeness' on issues of national security.[6] Every state has equal rights and status in achieving national security and no state should maintain national security at the cost of any other state by implementing unilateralism. States should cooperate with each other to better protect their respective national security. Sources of threat to security do not come from power and capability gaps, but from those policies formulated and implemented by hegemony, power politics, and expansionism.[7] With this concept, China tried to convince Central Asian states and Russia that national security in the contemporary world of US unilateralism can only be achieved through cooperation with each other, based on mutual trust and mutual benefit. It is also very important that such cooperation does not ostensibly target any third party. By promoting this concept, China seeks to legitimise its attempts at forging multi-issue cooperation against the 'three evils' through the SCO process. Its instrumental use of intellectual innovation helps to link the issues together.

The concept of a 'harmonious society' was initially established for domestic purposes as the Chinese government tried to end social conflicts during an era of social upheaval and transformation. However, the concept was quickly applied to foreign policy. It was first proposed by President Hu at the Asia-Africa summit in Jakarta, Indonesia, in April 2005. During Hu's state visit to Russia in July that year, the concept was written into the Sino-Russian Joint Declaration on 21st Century International Order. Hu further detailed the concept at the UN summit in September 2005. The Chinese government promoted the concept of a 'harmonious world' (*hexie shijie*) at the SCO when President Hu Jingtao first cited it as a regional approach at the SCO summit in 2006. The SCO again became a testing ground for promoting the norm of a 'harmonious world'. At the 2007 SCO summit in Bishkek, SCO leaders signed the 'Shanghai Cooperation Organisation Treaty on Long-term Good Neighbourly, Friendship and Cooperation'. Pan (2007: 3) remarks that the speed with which the treaty was prepared reflected the high degree of consensus shared by the signatory states.

China's intellectual leadership continues as it has advocated the concept of 'destiny community', surpassing that of 'interest community'. This concept was first proposed in the white paper on China's peaceful development, published by the Press Office of the State Council in 2011. It posits that a state should take into consideration concerns of other states while it is pursuing interests of its own and eventually work for mutual development. This call is based on the notion that there is only one world where all nations are bound together for the ultimate common destiny. This concept of destiny community has been promoted by China to the SCO context and beyond (Xu, 2014: 127–128).

Although China is unsure of the extent to which SCO partners share the idea, it actively projects intellectual ideas into the process as long as the ideas are not detrimental to the interests of the individual member states. The role of intellectual leadership helps maintain the regional organisation with some 'sustainable nutrients'.

Conclusion: international leadership in making

The Chinese role in the establishment and development of the Shanghai Cooperation Organisation marks a beginning of a new phase of Chinese diplomacy and foreign strategy. 'The SCO process, with its successful practice and evolution, symbolizes the transformation of Chinese diplomacy from its traditional focus on bilateral relations, towards the growing embrace of multilateral interactions' (Pan, 2008/2009: 59). More importantly, a paradigmatic shift is taking shape with the SCO process. Instead of sticking to traditional bilateral diplomacy, China has begun to be more used to multilateralism. It is shifting from its long-time passive response to international situations to active participation in international affairs. Not only to be more involved in existing institutions, it has also begun to initiate and lead construction of international organisation and cooperation framework.

China's Central Asian policy in general and its involvement in the SCO process are formulated in accordance with its overall foreign policy planning and strategic orientation. It is in conformity with general concepts of peaceful development and harmonious world (Zhao, 2007a: 19). The adjustment of Chinese foreign policy strategy towards more active participation in multi-lateralism reflects the relative distribution of power in China's favour. To better benefit from globalisation, in particular, in the economic field, China has to redefine its international position and global role. A more active approach should be more helpful to this end. Since the later 1990s, China has claimed to be a 'responsible great power' on the world stage. This suggests that China would be willing to cooperate with existing international norms and institutions, participate in international cooperation and maintain world and regional stability. Its policy towards the SCO and the Central Asia region is a concrete attempt made by China to act as a 'responsible great power' and even as a leader of regional cooperation framework.

It is usually the case that international negotiations take place 'under a veil of uncertainty'. Therefore, none of the stakeholders will be sure about attainment of benefits from various alternative options regarding the proposed institutional building and its further development (Young, 1991: 288). In the SCO process, the Chinese experience holds true of the proposition. Because of uncertainty, China takes an approach of 'crossing the river by feeling for the stones' (*Mo Zhe Shitou Guohe*) (Jia, 2007: 118). Since the inception of the SCO, China has tried to stress different functional aspects of the organisation. At the outset, Chinese officials appreciated the SCO as a forum for joint action against transnational terrorism. With the U.S. military presence after the Afghanistan War in 2001, China attempts at countervailing, if not ousting, the U.S. influence. When the issue of energy supply became demanding, it has given full attention to the SCO as a stepping stone for oil and gas in the region. It seems that China does not have a 'grand strategy' in the process, but evolves with changing circumstances over time (Zhao, 2007b: 137). However, adaptation itself is a feasible and often effective strategy when policymakers and strategists act in situation of uncertainty. Therefore, the Chinese trial approach is practical towards a more mature leadership in multilateral diplomacy, though it sometimes seems awkward.

Notes

1 The main ideas of this chapter are expressed in the author's previous publications on the topic, including Song (2011) and Song (2014).
2 *Renmin Ribao* [People's Daily], 11 December 2006.
3 For example, as a political strategy, Turkmenistan declared itself permanently neutral to ensure its independence and autonomy.
4 For more detailed information about Central Asian states' perception of China and the role of the SCO, refer to Dadabaev (2014).

5 The principles include equality, mutual benefit and mutual respect for territorial integrity and sovereignty in the regulations of international relations. For detailed information, please refer to http://www.fmprc.gov.cn/eng/ziliao/3602/3604/t18053. htm, accessed 2 March 2014.
6 Zongguo Guanyu Xin Anquanguan de Zhengze Wenjian (China's Position Paper on New Outlook on Security), Chinese Ministry of Foreign Affairs, 31 July 2002, http://www.mfa.gov.cn/chn//pds/ziliao/tytj/t4549.htm, accessed 20 July 2010.
7 'Wei Jianli Gongzhen Heli de Guoji Xinzhixu er Gongtong Nuli (Striving for a Just and Fair World Order)', *Renmin Ribao* [People's Daily], 24 April 1997.

References

Ambrosio, Thomas (2008) 'Catching the "Shanghai Spirit": How the Shanghai Cooperation Organization Promotes Authoritarian Norms in Central Asia', *Europe-Asia Studies*, 60(8), pp. 1321–1344.

Aris, Stephen (2009) 'The Shanghai Cooperation Organization: "Tackling the Three Evils"; A Regional Response to Non-traditional Security Challenges or an Anti-Western Bloc?' *Europe-Asia Studies*, 61(3): 457–482.

Breslin, Shaun (2009) 'Understanding China's Regional Rise: Interpretations, Identities, and Implications', *International Affairs*, 85(4), pp. 817–835.

Chung, Chien-peng (2004) 'The Shanghai Co-operation Organization: China's changing Influence in Central Asia', *The China Quarterly*, 180: 989–1009.

Chung, Chien-peng (2006) 'China and the Institutionalization of the Shanghai Cooperation Organization', *Problems of Post-Communism*, 53(5): 10.

Cohen, Ariel (2006) 'After the G-8 Summit: China and the Shanghai Cooperation Organization', *China and Eurasian Forum Quarterly*, 4(3): 53.

Dadabaev, Timur (2014) 'Shanghai Cooperation Organization (SCO) Regional Identity Formation from the Perspective of the Central Asia States', *Journal of Contemporary China*, 23(85): 102–118.

Gill, Bates (2001) 'Shanghai Five: An Attempt to Counter US Influence in Central Asia?' *Newsweek Korea*. http://www.brookings.edu/opinions/2001/0504china_gill.asp x (accessed 2 July 2011).

Hasenclever, Andreas, Peter Mayer and Volker Rittberger (1997) *Theories of International Regimes*. Cambridge: Cambridge University Press.

Jia, Qingguo (2007) 'The Shanghai Cooperation Organization: China's Experiment in Multilateral Leadership'. In Iwashita Akihiro (Ed.), *Eager Eyes Fixed on Eurasia: Russia and its Eastern Edge*, pp. 113–123. Sapporo: Slavic Research Center, Hokkaido University.

Karrar, Hasan H. (2009) *The New Silk Road Diplomacy: China's Central Asian Foreign Policy since the Cold War*. Vancouver, Canada: University of British Columbia Press.

Kavalski, Emilian (Ed.) (2009) *China and the Global Politics of Regionalization*. Surrey: Ashgate.

Kazantsev, Andrei (2008) 'Russian Policy in Central Asia and the Caspian Sea Region', *Europe-Asia Studies*, 60(6): 1080.

Kerr, David (2010) 'Central Asia and Russian Perspectives on China's Strategic Emergence', *International Affairs*, 86(1): 128–129.

Kerr, David and Laura C. Swinton (2008) 'China, Xinjiang, and the Transnational Security of Central Asia', *Critical Asian Studies*, 40(1): 113–142.

Lanteigne, Marc (2006/2007) 'In Medias Res: The Development of the Shanghai Co-operation Organization as a Security Community', *Pacific Affairs*, 79(4): 607.

Liang, Qiang (2006) 'Shanghe Zuzhi de Shuanghexin Kunao' [The Two Core Annoyances in the Shanghai Cooperation Organization], *Nanfeng Chuang (Window to the South)*, 12: 68–70.

Lo, Bobo (2008) *Axis of Convenience: Moscow, Beijing, and the New Geopolitics.* London: Chatham House.

Maksutov, Ruslan (2006) 'The Shanghai Cooperation Organization: A Central Asian Perspective', a SIPRI paper, p. 1.

Martin, Lisa (1992) 'Interests, Power, and Multilateralism', *International Organization*, 46(4): 766.

Ong, Russell (2005) 'China's Security Interests in Central Asia', *Central Asian Survey*, 24(4): 425–439.

Pan, Guang (2007) 'Bishkek: SCO's Success in the Hinterland of Eurasia', *China and Eurasian Forum Quarterly*, 5(4): 3.

Pan, Guang (2008/2009) 'A New Diplomatic Model: A Chinese Perspective on the Shanghai Cooperation Organization', *Washington Journal of Modern China*, 9(1): 55–72.

Sheives, Kevin (2006) 'China Turns West: Beijing's Contemporary Strategy towards Central Asia', *Pacific Affairs*, 79(2): 205–224.

Shlapentokh, Vladimir (2007) 'China in the Russian Mind Today: Ambivalence and Defeatism', *Europe-Asia Studies*, 59(1): 1–21.

Song, Weiqing (2011) 'Peaceful Rise from the Border: China's Practice of Diplomatic Leadership in Shanghai Cooperation Organization'. In Yufan Hao and Bill Kwokping Chou (Eds.), *China's Policies on its Borderlands and the International Implications*, Singapore: World Scientific, pp. 47–67.

Song, Weiqing (2014) 'Interests, Power, and Difficult Games of Shanghai Cooperation Organization', *Journal of Contemporary China*, 23(85): 85–101.

Sutter, Robert (2008) 'Durability in China's Strategy toward Central Asia – Reasons for Optimism', *China and Eurasian Forum Quarterly*, 6(1): 6.

Swanström, Niklas (2005) 'China and Central Asia: A New Great Game or Traditional Vassal Relations?' *Journal of Contemporary China*, 14(25): 569–584.

Wang, Jianwei (2005) 'China's Multilateral Diplomacy in the New Millennium'. In Yong Deng and Wang Fei-ling (Eds.), *China Rising: Power and Motivation in Chinese Foreign Policy*, pp. 159–200. New York: Rowman and Littlefield.

Wang, Xiaoyu and Tao Xu (2003) 'Lun Shanghai Hezuo Zuzhi Jincheng Zhong De ZongHe Anquan Linian' [The Concept of Comprehensive Security in the Process of Shanghai Cooperation Organization], *Eluosi Zhongya Dongou Yanjiu* [Russian, Central Asian and Eastern European Studies], 5: 52–57.

Xu, Wenhong (2014) 'Shanghai Hezuo Zuzhi yinggai Chengwei "Liyi Gongtongti" he "Mingyun Gongtongti"' ['Shanghai Cooperation Organization to become an interest community and a destiny community'], in Li Jingfeng, Wu Hongwei and Li Wei (Eds.), *Shanghai Hezuo Zuzhi Fazhan Baogao 2014* [2014 Annual Report on the Shanghai Cooperation Organization]. Beijing: Shehui Kexue Wenxian Chubanshe, pp. 127–144.

Yang, Shu (2009) 'Reassessing the SCO's Internal Difficulties: A Chinese Point of View', *China and Eurasia Forum Quarterly*, 7(3): 17–23.

Young, Oran R. (1991) 'Political Leadership and Regime Formation: On the Development of Institutions in International Society', *International Organization*, 45(3): 288.

Yuan, Jing-Dong (2010) 'China's Role in Establishing and Building the Shanghai Cooperation Organization (SCO)', *Journal of Contemporary China*, 19(67): 855–869.

Zhao, Huasheng (2007a) 'Zhongguo zhongya waijiao de lilun he shijian' [Theory and Practice of China's Foreign Policy toward Central Asia], *Guoji Wendi Yanjiu* [Studies of International Affairs], 3: 19–25, and 54.

Zhao, Huasheng (2007b), 'Central Asia in China's Diplomacy'. In Eugene Rumer, Dmitri Trenin and Huasheng Zhao, *Central Asia: Views from Washington, Moscow, and Beijing.* Armonk, NY and London: M.E. Sharpe.

3   Institutionalisation of the SCO

This chapter traces the evolution of the SCO from its origin as a border settlement mechanism to the informal coordination process of the 'Shanghai Five' and eventually to its current formalised incarnation. It also discusses developments in the consolidation of the SCO's organisational structure and functional divisions. Therefore, this chapter focuses on the regional SCO's institutionalisation process.

The 'Shanghai Five' as prelude

Although the SCO was officially established in Shanghai on 16 July 2001 when leaders of China, Russia and four Central Asian states signed the Declaration on the Establishment of the Shanghai Cooperation Organisation, the genesis of this regional organisation can be traced back to its predecessor the 'Shanghai Five', a group comprising all of the SCO members except Uzbekistan. In fact, China, Russia, Kazakhstan, Kyrgyzstan and Tajikistan signed the Treaty on Deepening Military Trust in Border Regions in Shanghai as early as April 1996. This event marked the beginning of the formalisation of regional cooperation among most of the SCO partners.

The 'Shanghai Five' process and succeeding SCO were formed as a result of prolonged border negotiations between China and the former Soviet Republics of Russia, Kazakhstan, Kyrgyzstan and Tajikistan. To some extent, the most fundamental aim of the long process has always been to maintain the border stability of the member states. The Soviet–Chinese border, which consists of a 4,300-kilometer eastern section from the eastern edge of Mongolia to the Tumen River bordering North Korea and a 3,200-kilometer western section from the western edge of Mongolia to the Tajik–Afghanistan border junction, was delineated mainly by the Russian Empire and the Qing Dynasty in the late nineteenth century (Iwashita, 2004: 261). More recently, China and the Soviet Union had three bilateral meetings about border demarcation issues in 1964, 1969 and 1987, respectively. The first two bilateral meetings yielded no results. At the third meeting, the two sides reached an agreement on the principles of border settlement.[1] With the collapse of the Soviet Union, the third bilateral meeting about border demarcation issues was forced to end early.

Before the collapse, China had to solve its territorial disputes with one country. Afterwards, it found that it had to deal with Russia and three new emerging states of Kazakhstan, Kyrgyzstan and Tajikistan. Due to this change, China held bilateral meetings with each of the states to consider border demarcation, troop reductions and confidence building in the border areas. The development of the negotiations led the heads of state of China and four other states to meet in Shanghai on 26 April 1996. From then on, the annual heads-of-state summit developed into an important mechanism and eventually into the 'Shanghai Five'.[2] At the first summit in Shanghai, the five states signed the Agreement on Confidence Building in the Military Sphere in the Border Areas, which stressed the importance of military confidence building and border issues with relevant measures and called for multilateral security dialogue in the region. This summit was the concrete result of China's bilateral discussions with four former Soviet Union countries after five years of examining border demarcation and troop reductions. The second 'Shanghai Five' summit was held in Moscow on 24 April 1997, at which the Treaty on Reduction of Military Forces in Border Regions was signed. This agreement substantiated the first agreement reached at the Shanghai summit one year before and provided some concrete measures for mutual confidence in the border areas.

Encouraged by the progress of the first two summits, the leaders of the five states began to explore possibilities for cooperation in broader areas beyond border demarcation and confidence building. Hence, the 'Shanghai Five' members widely accepted the annual heads-of-state summit as an effective multilateral platform. The third 'Shanghai Five' summit was held in Almaty, Kazakhstan on 3 July 1998, with the heads of states focusing their attention on promoting peace and stability in Central Asia and possible future economic cooperation. The joint statement of the Almaty summit advised that apart from the current heads-of-state summit, the 'Shanghai Five' should convene regular meetings of the Council of Heads of Government (Prime Ministers), the Council of Foreign Ministers and the 'Shanghai Five' specialists, as such regular meetings would be important and essential to security and cooperation in the Central Asian region and beyond.[3] The joint statement observed that all of the 'Shanghai Five' members were interested in developing economic cooperation particularly in terms of oil and gas pipelines, railways, highways and other transportation infrastructures. Finally and most importantly, the summit witnessed a shift in the emphasis of the 'Shanghai Five' on non-traditional security issues related to 'extremism', 'separatism', drug trafficking and other organised crime (Clarke, 2010: 126).

In August 1999, the leaders of the five states attended the annual summit in Bishkek, Kyrgyzstan. Not long before the summit, the incursion of the Islamic Movement of Uzbekistan into the Batken region of Kyrgyzstan shocked the entire Central Asia region. In response, the summit continued to focus on combating international terrorism, drug and weapons trafficking, illegal immigration and other transnational crimes, and ethnic separatism and religious extremism. Few concrete measures were advanced at the meeting. The joint statement simply reiterated some of the principles advanced by previous meetings, such as the cooperation of the 'Shanghai Five' in not targeting any other third state.

Compared with previous 'Shanghai Five' summits, the 2000 Dushanbe summit was special because Uzbekistan, another Central Asian state that was not part of the 'Shanghai Five', was invited to take part. The 'Batken Incident' proved that the absence of Uzbekistan in the 'Shanghai Five' represented a missing link in countering common threats in the region. As such, Russia played a major role in convincing Uzbek President Islam Karimov to attend the S-5 meeting in the Tajik capital of Dushanbe between 4 and 5 July 2000 (Clarke, 2010: 127). At the meeting, the 'three evils' of ethnic separatism, international terrorism and religious extremism were considered for the first time as the most serious threats to regional security. The formulation of the 'three evils' effectively laid a solid foundation for furthering cooperation, which led to the final establishment of the SCO.

The 'Shanghai Five' was also used as a multilateral venue for its members' mutual support of issues related to their essential national interests. For example, the joint statement released at the Dushanbe summit fully supported China's stance on Taiwan and Russia's policy towards Chechnya and strongly opposed the United States' planned deployment of theatre missile defence in the Asia Pacific region. Furthermore, the foreign ministers of the 'Shanghai Five' member states met for the first time along with their Uzbekistan counterparts.[4] They agreed to hold meetings no less than once a year to address mutual concerns in the region and world at large. It was also agreed at the first foreign ministers' meeting that a council of national coordinators composed of senior member state diplomats should be established as the operating organ in the 'Shanghai Five' framework.

In short, from 1996 to 2000, the 'Shanghai Five' paved the way for the success of the formalised SCO in a number of ways. Most importantly, the 'Shanghai Five' regularised the valuable mechanism of the heads-of-state summit, which brings together top leaders of China, Russia and most of the newly independent Central Asian states into a multilateral setting. Although bilateral discussions were more frequent and effective during the period, the nascent multilateral forum of the 'Shanghai Five' provided a unique opportunity for participating states to solve problems and achieve international visibility. During this period, China and Russia showed their dominant roles in initiating plans and mobilising resources for some premature rhetoric ambitions. Well-defined common concepts and actions currently remain largely absent from the SCO. For example, although the member states have articulated objections to neo-interventionism and power politics in international relations, they have failed to put them into practice. This suggests that intellectual and entrepreneurial leadership can only be exercised when a structural leadership investment has been sufficiently determined. Nevertheless, the 'Shanghai Five' took a crucial step towards greater formalisation and international visibility to ensure regional cooperation in Central Asia (Lanteigne, 2006: 609). After officially welcoming

Uzbekistan into the fold, the leaders of the six states met again in Shanghai in 2001 to sign the Declaration for the Establishment of the Shanghai Cooperation Organisation, which culminated in the formation of a new regional intergovernmental organisation in the Eurasian hinterland.

Creation of the SCO

The 'Shanghai Five' seemed to transition naturally into the SCO, as the original regional cooperation mechanism evolved from a coordination forum into a formal regional organisation. This shift was triggered by several factors, including the national interests and power relations of the partners and their relations and interactions within the wider context. However, the most immediate inspiration came from the Uzbek government's request to officially become involved in the 'Shanghai Five'. Unlike the other Central Asian states, Uzbekistan shared no common border with China and therefore had no practical basis for joining the 'Shanghai Five'. Nevertheless, the Uzbek government became increasingly interested in joining, probably due to the group's growing international visibility and effectiveness in handling regional security matters. Uzbekistani President Islam Karimov attended the Dushanbe summit in 2000 as an observer. In January 2000, the Uzbek leadership officially expressed its wish to join the group to the Chinese government, which was serving as its rotating president at the time. Some of the Central Asian states were concerned about the prudency of accepting a new member, as Uzbekistan had not participated in the previous agreements reached in 1996 and 1997. Supported by Russia, the Chinese government made great efforts to persuade other members of the importance of including Uzbekistan in the regional cooperation (Pan and Hu, 2006: 54). On 28 April 2001, the foreign ministers of the five member states held the second foreign ministers' meeting of the 'Shanghai Five' in Moscow. Due to the divergence of opinion on the Uzbek membership issue, no Uzbekistani officials were invited to attend as observers. After the joint efforts made by China and Russia, no other member state insisted on objecting to the membership of Uzbekistan. On 11 May 2001, President Karimov announced that Uzbekistan was ready to join the 'Shanghai Five' (Minzu, 2002: 158). On 10 and 11 June 2001, the national coordinators of the 'Shanghai Five' convened its meeting in Beijing, and the vice foreign minister of Uzbekistan participated as a formal member for the first time. This meeting finalised preparations for upgrading the informal border settlement mechanism to a formal regional organisation.

The matter of Uzbekistan's membership shows that the 'Shanghai Five' involved both convergences and divergences of national interest. Such was also the case in creating the SCO. For example, Chinese analysts implicitly suggest that Russia initially preferred to create the new organisation as a formal alliance, believing that it could be considerably undermined otherwise. In response, China insisted that it would benefit all of the partners in the organisation to follow the principles of non-alliance and non-confrontation and to avoid targeting any third country (Minzu, 2002: 156) Although China shared in the perceived threats Russia received from the West and particularly the United States, it avoided a confrontational approach in its first attempt at a regional cooperation initiative.

At the inaugural SCO summit on 14 June 2001 in Shanghai, China, the other 'Shanghai Five' members and Uzbekistan declared the establishment of the formalised SCO. Two important documents were adopted by the heads of state at the summit: the Declaration of the Establishment of the Shanghai Cooperation Organisation and the Shanghai Covenant on the Suppression of Terrorism, Separatism and Religious Extremism. In addition to announcing the establishment of the SCO, the Declaration defined the basic principles of the organisation. According to the Declaration, 'Shanghai Five' mechanisms such as the annual heads-of-state summit and other similar important mechanisms are reserved for the SCO. In particular, the Declaration stresses that the SCO embodies values known collectively as the 'Shanghai Spirit', which includes mutual trust, mutual benefit, equality, consultation, respect for diverse civilisations and the goal of common development. The 'Shanghai Spirit' provides a basis for the principles involved in managing relations between the six member states of the SCO. The 'Shanghai Covenant' document exhibited the SCO members' determination to crack down on the 'three evils'. In fact, the newly established organisation identified the rampant organised crime and terrorism in the region as the biggest threats and major targets. To promote cooperation and the development of the SCO, the two documents provide a legal basis for the establishment of new agencies, including the Council of National Coordinators and the SCO RATS.[5] For example, Article 10 of the 'Shanghai Covenant' stresses that 'the Parties will conclude a separate agreement and will adopt other necessary documents in order to establish and provide for functioning of a Parties' Regional Anti-Terrorist Structure with the headquarter in Bishkek, Kyrgyzstan, the purpose of which would be to effectively combat the acts referred to in Article 1 (1) of the Convention'.

The establishment of the SCO marked the beginning of a strategic readjustment of Chinese foreign policy and diplomacy. It demonstrated that China had shifted from passively joining international institutions and organisations to proactively initiating and leading new regional cooperation frameworks and from sticking to traditional bilateral diplomacy to accepting new multilateral diplomacy (Jiang, 2003: 46). China doubtlessly played an active and essential role in the formation of the SCO. Its leadership role is reflected on the political, economic and intellectual fronts (Zhao, 2008: 410–411). From a political perspective, China has always been determined to promote the development of the SCO. From an economic perspective, China has made essential contributions to the organisation via both its budget contributions and its economic support for various implementation programmes and projects. China also contributes intellectual resources by initiating many of the ideas, principles and norms, most vividly exemplified by the 'Shanghai Spirit'.

The SCO's formalisation process

Thus far, the SCO has witnessed three major stages in its formalisation process: the establishment of a basic institutional framework in the first period from 2001 to 2006; the furthering of institutional arrangements in the second period from 2007 to 2011; and the exploration of new areas for institutional improvement in the third period from 2012 to the present.

The first stage

Although the first SCO summit in 2001 produced two important documents, the newly created regional organisation had yet to establish its founding constitutional charter, a quite unusual situation in international diplomacy. The SCO members might not have been well experienced in creating an intergovernmental organisation. The task of approving an SCO charter was fulfilled at the second summit in St. Petersburg, Russia on 7 June 2002 with the adoption of the Charter of the Shanghai Cooperation Organisation. The Charter legalises the principles and mechanisms developed since the 'Shanghai Five' and provides a legal framework for further institutional development. In this way, the Charter defines the SCO as a composition of seven main organs: the Council of Heads of State, the Council of Heads of Government, the Council of Ministers of Foreign Affairs, Meetings of Heads of Ministries and/or Agencies, the Council of National Coordinators, the Regional Anti-Terrorist Structure (RATS)/Regional Counter-Terrorist Structure (RCTS) and the SCO Secretariat, the final two of which are permanent organs of the SCO. The decision to establish the permanent agencies of the SCO Secretariat and the RATS was essential to the SCO as a well-functioning international organisation. Without it, the SCO's identity as a real organisation would have fallen into question (Xu, 2003: 8). Article 14 of the Charter, 'Relationship with Other States and International Organisations', stipulates the SCO's willingness to provide the status of dialogue partner or observer to other states or international organisations. However, there is no mention of the future acceptance of new members. The organisation's operational framework began to take shape after the Charter was adopted.

The third SCO summit held in Moscow, Russia on 29 May 2003 sought to put several institutional arrangements into practice. For instance, the Council of Heads of State approved legal documents for permanent SCO agencies including the Secretariat in Beijing and the RATS in Bishkek. It stressed the urgency of the matter and stated that the permanent SCO agencies should start by the end of 2003. Upon the recommendation of the Council of Ministers of Foreign Affairs, the Council of Heads of States appointed Zhang Deguang from China as the first secretary general of the SCO Secretariat. A senior Chinese diplomat, Zhang had previously served as vice foreign minister and the Chinese ambassador to Russia and Kazakhstan. On 15 January 2004, the position of SCO Secretariat was officially instituted in Beijing. On 17 June

2004, the RATS was founded in Tashkent, Uzbekistan, but not in Bishkek, Kyrgyzstan as originally decided. The change of seat for the RATS/(RCTS) was largely a result of a persuasion game played by China and Russia to induce Uzbekistan to cooperate further with the SCO. The developments in the first years of the SCO's history formed the basic institutional establishment of the organisation.

Article 14 of the SCO Charter states that the SCO is willing to provide the status of dialogue partner or observer to other countries or international organisations interested in establishing close relations with the SCO. As a concrete step, the Council of the Heads of State adopted the Regulations on Observer Status at the Shanghai Cooperation Organisation at the 2004 heads-of-state summit held in Tashkent on 15 January 2004. The regulations detail the basic procedures of the application and entitlement of the rights and obligations as an observer within the SCO. The first observer status was given to Mongolia in 2004. Iran, Pakistan and India joined the rank the following year. This development showed that despite its short history, the SCO was beginning to expand its influence to its neighbouring areas.

The SCO started as a regional organisation specialising in addressing non-traditional security issues in Central Asia. Soon after its creation, the SCO began to initiate regional cooperation in the economic sphere. In 2003, the Council of the Heads of Government, which was composed of the prime ministers of the member states, passed the SCO Programme of Multilateral Trade and Economic Cooperation and approved the programme's action plan the following year. Implementing the programme became the main focus of economic cooperation in the SCO, and two important non-governmental organisations (NGOs) were subsequently created. At the Tashkent summit in 2004, the heads of state advised that the SCO should establish a development fund and a business council. The SCO Secretariat undertook these jobs and prepared the relevant documents to implement the proposal. At the Astana summit in 2005, the SCO member states agreed to strengthen the level of cooperation between banks by providing financial support for the implementation of regional cooperation projects. As a result, the Interbank Consortium, rather than the originally proposed development fund, was established on 26 October 2005 when the Council of Heads of Government officially announced its creation. The main goal of creating the Interbank Consortium under the SCO framework was to establish a funding and banking service mechanism for investment projects with the support of the governments of the SCO member states. The Business Council of the SCO was founded on 4 June 2006 in Shanghai. The goal of the Business Council is to promote economic cooperation in the region by providing a platform for business and financial circles from the respective SCO member states to build business links and dialogues. The Business Council also defines social aspects as an equally important area of future cooperation in the SCO. The civil societies in all of the SCO member states are either underdeveloped or heavily regulated. Business groups are among the few active parts within the domestic societies. Despite their substantial governmental backgrounds, both the Interbank Consortium and Business Council are officially non-governmental bodies under the SCO framework.

The first few years of the SCO witnessed the most rapid development of the newly born regional organisation and most particularly its important accomplishment of building an institutional arrangement that would facilitate multifaceted and multilevel cooperation between the member states. The SCO built a basic institutional structure that would help to run and support its basic operations (Zhao, 2008: 110). The framework was built in less than five years, covering a list of multilevel summits, agreements, joint statements, permanent executive bodies and two subsidiary NGOs. In addition, to avoid limiting itself to Central Asia and traditional political fields, the SCO began to expand its influences to its surrounding areas such as South and West Asia and extend its cooperation to other areas such as transportation, energy and environmental protection.

The second stage

After setting up the basic institutional infrastructure in the first five years, the SCO entered a more stable stage and became ready for further development. At the Bishkek summit held on 16 August 2007, the Council of Heads of State adopted the Treaty on Long-Term Good-Neighbourliness, Friendship and Cooperation between the Member States of the Shanghai Cooperation Organisation. According to the Treaty, the member states of the SCO were 'convinced that strengthening and deepening relations of good-neighbourliness, friendship and cooperation between the Member States of the Organisation corresponds to the fundamental interests of their peoples and contributes to peace and development in the SCO space and in the whole world'. Together with the SCO Charter, the Treaty stressed that the principles upheld by SCO members fundamentally underpinned the organisation. More importantly, it elaborated the organisation's values and norms, known collectively as the 'Shanghai Spirit'.

At the Dushanbe summit held on 28 August 2008, the Council of Heads of State adopted the Regulations on the Status of Dialogue Partner of the Shanghai Cooperation Organisation. This document along with the Regulations on the Status of Observer State of the SCO formed important keystones of the SCO's external communication and relations mechanisms. The Council also signed the Agreement on the Order of Organisation and Staging of Joint Anti-Terrorism Exercises by the Member States of the Shanghai Cooperation Organisation and the Agreement on Cooperation among the Governments of the Member States of the Shanghai Cooperation Organisation on Combating Illegal Circulation of Weapons, Ammunition and Explosives at the summit. These two important documents provided legal status to the member states that engaged in security cooperation by incorporating current practices such as joint military exercises.

In 2009, facing the global financial crisis, the SCO members announced the SCO Joint Initiative on Increasing Multilateral Economic Cooperation in the Fields of Tackling the Consequences of the Global Financial Economic Crisis when the leaders of the SCO member states issued the Yekaterinburg Declaration during the SCO summit. This joint initiative stressed the importance of increasing multilateral trade and economic cooperation and realising the Action Plan on Implementation of the SCO's Programme of Multilateral Trade and Economic Cooperation.

At the Tashkent summit held on 11 June 2010, the heads of state of the SCO adopted two documents, including the Rules of Procedure of the SCO and Statute on the Order Admission of New Members to the SCO. These two documents are very important to the SCO's administrative operations. The former stipulates the legal basis for the rules and procedures of various SCO bodies. The latter makes it possible for the SCO to consider accepting new members in the future. At a Council of Heads of Government meeting in 2010, then Chinese Premier Wen Jiabao called for serious consideration of the establishment of an SCO development bank in a joint effort to support infrastructure construction in the member states and particularly the Central Asian states, which were badly short on investments in their poor transportation and communication infrastructure (Chen, 2011: 108).

The SCO celebrated its 10th anniversary in 2011. The Council of Heads of State offered high remarks about the organisation's performance over the past 10 years. The Astana Declaration (2011) of the 10th Anniversary of the Shanghai Cooperation Organisation noted the following: '[I]n the course of 10 years the Shanghai Cooperation Organisation has successfully established and institutionalised effective mechanisms of interaction in various fields'. In the second stage of SCO formalisation, the member states further improved the institutional arrangement and more importantly began to implement activities under the SCO institutional framework. The effectiveness of the SCO implementation was generally mixed: although security cooperation was strengthened, economic and cultural cooperation required further improvement.

The third stage

After its first decade of development, the SCO entered another stage of institutional development. In the current stage, SCO members face the challenge of exploring new areas for further development. In 2012, the Council of Heads of State approved the Strategic Plan for the Medium-term Development of the SCO. The strategic plan stressed that the priority of the SCO in the near future should be maintaining security in Central Asia and that the SCO had no intention to become a military–political alliance. Meanwhile, the Council agreed to designate Afghanistan an SCO observer state and the Republic of Turkey a dialogue partner. The SCO currently has five observer states and three dialogue partners.[6]

The 2013 SCO summit was held in Bishkek and marked the first attendance of China's new top leader President Xi Jinping. Before attending the summit, President Xi proposed the 'Silk Road Economic Belt' in a speech delivered at Nazarbayev University in Astana during his visit to Kazakhstan. The SCO leaders at the summit welcomed the proposal. In fact, the Central Asian states were interested in the Chinese initiative, as they hoped it would offer an opportunity to receive Chinese investment and hasten infrastructure improvements (Chen, 2014: 25–26). China again proposed establishing an SCO development bank at the summit. Although ardently advocated by China and welcomed by the Central Asian states, the proposal met with an ambivalent attitude from Russia due to its concern about the increasing Chinese influence in its strategic backyard.[7] The SCO leaders approved the implementation plan of the Treaty on Long-Term Good-Neighbourliness, Friendship and Cooperation between the Member States of the SCO at the summit.

At the most recent SCO summit held in Dushanbe, Tajikistan on 11 and 12 September 2014, the SCO leaders signed a number of agreements related to the organisation's institutional development. The Decision of the Council of Heads of SCO Member States on a Standard Memorandum on the Obligations of Countries Applying to Join the SCO and the Decision of the Council of Heads of SCO Member States on Approving Procedures for Accession to the SCO received the most international attention and signified that the member states had reached a consensus on accepting new members in the coming years. It was widely believed that India, Iran, Mongolia and Pakistan would soon be admitted as full members of the SCO. The defence ministers of the SCO member states held a meeting in Sughd, Tajikistan on 1 April 2014. The national ministers exchanged their views related to issues such as enhancing regional peace, security and stability against the background of the withdrawal of American and Western forces from Afghanistan. Within this context, China initiated a proposal to establish an anti-terrorist centre as a joint military agency specialising in collective action against possible trans-boundary terrorist attacks. Russia supported the initiative.[8] Furthermore, the leaders approved the Decision of the Council of Heads of SCO Member States on the Draft SCO Development Strategy through to 2025, a decision that began formulating the organisation's roadmap for the next decade.

Organisation of the SCO

The SCO framework can generally be divided into meeting mechanisms and permanent institutions. The former includes different levels of SCO meeting, including meetings of the Council of Heads of State of the SCO and the Council of Heads of Government (Prime Ministers). The latter includes institutions with different functions, including the SCO Secretariat in Beijing and the regional Anti/Counter-terrorism Structure of the SCO in Tashkent. Based on their different levels and scopes, these different mechanisms constitute an institutional framework that ensures the SCO's operations. The Council of

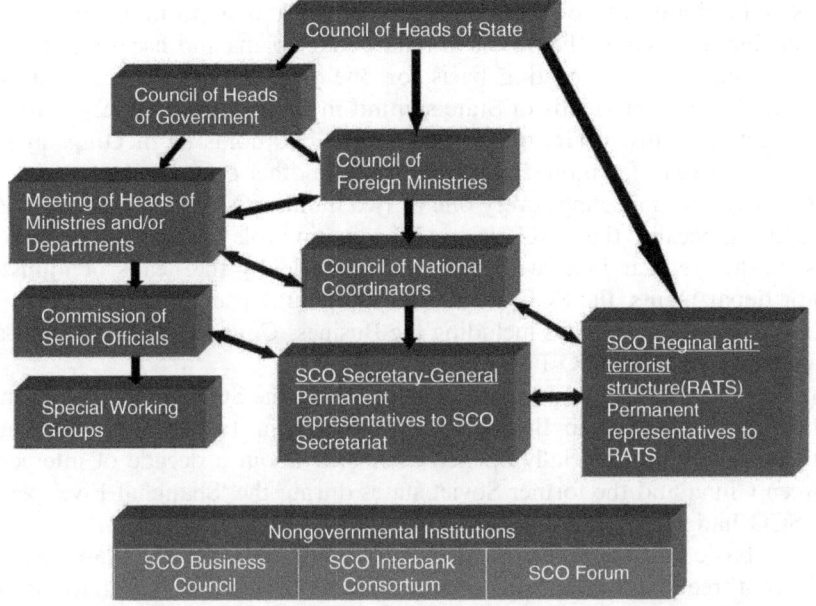

Figure 3.1 Organisational Structure of the SCO

Heads of State is the organisation's highest decision-making body. It convenes once a year to make major decisions and offer instructions for all of the important issues related to SCO activities. The Council of Heads of Government meets once a year to discuss multilateral cooperation strategies, prioritise directions, solve important and pressing issues related to economic cooperation and other areas, and adopt the SCO's annual budget. In a nutshell, the Council of Heads of State is responsible for addressing the SCO's strategies and overall issues while the Council of Heads of Government is the organisation's highest executive body.

In addition to the Councils of Heads of State/Government sessions, meetings are held by speakers of Parliament; secretaries of Security Councils; foreign ministers; ministers of defence, emergency relief, economy, transportation, culture, education, healthcare; heads of law enforcement agencies; Supreme Courts; Courts of Arbitration and prosecutors general. The Council of Ministers of Foreign Affairs operates in direct service of the Council of Heads of State. According to Article 7 of the Charter, '[T]he Council of Ministers of Foreign Affairs shall consider issues related to day-to-day activities of the Organisation, preparation of meetings of the Council of Heads of State and holding of consultations on international problems within the Organisations'. Therefore, the Council of Ministers of Foreign Affairs generally holds meetings one month before the summit of the Council of Heads of State. Senior official commissions and special working groups are usually established in service to the minister meetings. The Council of National Coordinators (CNC) of the SCO member states is in charge of coordinating interactions and important management responsibilities such as the SCO's annual budget plans and fiscal reports. The CNC is chaired on a rotating basis for one year by the member state and hosts the Council of Heads of State summit in that year. To better coordinate and direct the daily affairs of the SCO, the CNC holds its meetings at least three times a year, far more frequently than the other councils. In practice, the CNC convenes its meetings every one or two months (Xing and Sun, 2007: 61). In addition, because the CNC plays a coordinating role in the SCO framework, it establishes regular links with the meetings held by the heads of ministries and/or departments, the SCO Regional Anti/Counter-terrorism Structure, the SCO Secretariat and NGOs including the Business Council, the SCO Interbank Consortium and the SCO Forum.

In the second group of permanent institutions, the SCO has two permanent bodies: the Secretariat in Beijing and the RCTS in Tashkent. Analysts note that the former was officially opened after only about a decade of interaction between China and the former Soviet states during the 'Shanghai Five' period. The SCO had planned to establish a secretariat since its formation in 2001 to perform basic and necessary administrative functions, yet the plan was only achieved three years later, after being delayed by difficult negotiations over matters such as budget allocation, staff and working procedures. The idea to establish the RCTS was conceived in 1998 under the 'Shanghai Five' and finally became a reality in June 2004 (Zhao, 2005: 10). The location of the Secretariat in Beijing indicated the determination and resource advantages China enjoyed over its SCO partners. However, even more dramatic was the change in location of the RCTS. It was originally decided at the inaugural SCO summit in Shanghai in June 2001 that the SCO's anti-terrorist agency would be established in Bishkek, the capital of Kyrgyzstan. However, this decision, which was written into the 'Shanghai Covenant' to crack down on terrorism, was changed when China and Russia found that it induced Uzbekistan to become further involved in the SCO cooperation. The relocation of the RCTS to Tashkent shows how power politics work in international relations. This politics of location is also reflected in decisions made in relation to the location of other SCO institutions and agencies. In the SCO framework, NGOs are important supplements for intergovernmental cooperation. Three NGOs have been created and incorporated into the SCO, including the Business Council, SCO Interbank Consortium and SCO Forum. Of these, the Business Council, which was officially established in Shanghai in 2006, is a more permanent institution with a secretariat set up in Moscow. The SCO member states have tried to strike a balance when determining the locations of their different agencies and institutions.

In terms of role and status, the Secretariat and RCTS are the two most important SCO institutions. The SCO secretary general and RCTS executive committee director are both appointed by the Council of Heads of State for a period of three years.[9] Similar to other international organisation secretariats, the Secretariat in Beijing is a standing administrative body of the SCO. It comprises three departments responsible for political and security affairs; economic, trade and cultural affairs; and press and legal affairs. Article 11 of the Charter defines the Secretariat as a body that 'shall provide organisational and technical support to the activities carried out in the framework of SCO and prepare proposals on the annual budget of the Organisation'. In theory, the Secretariat and RCTS are responsible to the SCO rather than any of its member states. However, the member states' budget contributions decide the national affiliations of the officials at the Secretariat. For example, Russia provides 24 per cent of the SCO's budget and is therefore allocated seven posts in the Secretariat (Oresman, 2004: 2).[10]

Security cooperation takes priority over other issues under the SCO framework, and combating terrorism, separatism and extremism is of uppermost priority in the security cooperation. The Council of Heads of State adopted the Shanghai Convention on Combating Terrorism, Separatism and Extremism at the first summit in 2001, one year before the adoption of the SCO Charter. Hence, the Regional Anti/Counter-terrorism Structure holds a privileged position in the SCO framework. According to Article 3 of the Agreement Between the Member States of the Shanghai Cooperation Organisation on the Regional Anti-Terrorist Structure, the 'Regional Anti-Terrorist Structure shall be a permanent body of the SCO and is intended to assist in the coordination and collaboration of the Parties' competent agencies in combating terrorism, separatism and extremism, as these activities are defined in the Convention'. The basic purpose of the Regional Anti/Counter-terrorism Structure is to combat terrorism and related transnational crimes, while the top priorities currently are encouraging the sharing of security-related information and promoting the harmonisation of anti-terrorism policies. The internal body of the RATS includes the Council of Regional Anti/Counter-terrorism Structure and the Executive Committee.

Functions of the SCO

Cooperation in the SCO framework covers a wide range of issues related to security, economics, energy, various functional areas, education and culture. It has also developed institutional arrangements for external relations and NGO interactions.

Regional security is at the top of the SCO's agenda. In fact, cooperation in the security field and particularly the struggle against international terrorism have comprised the main areas of SCO activity since its establishment (Lukin, 2007: 142). Hence, strengthening security cooperation is the priority when the member states develop the SCO's institutional dimension. The security cooperation framework is supported by several institutional mechanisms. A number of regular meeting arrangements are made. The Council of Heads of State is the highest decision-making body involved in security cooperation and largely provides the general principles and guidelines. The SCO has several other institutional mechanisms of security cooperation, including the member states' security council secretaries, ministers of defence, emergency relief, heads of law enforcement agencies and joint military exercises. The SCO's two permanent bodies, including the Secretariat in Beijing and the Regional Anti/Counter-terrorist Structure based in Tashkent, play decisive roles in coordinating and combating terrorism, separatism and extremism. As a special security mechanism, the SCO's joint anti-terrorism military exercises have become a matter of routine to improve the member states' anti-terrorism abilities. In 2007, the presence of heads of states at military manoeuvres for the first time in the SCO's history demonstrated the growing significance of the organisation's military component and signalled their determination to take command of the security situation in the region (de Haas, 2009: 18). In 2008, the member states signed the Agreement on the Order of Organisation and Staging of Joint Anti-Terrorism Exercises by the Member States of the Shanghai Cooperation Organisation. As a concrete step, the joint anti-terrorism military exercise known as the Peace Mission is held almost annually. The exercise has had an influence on the region and attracted international attention.

The SCO has gradually developed its cooperation in economic areas. As an institutional framework, the meetings of the ministers of economy and transportation are mainly responsible for establishing economically related cooperation between the member states. At the ministerial level, the SCO established the Commission of Senior Officials and seven special working groups that are charged with specific responsibilities to ensure regional economic cooperation. These seven special working groups address customs cooperation; quality inspection; electronic commerce; investment promotion; the development of transit potential; fuel and energy; and telecommunications, respectively. In addition to the governmental arrangements, two NGOs are closely related to regional economic cooperation. The Business Council was officially designed to be an NGO within the SCO. It provides a platform for enterprises from the SCO member states to establish links and dialogues. The Business Council has its own well-defined organisational structure consisting of the Annual Session and the permanent Secretariat of the SCO Business Council headquartered in Moscow. The Interbank Consortium provides financial support to cooperation programmes under the SCO framework. The permanent body of the Interbank Consortium is its council, which convenes meetings at least once a year. The Interbank Consortium primarily comprises the designated development or commercial banks of the SCO member states. Its members include the State Development Bank of China, the Development Bank of Kazakhstan, the Bank for Development and Foreign Economic Affairs of the Russian Federation (Vnesheconombank), the National Bank for Foreign Economic Activity of the Republic of Uzbekistan, the Settlement & Savings Company of the Kyrgyzstan Republic (RSB Bank) and the State Savings Bank of the Republic of Tajikistan (Amonatbonk).

The SCO also developed an institutional framework for furthering cultural and educational cooperation. The Intergovernmental Agreement on Cooperation in the Field of Culture, which was signed by the SCO member states at the Bishkek summit in 2007, outlines the scope, mechanism and effective paths of the SCO's cultural cooperation and the dispute settlement mechanism. Under the SCO framework, cultural cooperation between the SCO member states is mainly administered through the non-permanent mechanism of meetings held at different levels. As in all other areas, the Councils of Heads of State/Government are concerned about the overall arrangement and processes of cultural cooperation. The ministers of culture, senior officials and expert working groups are in charge of implementing specific and concrete cultural cooperation programmes. The formation of cooperation mechanisms to address the SCO's educational matters was derived from the signing of the Intergovernmental Education Cooperation Agreement of the SCO Member States in 2006. The educational cooperation mechanisms comprise two parts: governmental and non-governmental mechanisms. Governmental mechanisms usually include the meetings held by the SCO member states' ministers of education and the expert working groups. The non-governmental mechanism usually includes the regular Forum of University Rectors and the SCO member states' education weeks. The latest attempt at improving educational cooperation was the establishment of the University of Shanghai Cooperation Organisation, first proposed by Russian President Vladimir Putin at the Bishkek Summit in 2007. However, due to the differences in education among the SCO member states, the SCO University merely operates as a network of the universities located in the SCO member states, which are selected by the states' respective governments.

The SCO gradually developed external relations by consolidating its internal institutional build-up. Under the SCO framework, external communication is made up of three mechanisms: the observer and dialogue partner mechanisms and the SCO-Afghanistan Contact Group. Article 14 of the SCO Charter, 'Relationship with Other States and International Organisation', states that the 'SCO may interact and maintain dialogue with other States and International Organisations' and that the 'SCO may grant to the State or International Organisations concerned the status of a dialogue partner or observer'. The SCO member states signed the Regulations on Observer Status at the Shanghai Cooperation Organisation in 2004 and Regulations on the Status of Dialogue Partner of the Shanghai Cooperation Organisation in 2008, officially institutionalising the observer and dialogue mechanisms, respectively. By the end of 2013, the SCO had five observer states, Afghanistan, India, Iran, Mongolia and Pakistan, and three dialogue partners, Belarus, Turkey and Sri Lanka.

In addition to the two conventional mechanisms, a special mechanism was made between the SCO and Afghanistan: the SCO-Afghanistan Contact Group. In 2009, the two parties signed the Protocol on Establishment of the SCO-Afghanistan Contact Group between the SCO and the Islamic Republic of Afghanistan. The Contact Group was established to combat terrorism, illicit drug trafficking and organised crime more efficiently given Afghanistan's countless ties with Central Asia and the considerable effects on the security of the region. The SCO has also established several official links with other international organisations. For instance, it has established different levels of official relations with the United Nations (UN), the Commonwealth of Independent States (CIS), the Eurasian Economic Community, the UN Economic and Social Commission for Asia and the Pacific, and the ASEAN.

The SCO has established platforms for non-governmental interactions, *inter alia*, the Business Council, Interbank Consortium and SCO Forum. The Business Council and Interbank Consortium have already been discussed according to the framework of regional economic cooperation. The SCO Forum, which was established in Moscow on 22 May 2006, is a multilateral academic mechanism and non-governmental advisory body comprising experts from the SCO member states. Each member state of the SCO designates one authoritative research institution as its national representative to participate in the SCO Forum. These research institutions include the China Institute for International Studies, International Institute for Modern Policy (Republic of Kazakhstan), Institute for Strategic Analysis and Assessment under the President of the Kyrgyzstan Republic, Center for East Asian and SCO Studies at the Moscow State University for International Relations, Center for Strategic Studies under the President of the Republic of Tajikistan, and Institute for Strategic and Interregional Studies under the President of the Republic of Uzbekistan. The SCO Forum is headed by the annual SCO Forum Meeting. Presidency of the Forum is determined on a rotating basis. The head of the national centre of the SCO member state hosting the forum meeting serves as the chairman.

Conclusion: leadership in SCO institutionalisation

The informal process of the 'Shanghai Five', which originated as a border settlement mechanism, was replaced by the formal SCO in 2001. The most important political legacy of the 'Shanghai Five' was the regular meetings of heads of state, which developed into the top decision-making body of the Council of Heads of State under the SCO framework. On 15 June 2001, five years after the first heads of state meeting, the SCO was established based on the 'Shanghai Five'. The newly established SCO includes all of the 'Shanghai Five' countries and one new member, Uzbekistan. In this sense, the 'Shanghai Five' may be considered the forerunner that laid the necessary groundwork for the SCO. In fact, the move to upgrade the 'Shanghai Five' to the formalised SCO was inspired by Uzbekistan's request to join the 'Shanghai Five' as an official member. This request was made in conformity with other members and particularly China's ambition to establish a multilateral organisation in Central Asia. At the Shanghai summit, the six states signed the Establishment Declaration of the Shanghai Cooperation Organisation, marking its official formation. Furthermore, the Shanghai Convention on Combating Terrorism, Separatism and Extremism was signed as the organisation's first document. Important issues such as the SCO Charter and its permanent agencies were settled as the organisation evolved over the following years.

The SCO has been institutionalised in a gradual, piecemeal and step-by-step manner. This is in sharp contrast to the processes of most other international organisations, which are usually well defined from the beginning in terms of their structures and functions. This distinctiveness reflects the configuration of national interests and power relations among the SCO partners and their domestic situations, relations with outside parties and positions in the wider international context. In other words, the SCO's institutionalisation process from before its inception to the present day has been based on the paths taken by the member states as a result of their interests and power statuses.

It is widely acknowledged that China plays a pivotal organisational leadership role in the SCO's institutionalisation process. China is an initiator, a leader and a supporter of the new regional organisation in this long-forgotten hinterland of the Eurasian continent. As a great power, China enjoys a formidable geopolitical edge over the Central Asian states. With its tremendous structural power, China is the *de facto* backbone of the organisation. Given its massive economic advantage, China is able to exercise its entrepreneurial power and take the lead in planning and implementing various initiatives and programmes. Finally, China has demonstrated its intellectual power by setting the various principles and norms of the new SCO. This has involved a learning process for China's international leadership, particularly in terms of its exercise of entrepreneurial power. From the 'Shanghai Five' period into the current SCO incarnation, China has practised its negotiation skills to influence the results of mutually acceptable deals and how issues are presented. On several occasions, China has managed to coordinate SCO partners and strike a balanced deal. Such was the case with the Uzbekistan membership and relocation of the RCTS.

The SCO's institutionalisation is a result of the efforts of leading states and a convergence of national interests. However, the institutionalised structure can wrap the SCO member states 'in an ever-thickening web of regular engagement and multiplying issues' (Chung, 2006: 13). The SCO is a little less than two decades old, even when the 'Shanghai Five' period is taken into account. Over the past two decades, the organisation has gradually established an institutional structure and operated in various areas and at different levels. However, it has yet to demonstrate its effectiveness in regional cooperation.

Notes

1 http://news.sina.com.cn/c/2004-12-03/09294420814s.shtml, accessed 16 December 2014.
2 http://www.fmprc.gov.cn/mfa_chn/ziliao_611306/wjs_611318/2159_611322/t8984.shtml, accessed 3 November 2014.
3 http://www.mfa.gov.cn/chn//gxh/zlb/smgg/t11143.htm, accessed 3 November 2014.
4 http://www.fmprc.gov.cn/mfa_chn/ziliao_611306/zt_611380/ywzt_611452/2391_612234/2409_612250/t11355.shtml, accessed 3 November 2014.
5 The English translation was later changed to the Regional Counter-terrorism Structure (RCTS), probably due to the unfortunate association accompanying the original acronym.

6 The observer states include Afghanistan, India, Iran, Mongolia and Pakistan. The dialogue partners include Belarus, Sri Lanka and Turkey.
7 http://sputniknews.cn/china/20131023/43894142.html, accessed 15 February 2015.
8 'Eluosi Fangzhang Ceng Eluosi Zhichi Zhongguo Jianli Shanghe Zuzhi Fangkong Zhongxin de Zhuzhang (Russian Defense Minister says that Russia Supports China's Proposal on Establishing the SCO Anti-terrorist Centre)', http://mil.news. sina.com.cn/2014-04-03/1539772140.html, accessed 22 February 2015.
9 http://www.sectsco.org/EN123/brief.asp, accessed 3 November 2014.
10 According to their agreement, China and Russia each contribute 24 per cent of the SCO budget, Kazakhstan contributes 21 per cent, Uzbekistan 15 per cent, Kyrgyzstan 10 per cent and Tajikistan 6 per cent.

References

Chen, Yurong (2011) '2010nian Shanghai hezuo zuzhi chengyuanguo zhengfu shounao lishihui huiyi' [The 2011 meeting of the Council of Heads of Government of the SCO]', *Annual Report on the Shanghai Cooperation Organization (2011)*, pp. 105–111. Beijing: Social Sciences Academic Press.

Chen, Yurong (2014) '2013nian Shanghai hezuo zuzhi yuanshou lishihui huiyi' [The 2013 meeting of the Council of Heads of State of the SCO], *Annual Report on the Shanghai Cooperation Organization (2014)*, pp. 19–27. Beijing: Social Sciences Academic Press.

Chung, Chien-peng (2006) 'China and the Institutionalization of the Shanghai Cooperation Organization', *Problems of Post-Communism*, 53(5): 3–14.

Clarke, Michael (2010) 'China and the Shanghai Cooperation Organization: The Dynamics of "New Regionalism", "Vassalization", and Geopolitics in Central Asia'. In Emilian Kavalski (Ed.), *The New Central Asia*, pp. 117–147. Singapore: World Scientific Publishing.

De Haas, Marcel (2009) 'The Shanghai Cooperation Organization's Momentum Towards a Mature Security Alliance', *Scientia Militaria*, 36(1): 14–30.

Iwashita, Akihiro (2004) 'The Shanghai Cooperation Organization and its Implications for Eurasian Security: A New Dimension of "Partnership" after the Post-Cold War Period', *Slavic Eurasia's Integration in to the World Economy and Community*, pp. 259–281. Slavic Research Center, Hokkaido University.

Jiang, Yi (2003) 'Zhongguo de Duobian Waijiao yu Shanghai Hezuo Zuzhi' [China's multilateral diplomacy and Shanghai Cooperation], *Eluosi Zhongya Dongou Yanjiu* [Studies of Russia, Central Asia and Eastern Europe], 5: 46–51.

Lanteigne, Marc (2006/7) '"In Medias Res": The Development of the Shanghai Cooperation Organizations as a Security Community, *Pacific Affairs*, 79(4): 605–622.

Lukin, Alexander (2007) 'The Shanghai Cooperation Organization: What Next?' *Russia in Global Affairs*, 5(3): 140–156.

MinzuyuZongjiaoYanjiuZhongxin (Ethnic and Religious Studies Center, China Institute of Contemporary International Relations) (2002) *Shanghai Hezuo Zuzhi: Xin Anquanguan yu Xinjizhi* [Shanghai Cooperation Organization: New Type of Security View and New Mechanisms]. Beijing: Shishi (Current Affairs) Press.

Oresman, Matthew (2004) 'SCO Update: The Official Lunch of the Shanghai Cooperation Organization', *China and Eurasian Forum*, 2(1): 1–4.

Pan, Guang and Jian Hu (2006) *21 Shiji de Diyi ge Xinxing Quyu Hezuo Zuzhi: dui Shanghai Hezuo Zuzhi de Zonghe Yanjiu* [The First New Type Regional

Cooperation Organization: a Comprehensive Study of the Shanghai Cooperation Organization]. Beijing: Party School of Chinese Communist Party Press.

SCO Secretariat (2001a) *Declaration on the Establishment of the Shanghai Cooperation Organizations.*

SCO Secretariat (2001b) *The Shanghai Convention on Combating Terrorism, Separatism and Extremism.*

SCO Secretariat (2002) *Charter of the Shanghai Cooperation Organization.*

Xing, Guangchen and Zhuangshi Sun (2007) *Shanghai Hezuo Zuzhi Yanjiu*[Studies of Shanghai Cooperation Organization]. Changchu, China: Changchun Press.

Xu, Tao (2003) 'Lun Shanghai Hezuo Zuzhi de Jizhihua' [On Institutionalization of the SCO], *Xiandai Guoji Guanxi* [Contemporary International Relations], 6:. 7–13.

Zhao, Huasheng (2005) 'The SCO in the Last Year', *China and Eurasian Forum*, 3(2): 10–12.

Zhao, Huasheng (2006) 'The Shanghai Cooperation Organization at 5: Achievement and Challenges Ahead', *China and Eurasia Forum Quarterly*, 4(3): 105–123.

Zhao, Huasheng (2008) *Zhongguo de Zhongya Waijiao* [China's Central Asian Diplomacy]. Beijing: Shishi (Current Affairs) Press.

4 International politics of the SCO

This chapter addresses factors external to the SCO, including the foreign policy orientations of the SCO member states, international responses to the SCO and interactions between SCO members, particularly China and interested non-member states. Many analysts argue that the SCO is essentially an inward-looking organisation that concentrates on managing internal relations and developing cooperation between its member states. However, factors external to the SCO cannot be neglected. Since the organisation's inception, its implications have extended beyond Central Asia and it has increasingly developed links with other states and organisations alike. In this way, it has notably promoted its international visibility and participation. This chapter addresses the SCO's relations with not only the observer and dialogue states, including Afghanistan, India, Iran, Mongolia and Pakistan, but also countries with strong stakes and interests, particularly, the United States. It also considers the SCO's partici-pation in major international organisations such as the UN and contact with other international organisations such as the CIS and ASEAN.

International orientations of the SCO members

As both China and Russia are great powers with a global outreach and focus, Central Asia comprises only one part of their foreign policy priorities. China was traditionally an East Asian state whose foreign policy concerns extended to its near neighbourhood. It has substantial bilateral relations with its neigh-bouring countries in Northeast and Southeast Asia. It has also developed modest relations with developed countries in the West, largely for economic purposes, and third world countries in Africa and Latin America for moral support of its world politics, particularly during the Cold War. Only with its rise in recent years has China become much more ambitious in its efforts to reach out internationally. This is most exemplified by its 'go global' strategy along with both its business and political efforts.[1] As stated earlier, China's policy towards Central Asia has been developed and implemented against this backdrop over the past years. The recent 'One Belt, One Road' initiative confirms China's strategy of expanding its power and influence through its use of economic statecraft. Central Asia has become a core area in this grand strategy.

Although it inherited most of the Soviet legacies and remained a major global power, Russia has retreated considerably from the power status it held during the Cold War. Russian strategists make it a priority to retain the traditional sphere of influence belonging to the former Soviet space. As such, Russia considers Central Asia an area key to its old empire mentality and part of its strategic backyard, with the main objective of maintaining its influence in the region. Russia has many major policy considerations in Central Asia that involve strengthening its economic and strategic interests, coordinating with great powers and countering the roots of domestic problems such as organised crime and trans-boundary Islamic extremism (Kazantsev, 2008: 1073). To develop and consolidate their national interests in the region, China and Russia have a strong motivation to manage their relations with the Central Asian states in a multilateral setting through bilateral diplomacy.

As China and Russia are the two most powerful states in the SCO, Sino-Russian relations are doubtlessly important. The two countries must manage their relations with the other member states for the SCO to function properly and continue developing. Furthermore, they must deal with outside powers, particularly the United States. Driven by the calculation of state interests China and Russia have steadily developed their bilateral relations since the end of the Cold War. It is fortunate that the two countries share some 'striking similarities' in the ideological foundations that underpin their respective world outlooks and global roles (Kuchins, 2007: 325). Since the turn of the century, China and Russia have engaged in big-scale cooperation in many areas. The two countries have had close consultations and cooperated in multilateral forums such as the UN and the nascent BRICS forum. On 20 May 2014, they further promoted their strategic partnership to its highest status as a 'comprehensive strategic cooperative partnership'.[2] Both countries maintain certain levels of suspicion and distrust. However, motivated by their common perception of Western threats, Chinese and Russian policymakers are strongly interested in strengthening their bilateral cooperation.

By the time the Soviet Union officially collapsed on 25 December 1991, the Central Asian countries had already declared their formal independence, as the Soviet central government in Moscow had already lost its effective control.[3] On 2 March 1991, all five of the newly independent Central Asian states were accepted as new member states in the UN, marking their international recognition. For quite some time, these landlocked states located in the hinterland of the Eurasian continent were not well known to the outside world, and the international community paid them little attention. Meanwhile, the Central Asian countries struggled with many domestic problems that challenged the stability of their regimes. Among the major domestic issues, the Central Asian states had to develop foreign strategies and implement foreign policies. These were difficult tasks for the young states, as they created internal and external difficulties in their state-building processes.

The Central Asian states must make several major considerations while formulating their foreign policy strategies. These include ensuring state security and national defence, creating a favourable environment for their domestic stability and development, managing relations with neighbouring countries in the region, and participating in the international community (Pan and Hu, 2006: 18–20). Ensuring state security is the most important priority, as the states are located in a region prone to domestic and foreign threats. These threats are largely derived from religion-based terrorism and organised crime, with Afghanistan a major source of the problem. The states must also stabilise an external environment to maintain their domestic politics and encourage their social and economic development. This entails managing their relations with neighbouring countries in the region and with great power states that have stakes and a presence in the region. Relations between the Central Asian countries are complicated because they were closely intertwined with one another due to their historical legacies and other practical factors. In fact, the countries are socially and economically interdependent. Most acutely, the various countries across the region are home to many trans-boundary ethnic groups. This poses governance problems in relation to not only the countries' domestic policies, but also their foreign relations. Finally, the Central Asian states aspire to participate in the international community to achieve international recognition, prestige and influence.

Despite some noticeable differences in foreign policy orientation, the Central Asian states generally adopt a multi-vector strategy when developing relations with major power states. Kazakhstan is a representative case (Ipek, 2007). A landlocked country rich in oil and gas, Kazakhstan must overcome several challenges to cope with its foreign relations, including attracting foreign investment to explore its natural resources and economic development, securing export markets for its energies and managing relations with its neighbouring countries in the region. It is well noted that Kazakh leaders adopt a viable foreign strategy to maintain good relations with the great powers in its neighbourhood (Russia and China) and Western powers, *inter alia*, the United States and European Union countries. Other Central Asian states such as Kyrgyzstan, Tajikistan, Turkmenistan and Uzbekistan are subject to similar determinants and find themselves in similar situations. These countries more or less adopt balanced strategies when dealing with the great powers. The Turk-men leadership adopts a permanent neutral state strategy, strictly prohibiting itself from entering any multilateral agreement in the international community. In the other Central Asian states, SCO cooperation is perceived as an effective mechanism to manage relations between the states and protect their interests in the region by aligning with the two major powers of China and Russia.

The SCO primarily allows its members to engage in multilateral cooperation. It is also intended for use as an instrument to exert an international influence. However, this does not mean that the SCO has no implications for or relations with other parties. On the contrary, in pressing situations, it calls for reactive and proactive participation in regional and world affairs.

In the Central Asian region, the SCO is facing complications, such as competition with other multilateral arrangements. There are currently quite a few multilateral organisations operating in the region, including the CIS, CIS Collective Security Treaty Organisation (CSTO), Eurasian Economic Union (EAEU) and Asian Security and Mutual Trust Agreement (CICA), all of which lack good coordination and interaction. These organisations may overlap and compete with the SCO in certain ways (Jiang, 2003: 50). The CSTO provides a clear example (Frost, 2009). It was established in May 2002 out of the Collective Security Treaty of the CIS, which was launched almost immediately after the collapse of the Soviet Union. Except for China, the member states of the CSTO largely overlap those of the SCO and include Armenia, Belarus, Kazakhstan, Kyrgyzstan, Russia and Tajikistan. In many ways, the CSTO, which is headquartered in Moscow, is intended to be a conventional organisation of collective security. It has the primary objective of fighting against all kinds of security threats targeting the member states. In terms of security cooperation, the CSTO has made far more progress than the SCO. The CSTO's Central Asian Collective Rapid Deployment Force (RDF) has been in place since January 2004, with Central Asian CSTO members and Russia contributing troops (Du Mont, 2004: 10), a move never envisaged by the SCO. In fact, Central Asian analysts have characterised the CSTO as the main competitor to the SCO's credentials in the region. The SCO has thus faced an obstacle to security cooperation. This is particularly the case for China, which must find ways to persuade its partners to devote more attention and resources to the SCO, a project of its own initiative.

Many analyses mention the difficult coordination and possible competition between China and Russia in the SCO. However, the two states have much in common, as they both perceive the same threats. Furthermore, power relations between China and Russia have increasingly tilted towards the Chinese side given its significant rise in recent decades. This is an unprecedented situation, as Russia had enjoyed power primacy over China since the nineteenth century, with its power asymmetry reaching its highest point after the end of World War II. The radical change in power relations between the two neighbouring giants has entailed necessary readjustment on both sides, particularly the Russian side. The recent American 'rebalancing of Asia' strategy and the Ukraine crisis have driven the two neighbouring powers even closer. Despite the deep-rooted caution adopted by the Russian leadership and its people towards China, its relationship with China has significantly improved since the Cold War (Kuchins, 2007). To a large extent, the SCO's international position and capabilities are determined by the status and coordination of its member states, particularly China and Russia.

International responses to Central Asia and the SCO

Despite its location in the hinterland of the Eurasian continent, Central Asia has increasingly attracted attention from various actors in the outside world, including great global powers, regional powers, international organisations and NGOs. In particular, the United States-led war in Afghanistan in 2001 suddenly brought the long-neglected region into the international spotlight.

Interested parties have followed changes and developments in Central Asia due to the region's increasing visibility and importance in recent world affairs. They have necessarily noticed the various practical and strategic implications brought about by regional organisations such as the SCO.

International responses to developments in Central Asia and the SCO have been mixed, with different perceptions, views, positions and policies from a variety of international actors. Some are more interested in practical issues of oil and gas in the region; some are more anxious about their geopolitical stakes in Central Asia; and others are more concerned about the regional and national stability of the Central Asian countries, including their social and economic development, human rights, organised crime and democracy and regime stability. In general, there are two groups of actors that follow SCO developments closely. The first includes countries that have a big interest in or a potential to join the SCO due to their geographical proximity and state interests. They are driven more by practical and strategic considerations. They are joined mostly by countries located in the neighbourhood or even within the region, including Afghanistan, India, Iran, Mongolia and Pakistan. The list of the second group includes other countries that may not be located nearby but have substantial stakes in the region, including the United States, Japan, South Korea, Turkey and some EU countries. The latter group of actors is more motivated by diverse economic, energy, security, strategic, democratic and human rights considerations.

When discussing the geopolitical and strategic position of Central Asia, one may easily recall the 'Great Games' of the region in the nineteenth century. Its geographic position in the heartland of the Eurasian continent determined the re-emergence of power politics in the region after the collapse of the Soviet Union, which created a power vacuum in this forgotten land throughout most of the twentieth century. Several great and regional powers currently coexist in Central Asia (Deyermond, 2009). These include the United States, the world hegemon; Russia, a declining yet formidable regional power; and China, a rapidly rising power that has gradually exerted its influence from the regional to global levels. A group of other regional powers including India, Iran and Turkey have also joined this geopolitically and strategically significant game and have respective interests that may converge or collide. This is necessarily reflected in the real politics of cooperation and competition in the region. In the contemporary era, power games in Central Asia are driven by their substantial economic significance to outsiders, mainly due to the energy, natural resources and long-run market potential they offer. SCO development has implications for interested parties. For example, India, Japan and South Korea are interested in developing economic relations with Central Asian countries mainly based on their energy and natural resources and market potential.

Among the first group of states, attitudes towards the SCO are generally positive. All of the states including Afghanistan, India, Iran, Mongolia and Pakistan are interested in becoming involved with the SCO in some way, although their concrete approaches and substantiality may differ. Pakistan's long-time foreign policy has focused on developing its relations with the Islamic world and China. It has also maintained a foreign policy tradition of good working relations with the West since the Cold War, although its strategic value seriously declined after the end of the Cold War. Despite being a South Asian country, it has strong links with Central Asia mainly due to its geographic proximity to Afghanistan and religious affinity with Central Asian countries. From the beginning, Pakistan showed a strong interest in participating in the 'Shanghai Five' and later the SCO. Its enthusiasm to join the club was motivated by political, economic and security considerations (Xing and Sun, 2007: 212–213). An SCO membership may help Pakistan further strengthen its relations with its *de facto* ally of China in an institutionalised setting and manage its relations with long-time rival India, indicating its interest in Central Asia and the SCO. Indeed, membership would be useful for Pakistan to stabilise its increasingly serious domestic situation arising from home-based and transboundary terrorism. Furthermore, the SCO may also help Pakistan's economic development by exploring the potential of economic development with the Central Asian states, which share similar cultural and religious backgrounds. Iran is also enthusiastic about joining the SCO, and its policymakers have been watching the organisation's development with strong interest.

At the beginning of the SCO process, Mongolia showed a somewhat ambiguous attitude towards the organisation. Since the end of the Cold War, Mongolia has broken away from its original *de facto* satellite state status of the Soviet Union and has begun searching for a foreign policy strategy to complement its democratisation. In 1994, its National Congress issued the blueprints of the Mongolian foreign policy, deciding that it would adopt an open, nonalliance and multi-vector peace-loving foreign policy (Xing and Sun, 2007: 209). As a fundamental strategy, Mongolia is determined to achieve a balanced diplomacy with its two giant neighbours Russia and China. Meanwhile, it attaches great importance to its relations with Japan, South Korea and particularly the United States, which it has nicknamed its 'third neighbour'. Mongolia has no substantial stake in and is not motivated by Central Asia or the SCO and shares no border with the Central Asian states. Indeed, the Alta Mountains hinder smooth transportation between the regions. Furthermore, the SCO has made countering terrorism based on Islamic fundamentalism its main goal. Mongolia is not experiencing the terrorist problems suffered by the Central Asian states. It also sees little economic benefit in the SCO process. However, its modest involvement in the SCO helps it to facilitate interactions with a group of neighbouring countries within a multilateral network, strengthen its relations with China and Russia and improve its international visibility.

Despite their interest in the SCO, India and Afghanistan were not expected to join the organisation in the near future because they realised that the time for their membership had not yet arrived. There is a longstanding tradition in Indian foreign policy to develop independent great-power diplomacy and actively exercise its influence in the international arena. One is easily reminded of India's role as a leading state in the 'Non-alignment Movement' during the Cold War. Recognised widely as a major emerging power, India has become increasingly assertive in international affairs in recent years. It perceives Central Asia as a neighbourhood of strategic importance because the region has substantial implications for its economic, strategic and security-related stakes. In addition, India considers China its major competitor and does not want to lag far behind in exercising its influence in the region. However, the Indian bid for SCO membership must overcome the Chinese obstacle. In contrast, Afghanistan does not aspire to be part of the important regional organisation soon because it realises that its internal turmoil hinders it from active participation and achieving international recognition.

Despite its location, the United States has considerable interest in the region due to its global reach. After its war in Afghanistan, the United States became particularly interested in the region because it was crucial to its success. The geographic position of Central Asia is an important strategic consideration for American policymakers, who perceive the region as an important crossroads in the Eurasian continent that faces other great powers such as China and Russia. The United States' most immediate concern is its war in Afghanistan and finding a lasting solution to ensure the stability of the country. American analysts have suggested possible strategic options such as promoting an American vision of central regionalism, reconciling the promotion of democracy with security concerns and adopting a pragmatic approach to Islam (Maynes, 2003: 129–132). More specifically, the United States may consider establishing a greater Central Asia partnership for cooperation and development (Starr, 2005). However, these strategic blueprints are difficult to achieve given the United States' geographic distance and its decline in power on a global scale.

Although the United States is more motivated by strategic and security-related concerns, other states in the second group are interested in Central Asia and the SCO for many reasons. Both are poor in natural resources and have export-oriented economies. Japan and South Korea are more interested in Central Asia due to practical economic considerations such as energy and market potentials. Furthermore, Japan has strategic concerns about its competition with China in the region. Frustrated by its long yet hopeless attempt at obtaining EU membership and Western criticism against its human rights record, Turkey has changed its strategic orientation from Europe to Central Asia, where it finds more cultural and religious affinity. Turkey has re-established its ambition to be the big brother in the Turkic world. In more recent years, the Turkish leadership has shown increasing interest in the SCO and even sought formal membership (Wang, 2014: 406). In contrast, the EU and European countries are more motivated by their political values and beliefs. Driven by a desire to export their model of development and governance, they are more concerned about the social and regime stability in Central Asian countries. In the West, the SCO is popularly interpreted as a multilateral effort of a group of authoritarian states to defend themselves against regional and global trends of democratisation. Led by the two most powerful auto-cratic states in China and Russia, the leaders of the Central Asian states have become bold enough to reject the West's promotion of democracy (Ambrosio, 2008). They are thus more worried about the SCO's obstructing role in their efforts to promote democracy and human rights in the region.

The SCO's international interactions

The SCO conducts its external relations with three types of actors: the United States and other Western countries, a group of neighbouring countries and some intergovernmental organisations. It takes time for SCO members to converge on positions and policies towards the United States. In general, members are cautious about the intentions and policies of the West. When necessary, they may adopt a soft-balancing strategy against perceived threats from the United States (Song, 2013). In their relations with some neighbouring countries, SCO members are more confident and flexible and engage to varying degrees. The SCO has managed to develop official relations and working contacts with several international and regional organisations.

When the SCO was established in 2001 after a decade of cooperation during the less-organised 'Shanghai Five' period, very few analysts were devoting serious thought to its international capabilities and influence. The organisation was basically thought to offer multilateral cooperation between a group of inward-looking countries largely concerned about their various internal problems and trans-boundary issues across Central Asia. Most of the member states also held this view. The member states usually declare their common positions on major international issues in joint declarations and communiqués issued after SCO summits and meetings of government heads and foreign ministers.

However, the SCO's low-profile position must change in response to externally imposed upheavals. Soon after its establishment, the SCO's international capabilities were tested when the Unites States war in Afghanistan, a direct response to 9/11, broke the quietness of Central Asia overnight. The region suddenly became the frontier of a new type of major conflict and a venue for great power games. The SCO was ill prepared to respond. In fact, its member states did not have enough time to obtain a well-coordinated position and instead responded on a more individual basis. The Central Asian states had little choice but to adopt a more accommodating attitude towards the Unites States' entry into the region. Countries such as Uzbekistan considered it an opportunity to get closer to the world hegemon and balance Russia and China's power in the region. Vladimir Putin assumed the Russian presidency, and the Russian leadership sought a strategic retreat and compromise and adopted a cooperative policy towards the American presence in Central Asia. After the United States' declaration of war in Afghanistan, Russia provided a full range of support such as information sharing, admission of its territorial area and logistic assistance. This surprised Chinese policymakers and analysts, who complained that the Russian policymakers did not have a correct understanding of the real intention of the United States (Wang, 2007: 68).

However, the Russian and Central Asian leaders drastically changed their perception of the United States' intention after the outbreak of the so-called 'Colour Revolution' in several former Soviet republics, particularly in Central Asia. During the 'Colour Revolution', the opposition successfully stirred up social resentment and anger in a time of social and economic difficulty. Various non-violent social activities such as demonstrations, protests and strikes were organised to put pressure on the domestic regimes and force a regime change. This massive wave spread across the former Soviet world from Georgia to Ukraine and Kyrgyzstan in Central Asia. In Kyrgyzstan, the Akayev regime was toppled during the Tulip Revolution in April 2005, surprising both China and Russia in addition to the other authoritarian regimes in the region. During this wave, the social movement against the Kalimov regime in Uzbekistan finally led to the Andijan Incident in May 2005, which was strongly criticised by the Western governments.

China spent a great deal of time monitoring the growing dispute between Russia and the United States after the short honeymoon following the United States-led war in Afghanistan. When relations between Russia and the United States became tense and the 'Colour Revolution' broke out, China thought the time had finally come to persuade its SCO partners to form a united front. The SCO began to stand up and say 'no' to the American presence in Central Asia. The 2005 SCO summit in Astana caught the world's attention courtesy of a joint declaration made by the member states that called for the United States to draw up a schedule for the withdrawal of American forces from military bases in Central Asia. Evidence suggests that this was primarily an Uzbek initiative and a counterattack against American and Western criticism of the Uzbek government's actions during the Andijan Incident. China and Russia supported the declaration and refused American military presence in the region (Oresman, 2005: 7). However, Rumer (2006: 3) suggests that Russia was in fact the strongest advocate of the call for American withdrawal. The same analyst argues that although the SCO was limited in its collective capabilities, its influence was considerable and its biggest members – China and Russia – had the ability to undercut American initiatives in the region (Rumer, 2006: 2).

In fact, the SCO member states and particularly China use the organisation to exhibit soft-balancing behaviour against the United States (Song, 2013). China aims to expand its security and power in Central Asia primarily through the SCO. However, China's rise in the region is taking place within an international system dominated by the United States. Perceiving a threat from the hegemon, China makes instrumental use of the SCO to soft balance American influence in the region. It uses three major soft-balancing tactics through the SCO, including pursuing collective action such as joint military exercises and statements, promoting institutional norms known primarily as the 'Shanghai Spirit' and competing for supporters through various means of engagement. Soft balancing is a security strategy adopted to undermine, frustrate and increase the cost of unilateral action for the stronger state rather than confront it directly via the traditional balance of power. It is a natural strategic option for China and its SCO partners given the power gap separating them from the United States (Song, 2013). However, soft balancing may turn into hard balancing. Some evidence shows that the aggressive policies of the United States and other Western countries have pushed China and Russia closer together in recent years.

Nevertheless, the SCO does not always sustain a united front. Divergences do occur, such as when Russian troops invaded Georgia on the opening day of the Beijing Olympics on 8 August 2008. Russia did not succeed in securing an endorsement from the SCO partners for its aggressive action. The SCO was also unable to take more concrete actions in recent situations such as the global financial crisis and the Crimean and Ukrainian crises.

Another major external dimension of the SCO is the way it manages relations with other powers and states, usually those within geographical proximity such as India, Iran, Mongolia, Turkey, Pakistan and Japan. All of these countries have an interest in being affiliated with the SCO, and some are even enthusiastic to be part of the organisation. SCO members have instruments at their disposal to associate these interested states. At the SCO Tashkent summit in 2004, the organisation adopted the Regulations on the Observer Status of the Shanghai Cooperation Organisation, a document that provides the procedures for becoming an observer of the SCO and the corresponding rights and duties. In particular, it stipulates that observer status can only be granted to a state or an international governmental organisation if it accepts the principle of 'respect for the sovereignty, territorial integrity and equal rights of the member states, recognition of the main objectives, principles and actions of the Organisation'. Although an observer does not have the right to make decisions, it has the right to attend open meetings of the Councils of Heads of State/Government/ Ministers of Finance and other ministerial conferences and participate in discussion under certain rules. Bestowing observer status is helpful for accommodating requests while keeping the SCO stable. Afghanistan, India, Iran, Mongolia and Pakistan are currently observer states in the SCO.

Furthermore, SCO members created the status of 'dialogue partner' to associate states that are distant from the region but acceptable for maintaining close relations. At the summit in August 2008, the SCO approved the Regulations on the Status of Dialogue Partner of the Shanghai Cooperation Organisation, which states that a state or an international organisation may be granted the status of dialogue partner if it wishes to establish an equal mutually beneficial partnership with the organisation and cooperate in specific and mutually agreed upon activities. The dialogue partner is entitled to participate in the meetings of ministry/department heads and senior officials and in the working groups of the SCO member states responsible for the areas of cooperation outlined in the memorandum. Moreover, it is entitled to make statements about issues related to their partnerships. Bestowing dialogue partner status offers the SCO and particularly its leading states (China and Russia) another useful way to conduct external relations. Belarus, Turkey and Sri Lanka are currently dialogue partners in the SCO.

Over the years, the SCO has tried to contribute to regional peace and stability. This is best exemplified by the SCO-Afghanistan Contact Group. On 4 November 2005, the SCO and Afghanistan signed the Protocol on Establishment of the SCO-Afghanistan Contact Group between the Shanghai Cooperation Organisation and the Islamic Republic of Afghanistan. The Contact Group consists of permanent representatives of member states to the SCO Secretariat, secretariat officers and senior diplomats of the Afghani Embassy to China in Beijing. When necessary, meetings of the Contact Group involve representatives of other SCO bodies and experts from the SCO member states and Afghanistan. The Contact Group conducts its activity in the form of consultations. As a follow-up measure, the Special Conference on Afghanistan was convened under the auspices of the SCO in March 2009. The SCO member states and Afghanistan issued a joint statement and a plan of action for combating terrorism, illicit drug trafficking and organised crime in March 2009. To strengthen its relations with Afghanistan, SCO leaders decided to accept the country as an SCO observer state at the Beijing summit in June 2012. Analysts believe that both Afghanistan and the SCO member states are preparing for more substantial security cooperation to meet the NATO withdrawal in 2015. It would not be farfetched to say that Afghanistan may join the SCO as a formal member.

Realising the utility of more international visibility, SCO members have gradually aspired to pursue more international participation, including contacts with other international and regional organisations. At a summit in Tashkent, Uzbekistan in 2004, leaders of the SCO member states presented a proposal to representatives of international and regional forums to establish a partnership network of multilateral associations.[4] The SCO has established more institutionalised contacts with the CIS and other Russian-led regional organisations, the ASEAN and the UN (Zhao, 2005: 11). There are a number of Russian-led regional organisations in the former Soviet space. Some of the most important include the CIS, Eurasian Economic Community/Union and CSTO. The memberships of these three organisations and especially the CSTO more or less overlap with the SCO. However awkward, they are the most convenient targets for the SCO's international relations. In fact, these organisations engage in a kind of mutual consumption to ensure their international visibility. An institutionalised coordination mechanism has been established and representatives of the four organisations meet regularly. Concrete cooperation has been established in recent years. For example, the SCO and CIS endorsed the domestic election of Uzbekistan as an independent observer.[5] The SCO and CSTO have begun cooperating on non-traditional security issues that are mostly related to terrorism. Although analysts initially described the two organisations as major competitors, the possibility of a merger has been discussed.[6]

The SCO and ASEAN share many similarities. Their member states are connected by geographical proximity. In particular, China serves as the linking state between the blocks. In addition to their mutual concern for regional security, the two organisations have similar aims and tasks in the political, economic, environmental and humanitarian arenas. More fundamentally, both organisations, which are composed of non-Western states, uphold similar underlying principles, advocate cooperation based on mutual respect and sovereignty equality and avoid targeting outside parties. The secretariats of the SCO and ASEAN signed an MOU in Jakarta on 21 April 2005, in which they expressed a common interest to cooperate in a number of functional areas with priority given to countering transnational crimes such as terrorism, drug trafficking, human trafficking, money laundering and arms smuggling. However, the methods of cooperation are quite modest, as they largely involve sharing information and best practices and mutual consultation on the sidelines of current meetings.[7]

The UN has become the major target of the SCO. Given the international status of China and Russia, its efforts have paid off. In December 2004, the SCO was granted observer status by the UN General Assembly. The SCO was invited to attend the 2005 World Summit in New York to celebrate the 60th anniversary of the UN. SCO Secretary General Zhang Deguang delivered a speech emphasising the SCO's principles of conducting international relations as 'non-alignment, non-direction against other states and regions' and 'outside openness'.[8] On 8 April 2010, the SCO and UN issued the Joint Declaration on SCO/UN Secretariat Cooperation under the names of Muratbek Imanaliev and Ban Ki-moon, the secretaries general of the respective organisations. In the Joint Declaration, the two expressed mutual respect and support and reiterated that 'the primary responsibility for the maintenance of international peace and security rests with the United Nations Security Council, in accordance with the Charter of the United Nations'.[9] The two organisations are quite comfortable with each other due to their shared premise of traditional sovereign state cooperation. Indeed, the SCO has worked in cooperation with the UN Economic and Social Commission for Asia and the Pacific, Office on Drugs and Crime and Development Programme.

Politics of SCO enlargement

Membership is a key issue in the SCO's external relations, in which interest and power play significant roles. As discussed earlier, China, Russia and the Central Asian states treat the SCO pragmatically. China uses the SCO as a vehicle to expand its influence in its immediate neighbourhood, where it has no solid historical or cultural foundations. China is not generally interested in inviting new members to join because it is more concerned with consolidating its cooperation with current members, particularly the Central Asian states. Commenting on the Regulations on Observer States of the SCO in June 2004, SCO Secretary General Zhang Deguang stated that the priority of the SCO was not enlargement but more substantive international cooperation and development.[10]

The Central Asian states consider the SCO as a mechanism to promote their international status, help stabilise their political regimes and provide economic benefits, all with the help of the two great powers (China and Russia). In principle, they are passive and cautious about accepting new member states into the organisation simply because expanding the SCO by bringing in new states would dilute their position and leverage in the SCO. Russia takes a pick-and-choose approach within the organisation, a pragmatic approach it also adopts for the issue of enlargement. This implies that Russia is more flexible on the issue and may selectively welcome the participation of other states when it perceives doing so to have potential benefits.

The politics of enlargement were reflected in the process of upgrading the 'Shanghai Five' to the SCO. Uzbekistan's accession to the regional organisation was made possible only with the joint support of China and Russia. Although the other three Central Asian states were reluctant to accept Uzbekistan's membership, they could not resist the strong will of the two 'big brothers'. These politics of enlargement continued after the SCO was founded in 2001. However, the member states' positions are not as divergent on the matter compared with their positions on security, economics and other functional areas.

Soon after the founding of the SCO, a few countries expressed an interest in becoming involved with the new organisation to varying degrees of enthusiasm. Some aspired to become members, some were interested in only a few elements of cooperation under the SCO framework, and some simply wished to be informed of new developments. To accommodate the varying demands articulated by other states, the SCO approved a regulation related to the status of its observer states at the Tashkent summit in June 2004. It was at this summit that Mongolia became the first observer state. The SCO granted the same status to Pakistan, India and Iran at the summit held in Astana, Kazakhstan in July 2005.

Although Mongolia was the first state to be granted observer status, it is largely unmotivated to join the SCO as a full member. In contrast, all of the other observer states including the newest observer state Afghanistan have expressed their strong intention to become full members. Pakistan and Iran are particularly enthusiastic about SCO membership. The former has harboured hopes of becoming an SCO member for a long time. Pakistan applied to join the 'Shanghai Five' as early as November 2000, before the SCO's official establishment. Since then, Pakistani heads of state and government have attended almost every SCO summit to show their sincerity towards and strong interest in the organisation. Pakistan's leaders have repeatedly sought to join the SCO through China's support. During his visit to China in February 2006, President Musharraf of Pakistan told SCO Secretary General Zhang Deguang that Pakistan wished to join the organisation to facilitate closer cooperation under the SCO framework.[11] There are many reasons behind

Pakistan's enthusiasm to become an SCO member. It has strong political, economic and security motivations. It also believes that SCO membership may strengthen its ties with China, a longstanding 'all weather' ally. However, it would not be easy for Pakistan to seal its bid for SCO membership. Although China would be happy to see its close friend as part of the organisation, it clearly understands that the admission of Pakistan *alone* would be unacceptable to Russia. In turn, China would refuse to accept the admission of India alone. If both were admitted to the organisation, the Indo-Pakistani rivalry would probably undermine the solidarity of the SCO.

Iran's enthusiasm to join the SCO became widely known when Iranian President Ahmadinejad attended the SCO summit in Shanghai in June 2006. Since then, Iran has not been satisfied with its observer status. It officially applied for SCO membership in 2008 (Wang, 2009: 287) and has a strong geopolitical motivation to join the organisation (Akbarzadeh, 2015). It considers the SCO, with its anti-Western leanings, as an ideal organisation in which it may play an active role, an opportunity to escape Western-imposed isolation and a possible counterweight against the United States in the region. Moreover, it considers that such an organisation, which largely comprises Islamic states and is located in its immediate neighbourhood, may help to raise Iran's international visibility and expand its overall influence. Iran also foresees a rosy future of economic cooperation, particularly in the energy sector. However, China and most of the other SCO members including Russia are unwilling or reluctant to grant Iran membership at the cost of confronting the United States, which strongly opposes such a move.[12] Therefore, SCO members consider Iran's current observer status to be appropriate. Iran can use its status as a tool to show its courage in the face of United States domination in the region and beyond. However, its observer status may be considered a less straightforward attempt by some SCO members to counter the American power through long-term unification with its enemy. The SCO partners have more or less reached a consensus on this sensitive issue.

Although not as enthusiastic as Pakistan and Iran, India has also shown a strong interest in becoming a full SCO member. It first expressed this interest during Kazakh President Nursultan Nazarbayev's visit to India in August 2001, immediately after the organisation was established. In a press interview in June 2002, the Indian ambassador to Russia stated that India fully supported the SCO principles and wished to join the organisation (Wu, 2009: 303). India's interest in the SCO is the result of a strategic calculation of Central Asia's value to its national interests.[13] It perceives the SCO as a vehicle to strengthen its cooperation with the Central Asian states in the energy, transportation, economy and trade sectors. More generally, participation in the SCO may help India expand its influence in the region. Analysts believe that Russia supports India's bid to join the SCO.[14] Russian policymakers feel that it would be easier to constrain China's influence on the SCO with India as a full member. On China's part, it has no reason to welcome a potential competitor into an organisation in which it plays a leading role. Therefore, to oppose

India's campaign for membership, China may argue that to accept India alone and exclude Pakistan would be unfair and that to grant membership to both may undermine the solidarity of the organisation by inciting a rivalry (Zhao, 2006: 25–26).

Nevertheless, other states await their opportunity to be granted similar status or even full membership. This list of states includes countries in the region and many outside nations. The United States informally requested observer status in 2005. Despite the absence of any geographical criterion for full membership in the SCO charter, China and Russia turned the request down based on the pretext that the United States did not geographically belong to the region.[15] It is believed that Japan and South Korea are also interested in becoming observer states. Their chances are also considered slim, as their bids would be subject to the consent of the two big powers. However, China and Russia were more flexible when Belarus and Sri Lanka applied for full membership. Although not all of the SCO member states were opposed to their intended involvement with the organisation, it seems inappropriate that they were accepted as observer states given their considerable geographical distance from the SCO region. In 2009, Belarus and Sri Lanka were finally admitted as so-called dialogue partners, a mechanism China and Russia invented specifically to accommodate requests from outsiders.[16]

Although China and most of the other member states are not actively interested in enlarging the organisation in the near future, the SCO approved two documents relating to the procedures for admitting new members at the Tashkent summit in June 2010: the Rules of Procedure and the Statute on the Order of Admission of New Members to the SCO. The stance reflected in these two documents mainly represents a passive Chinese response to the enthusiastic membership requests expressed by some states. It by no means implies that SCO members have a specific enlargement plan in mind, let alone that they have reached a consensus. It only reconfirms that it is quite easy to establish a formal multilateral agreement, which in this case relates to the procedural documents for the admission of new members. However, whether this agreement has a real effect is another matter. China has a less difficult game to play in this area, as its partners do not treat the issue as a priority.

More recently, however, there have been some new dramatic developments on the issue of membership enlargement. At the Dushanbe summit in September 2014, the SCO concluded a new agreement for accepting new members: the Order for Granting the Status of SCO Member State and Revised Model Memorandum of Commitments by the Applicant State for Obtaining SCO Member State Status. The SCO leaders considered this order an important step towards ensuring the future development of the SCO and improving the legal framework and future expansion of the organisation.[17] The SCO member states and particularly China may be undergoing strategic changes. China has attempted to stabilise relations with India, as it is facing more acute issues with other countries. In addition, Mongolia and Afghanistan, which are the countries considered most acceptable to the SCO members for admission, have shown more interest in joining the organisation. Observers would not be surprised when a number of new states are admitted in the near future.

Conclusion

Some analysts argue that the United States and CIS/CSTO are the two most important issues to consider when examining the SCO's external relations. The former presents an external challenge to the unity of the SCO members, and the latter presents a more internal problem that hinders the development of the organisation. Although this view sounds simplistic, it identifies two related problems influencing the SCO's effectiveness. When China and Russia have a common perception and position of external threats, the SCO and CSTO are more likely to converge.

The international situation is changing due to changes in power and inter-est. The United States and its Western allies began their military withdrawal from Afghanistan in October 2014. Mr Ashraf Ghani Ahmadzai notably chose China as the first country to visit in October 2014, only one month after he became the Afghan president. Analysts believe that the new Afghan government is trying to strengthen its ties with China to help its economic development and national security.[18] Chinese analysts proclaim that China will have a more active role to play in the Afghanistan peace-making process (Wu, 2014: 63–65). With the American retreat from Central Asia, one can expect the SCO to assume a bigger role, assist the Afghan government with its security and take on the major responsibility of regional security. Both the SCO members and Afghan government are well aware of the changes, and the two sides have already established frequent contact to increase their cooperation in security and other areas.

This reflects a defining reality in contemporary world politics: the power relations among the major states are transforming. The United States has gra-dually been losing the power supremacy it enjoyed in the years immediately following the Cold War. Meanwhile, China and a group of emerging powers are rising against the backdrop of the decline of certain traditional Western powers. This is affecting the SCO's development, as China and Russia are more determined to exercise their structural, entrepreneurial and intellectual leadership together when relations go tense during the transition between the traditional and emerging powers. The recent developments of the SCO have demonstrated its salience in the international arena.

Furthermore, China has expanded its 'go west' strategy to an even more ambitious grand strategy: the newly coined OBOR strategy. In other words, its Central Asian strategy, including its SCO policy, has been incorporated into this new strategy of economic statecraft. The China-led 'Silk Road Economic Belt' and the twenty-first-century 'Maritime Silk Road' initiatives reflect China's plans for power expansion based on its current economic power and influence. Although the success of these initiatives is unclear, it is certain that China will invest more of its resources in the SCO and Central Asia as part of its grand strategy. Additional international political dynamics will appear in the SCO process in the coming years.

Notes

1 'China Go Global', http://www.oecd.org/china/china-go-global.htm, accessed 9 February 2015.
2 http://news.sina.com.cn/c/2014-05-20/194530178276.shtml, accessed 4 February 2015.
3 Kyrgyzstan was the first to declare its independence on 31 August 1991, followed by Uzbekistan on 1 September 1991, Tajikistan on 9 September 1991, Turkmenistan on 27 October 1991 and Kazakhstan on 16 December 1991.
4 'SCO-ASEAN Cooperation for Mutual Interests', http://en.sco-russia.ru/coopera tion/20140905/1013179818.html, accessed 20 January 2015.
5 'SCO, CIS Observers say Uzbekistan Parliamentary Elections Democratic', http://itar-tass.com/en/world/768408, accessed 20 January 2015.
6 'SCO-CSTO Merger Raised at Dushanbe Conference', http://www.cacianalyst.org/p ublications/field-reports/item/12983-sco-csto-merger-raised-at-dushanbe-conference. html, accessed 20 January 2015.
7 www.asean.org/archive/ASEAN-SCO-MOU.pdf, accessed 20 January 2015.
8 'Speech by the Secretary General of the Shanghai Cooperation Organisation Zhang Deguang at the 60th High-level Preliminary Meeting of the United Nations General Assembly (New York, September 16, 2005)', http://www.un.org/webcast/ summit2005/statements.html, accessed 20 January 2015.
9 'Joint Declaration on SCO/UN Secretariat Cooperation', http://www.sectsco.org/ EN123/show.asp?id=198, accessed 20 January 2015.
10 *Renmin Ribao* [People's Daily], 16 June 2004.
11 'Pakistan President Keen to Further Ties with SCO,' *People's Daily Online*, last modified 21 February 2006, available at: http://english.peopledaily.com.cn/200602/ 21/eng20060221_244511.html (accessed 5 July 2011).
12 'Ahmadinejad Calls for Regional Security Alliance to Counter US Influence,' *Associated Press*, last modified on 15 June 2011, available at: http://www.guardian. co.uk/world/2011/jun/15/ahmadinejad-sco-united-front-against-us (accessed 6 July 2011).
13 Meena Singh Roy, 'Dynamics of Expanding the SCO' (IDSA Comment), *Institute for Defense Studies and Analyses*, last modified on 4 April 2011, available at: http:// www.idsa.in/idsacomments/DynamicsofExpandingtheSCO_msroy_040411 (accessed 6 July 2011).
14 Ibid.
15 Meiguo Yitu Lijian Shanghai Hezuo Zuhzhi (US Intentions to drive a wedge between members of the Shanghai Cooperation Organisation), see http://news.sina. com.cn/c/sd/2009-09-14/070018644233_6.shtml, accessed 6 July 2011.
16 According to the author's interview with a Chinese analyst from the Institute of Eurasian Studies, Chinese Academy of Social Sciences in March 2010, the SCO's 'dialogue partner' status was initiated by China and Russia and was originally intended to accommodate American and Japanese requests for a greater level of engagement with the organisation.
17 Dushanbe Declaration of the Heads of SCO Member States, http://www.scosumm it2014.tj/index.php/ru/glavnoe-menyu/arkhiv-novostej/262-dushanbe-declaratio n-of-the-heads-of-sco-member-states, accessed 6 February 2015.
18 'Afuhan Zongtong shoufang Xuan Zhongguo, Waimei Cheng Afuhan Jingkao Lingju (Afghan President Paid First China Visit, Foreign Media Say Afghanistan

Relies Greatly on its Close Neighbour)', http://world.huanqiu.com/exclusive/ 2014-10/5184437.html, accessed 14 February 2015.

References

Akbarzadeh, Shahram (2015) 'Iran and the Shanghai Cooperation Organization: Ideology and Realpolitik in Iranian Foreign Policy', *Australian Journal of International Affairs*, 69(1): 88–103.

Ambrosio, Thomas (2008) 'Catching the "Shanghai Spirit": How the Shanghai Cooperation Organization Promotes Authoritarian Norms in Central Asia', *Europe-Asia Studies*, 60(8): 1321–1344.

Deyermond, Ruth (2009) 'Matrioshka Hegemony? Multi-levelled Hegemonic Competition and Security in Post-Soviet Central Asia', *Review of International Studies*, 35(1): 151–173.

Du Mont, Malia K. (2004) 'That Other Central Asian Collective Security Organization – The CSTO', *China-Eurasian Forum*, 2(1): 8–11.

Frost, Alexander (2009) 'The Collective Security Treaty Organization, the Shanghai Cooperation Organization, and Russia's Strategic Goals in Central Asia', *China and Eurasian Forum*, 7(3): 83–102.

Ipek, Pinar (2007) 'The Role of Oil and Gas in Kazakhstan's Foreign Policy: Looking East or West?', *Europe-Asia Studies*, 59(7): 1179–1199.

Jiang, Yi (2003) 'Zhongguo de Duobian Waijiao yu Shanghai Hezuo Zuzhi' [China's Multilateral Diplomacy and Shanghai Cooperation], *Eluosi Zhongya Dongou Yanjiu* [Studies of Russia, Central Asia and Eastern Europe], 5: 46–51.

Kazantsev, Andrei (2008) 'Russian Policy in Central Asia and the Caspian Sea Region', *Europe-Asia Studies*, 60(6): 1073–1088.

Kuchins, Andrew (2007) 'Russia and China: The Ambivalent Embrace', *Current History*, 106(702): 321–327.

Maynes, Charles W. (2003) 'America Discovers Central Asia', *Foreign Affairs*, 82(2): 120–132.

Oresman, Matthew (2005) 'The Shanghai Cooperation Organization Summit: Where Do We Go from Here?', *China-Eurasian Forum*, 3(2): 5–9.

Pan, Guang and Jian Hu (2006) *21 Shiji de Diyi ge Xinxing Quyu Hezuo Zuzhi: dui Shanghai Hezuo Zuzhi de Zonghe Yanjiu* [The First New Type Regional Cooperation Organization: A Comprehensive Study of the Shanghai Cooperation Organisation]. Beijing: Party School of Chinese Communist Party Press.

Rumer, Eugene (2006) 'China, Russia and the Balance of Power in Central Asia', Strategic Forum, Institute of National Strategic Studies, National Defense University, No. 223.

Song, Weiqing (2013) 'Feeling Safe, Being Strong: China's Strategy of Soft-balancing through the Shanghai Cooperation Organization', *International Politics*, 50(5): 664–685.

Starr, S.Frederick (2005) 'A Partnership for Central Asia', *Foreign Affairs*, 84(4): 164–178.

Wang, Feng (2009) 'Yilang de xianzhuang yu fazhan qushi' [The Current Situation of Iran and its Development Tendency]. In Xing Guangcheng (Ed.), *Shanghai Hezuo Zuzhi Fazhan Baogao 2009* [2009 Annual Report on the Shanghai Cooperation Organization], pp. 273–288. Beijing: Shehui Kexue Wenxian Chubanshe.

Wang, Mingchang (2014) 'Duihua Huobanguo yu Shanghai Hezuo Zuzhi' [Dialogue Partners and the Shanghai Cooperation Organization], *Shanghai Hezuo Zuzhi Fazhang Baogao (2014)* [Annual Report on the Shanghai Cooperation Organization 2014], pp. 399–408. Beijing: Social Sciences Publishing Press.

Wang, Xiaoquan (2007) 'Eluosi dui Shanghai Hezuo Zuzhi de Zhengce Yanbian' [Evolution of Russian Policy towards the Shanghai Cooperation Organization]', *Eluosi Zhongya Dongou Yanjiu* [Journal of Russia, Central Asia, and Eastern Europe], 3, pp. 67–75.

Wu, Hongwei (2014) '2014nian Meiguo Cong Afuhan Chejun yu Zhongguo de Zuoyong' [The American Military Withdrawal in 2014 and China's Role]', *Annual Report on the Shanghai Cooperation Organization (2014)*, pp. 58–65. Beijing: Social Sciences Academic Press.

Wu, Zhaoli (2009) 'Yindu de xianzhuang yu fazhan qushi' [The Current Situation of India and its Development Tendency]. In Xing Guangcheng (Ed.), *Shanghai Hezuo Zuzhi Fazhan Baogao 2009* [2009 Annual Report on the Shanghai Cooperation Organization], pp. 289–305. Beijing: Shehui Kexue Wenxian Chubanshe.

Xing, Guangchen and Zhuangshi Sun (2007) *Shanghai Hezuo Zuzhi Yanjiu* [Studies of Shanghai Cooperation Organization]. Changchu, China: Changchun Press.

Zhao, Huasheng (2005) 'The SCO in the Last Year', *China-Eurasian Forum*, 3(2): 10–12.

Zhao, Huashen (2006) 'Dui Shanghai Hezuo Zuzhi fazhan qianjing de jidian kanfa' [Some Thoughts on the Prospects of the Shanghai Cooperation Organization], *Guoji Wenti Yanjiu* [Studies of International Issues], 3, pp. 23–27.

5 Security and political cooperation

This chapter examines the SCO's security and political cooperation. Beyond formalisation and institutionalisation, SCO member states have expanded the scope of security cooperation from issues of border settlement, military confidence building and regional stability to issues of international terrorism, trafficking, weapons proliferation and political and foreign strategic cooperation. The SCO's cooperation involves various military, public security, justice and political actors and departments. Development of member states' cooperation in this area is described using major variables of power and interest previously discussed. When members states' interests converge, particularly China and Russia's, the SCO can more easily promote political and security cooperation and take collective action.

The background

The breakup of the Soviet Union has had global consequences. Moreover, its effect on the former Soviet space was immediate and intense, bringing about an overall political and social transformation (Tsepkalo, 1998). Central Asia is part of the former Soviet space and bears much of its legacies and aftermath. It has been part of a special security situation during the post-Soviet era in several ways. The region is composed of a group of newly independent states that share complicated historical, ethnical and social relations. It is susceptible to various forms of traditional and non-traditional security threats, which are exacerbated by complicated domestic, regional and international challenges. Furthermore, the independence of the Central Asian states has triggered a renewed round of competition between the external powers in the region. This competition has had tremendous geopolitical significance, connecting some of the most important powers both within and far beyond the region. The countries in the region must cope with several pressing challenges simultaneously.

In the early 1990s, the Central Asian republics launched their respective state-building processes, and major institutions were established almost overnight. Since then, domestic politics in Central Asian states in general have been replete with ruthless political control, cronyism and corruption (Yang, 2005: 104–105). Ruled first by medieval regimes and then by totalitarian regimes for hundreds of years, these new states have no democratic tradition. In theory, constitutional principles and rules are officially promulgated and elections are held regularly across the countries. However, in practice, the Central Asian republics are mostly ruled by authoritarian presidentialism, with single rulers remaining perennially in power and ruling dominantly and sometimes brutally. Although Kyrgyzstan has adopted a more established democracy, it is undermined by chronic domestic instability and conflict.

For historical reasons, Central Asian countries are usually multi-ethnic societies. After achieving independence, the governments of the Central Asian republics adopted policies to upgrade the status of the dominating ethnic group that was superior to other groups in their respective societies, raising resentment among the latter. For example, Russia and most of the Central Asian republics have disputed the issue of dual citizenship for ethnic Russians. Their official language policy has become a fault line in the establishment of social harmony (Yang, 2005: 234–235). Furthermore, ethnic-related and other types of conflicts troubled all of the Central Asian republics such as Turkmenistan until recently (Shi, 2013: 361–368). Religious revival has had a profound effect on Central Asian societies. After achieving independence, the governments of the region encouraged the restoration of Islam out of various considerations. Islam has been used ideologically to enhance a sense of national autonomy and unity to better separate Central Asia from its Soviet past. In practical terms, religion has been used to attract investment and aid from more prosperous Muslim-dominated neighbouring countries such as Iran, Saudi Arabia and Turkey (Yang, 2005: 237–239). This has triggered some negative consequences, including Islamic fundamentalism, extreme political forces and religious-related terrorism (Yemelianova, 2007).

Indeed, Central Asia faces a variety of non-traditional security threats.[1] Apart from religiously motivated terrorism, organised crimes of various types such as drug and human trafficking are serious threats. Trafficking and cultivation in drugs and other narcotics is a serious and rampant problem across the region. Tajikistan is a major transit country for Afghan narcotics bound for Russian and to a lesser extent Western European markets. Tajikistan seizes roughly 80 per cent of all of the drugs captured in Central Asia and is third worldwide in seizures of opiates, including heroin and raw opium. It is also a significant consumer of opiates. Kazakhstan, Kyrgyzstan and Uzbekistan are other smaller-scale transit countries for Afghan and Southwest Asian narcotics bound for the same markets of Russia and Western Europe and serve as transit points for heroin precursor chemicals bound for Afghanistan. They are also major consumers of opiates. Furthermore, narcotics such as cannabis and opium poppies are cultivated in Central Asian countries for domestic and foreign markets. Besides, human trafficking is another acute issue in the region. Turkmenistan and Uzbekistan are source countries for children and women who are subject to sex trafficking both domestically and in Central Asia, the Middle East, Asia and Europe. In addition, men and women are forced into labour in the domestic service, agriculture, construction and oil industries within and beyond the region.

Independent from the former Soviet Union, Central Asian republics have yet to solve a few of the problems they face. The nations' perceptions of threat are deep-rooted and persistent (Nourzhanov, 2009: 98–99). The first issue that most Central Asian republics face is that of border demarcation with neighbouring countries. Kyrgyzstan is a typical country in this sense. Although it reached an agreement on boundary demarcation with Kazakhstan in 2001, the agreement has yet to be ratified through domestic procedures. The conclusion of Kyrgyzstan's border negotiation with Tajikistan has been delayed due to disputes in Isfara Valley. Furthermore, Kyrgyzstan's 130-km-long border with Uzbekistan is hampered by serious disputes over enclaves and other areas. In a similar vein, Kazakhstan began border demarcation negotiations with Uzbekistan in 2004, Turkmenistan in 2005 and Russia in 2007. Apart from field demarcation, its creation of a seabed boundary with Turkmenistan in the Caspian Sea remains unsolved. Although Kazakhstan along with Azerbaijan and Russia ratified Caspian seabed delimitation treaties based on their equidistance, Iran continues to insist on a bigger portion of the sea. Negotiations over border demarcation and the clearance of minefields between Tajikistan and Uzbekistan are on-going.

Matters of trans-border ethnic groups and disputes over natural resources in the region further complicate the issue of border demarcation. In Kyrgyzstan, the Kyrgyz are the dominating ethnic group, making up about 70 per cent of the population. The Uzbeks account for about 15 per cent and are concentrated in Ferghana Valley in the south. The Russians have a significant presence in the north and in the capital city of Bishkek. There is tension between the Kyrgyz and Uzbek communities in the south over land and housing resources. Water-sharing difficulties surrounding the Amu Darya River have created problems for some Central Asian countries, particularly Uzbekistan and Turkmenistan, which are both facing prolonged drought and a cotton monoculture. Kazakhstan is a multi-ethnic society, with Kazakh making up about 63 per cent of the population, Russians making up 23 per cent and the remainder comprising other smaller ethnic groups. The country generally enjoys harmony between the different ethnicities but has yet to develop a cohesive national identity. The trans-ethnic group issue is also present in Tajikistan, where ethnic Uzbeks form a substantial minority. In addition, the issue of cross-border ethnic groups causes problems for most Central Asian states and problematises their relationships. Kazakhstan and Uzbekistan are so at odds over the issue of cross-border ethnic groups that their border has practically been blocked.

Afghanistan has become a major source of the many perennial problems troubling the Central Asian region. The Soviet invasion of Afghanistan in 1979 marked the beginning of the country's domestic turmoil. After the Soviet withdrawal in 1989, the country entered into a destructive civil war fought between different factions. In 1996, the Taliban regime based on Islamic fundamentalism successfully controlled Kabul, the capital and much of the country. After the US-led war in Afghanistan in 2001, the country launched a process of state reconstruction towards democracy. However, this process suffered under the actions of resurgent rebels and provincial instability. The long-time civil war and domestic conflicts brought many problems to the country, the region and beyond. By 1999, Afghanistan was the largest producer of opium and a major source of illegal drugs in the region and as far abroad as Europe. This trend has continued and Afghanistan is now the world's number one opium producer (Yu, 2008: 165; Chouvy, 2006). Furthermore, Afghanistan is a source of religiously based terrorism that has had immediate consequences for its neighbours in Central and South Asia and China.

In comparison, China and Russia are two great powers with strong geographical, historical and practical linkages with Central Asian countries. Several big issues arose when the new republics emerged in the region after the collapse of the Soviet Union. The republics had to stabilise border areas, normalise bilateral relations and cope with trans-boundary issues with their giant neighbours. China and Russia share problems similar to those of their Central Asian neighbours. Both countries are multi-ethnic and suffer from domestic instability mostly in their frontier areas. In fact, China's Xinjiang region is a part of Central Asia and has substantial links with the Central Asian states. In recent years, the region of Xinjiang has been struggling with constant conflicts and terrorist attacks instigated by the religious fundamentalism and ethnic separatism of its Muslim-dominated Uighur population (Kerr, 2008; Hao and Liu, 2012). Russia's internal ethnic problem is more apparent in its problematic North Caucasian region, where the issue of Chechnya still lingers. Although the countries have their respective problems, their implications extend beyond the regional. Indeed, these countries face several challenges such as the various types of organised crime and religious extremism in Central Asia, the issue of East Turkestan in China's Xinjiang and religious separatism in Russia. In particular, the issue of international terrorism has become more acute due to its immediate political significance. These common challenges have inspired the leaders of these countries to make a collective arrangement and achieve unity and enhanced capability.

Due to its geopolitical significance and preservation of tremendous natural resources, Central Asia was restored as a venue for the 'Great Game' played during the post-Cold War era, with major powers competing against one another for interest and influence. China is pursuing its sphere of influence in Central Asia while addressing its concerns about the encirclement strategy by the US. Fearful of the continuing decline of its influence, Russia is keen on maintaining its traditional strategic backyard. Driven by strategic and moral considerations, Western states, *inter alia*, the US and European states, have also reached the region by pressing political reforms, influencing the civil societies and establishing a direct military presence. The re-emergence of the 'Great Game' in the region became the focus of a great deal of research, particularly after the US and NATO's war in Afghanistan (Menon, 2003; Berman, 2004). Central Asia is fated to be a regional dynamic security complex that attracts many powers both within and outside the region.

Operation and activities

Major stages

Development of the SCO has been triggered by the necessity of cooperating in security and political matters in Central Asia. It is no exaggeration to say that the entire SCO institutionalisation process centres on security and political cooperation, from the informal 'Shanghai Five' process to the SCO's official inception and its further development of regular meetings, permanent institutions and various activities. Security and political cooperation in the SCO has continually expanded in terms of issue content. This has included activities such as managing bilateral relations via border demarcation, borderland arms reduction and confidence building; non-traditional security threats from trans-boundary terrorist activities to cross-border organised crime; and managing regional security and balancing power games.

Issues affecting traditional inter-state relations such as border demarcation, borderland arms reduction and confidence building dominated the security and political cooperation agenda during the 'Shanghai Five' period and were especially important to China and the Central Asian states. When the Central Asian states became newly independent at the beginning of the 1990s, some analysts in Central Asia considered China a potential threat to their national security (Yang, 2005: 194–195). China successfully used the 'Shanghai Five' process to assuage suspicion of its young smaller neighbours and stabilise its bilateral relations with these countries and Russia in a more institutionalised setting. When the 'Shanghai Five' group was created on 26 April 1996, the heads of states of China, Kazakhstan, Kyrgyzstan, Russia and Tajikistan signed the Treaty on Deepening Military Trust in Border Regions in Shanghai. On 24 April 1997, the same countries signed the Treaty on Reduction of Military Forces in Border Regions at a meeting in Moscow. These documents marked the achievement of the states in building and enhancing mutual confidence.

After the SCO was launched, attention shifted to countering religiously motivated terrorism. The Shanghai Convention on anti-terrorism, in which types of terrorism are well defined, was signed at the inaugural SCO summit in Shanghai in June 2001. In the following years, the SCO adopted a broad definition of comprehensive security that covered a wide range of issues. At the Tashkent summit in June 2004, the SCO leaders signed agreements under the Shanghai Cooperation Organization on Cooperation in Combating Illegal Trafficking of Narcotics, Psychotropic Drugs and Their Precursors. This document provided a legal framework for the SCO member states to cooperate in combating the trafficking of illegal narcotics, which was worsening in the region mainly as a result of the Afghanistan problem. At the Astana summit in 2005, the SCO member states signed agreements on fighting the three 'evil forces' of terrorism, separatism and extremism and on providing mutual help in the form of emergency relief during disasters, which specified the more detailed approaches and procedures of cooperation involved in the anti-terrorism effort and disaster rescue and relief operations. At the 2006 Shanghai summit, the SCO leaders issued the Statement of Heads of State of Member States of Shanghai Cooperation Organization on International Information Security, extending the SCO's security cooperation into the newly emerging area of cyber security. Chinese analysts have extolled this statement as the first joint effort of an international organisation to combat threats to cyber security (Yu, 2008: 328–330). With this statement, the SCO leaders provided a necessary legal basis for its cyber security cooperation.

Holding various regular meetings is an important part of the institutional structure of the SCO's security and political cooperation. This includes meetings that address national defence, public security/civilian affairs/law enforcement, supreme courts and prosecurates. In this context, the regular meetings of national defence ministers are the key mechanisms used to regulate and implement the SCO's security cooperation. The first meeting of the defence ministers was held in March 2000, during the 'Shanghai Five' period. The ministers of national defence met in Astana, Kazakhstan in March 2000 in accordance with the guidelines provided by the 'Shanghai Five' Bishkek summit held in August 1999. In a joint communiqué, the ministers announced that it was important to hold regular meetings of the national defence ministers to strengthen mutual trust, engage in friendly cooperation in the military spheres and maintain peace, stability and development in the region. All of the parties agreed that the departments of national defence of the 'Shanghai Five' states would explore detailed measures for jointly fighting against international terrorism, cross-boundary organised crime and disaster rescue and relief and organise joint military exercises, seminars and training to address related issues. In the joint communiqué, the national ministers also criticised hegemony and power politics for threatening world peace and stability. More specifically, they expressed their objection to the interference in internal affairs of any other state in the name of protecting ethnic, religious interests and human rights and their concerns about the plan of the US to install the Theatre Missile Defense system (TDM) in Asia-Pacific, which threatened to destabilise the stability and security of the region.[2] The statement of the ministerial meeting aimed to achieve several objectives, including establishing the internal solidarity and mutual trust of the 'Shanghai Five' member states, which agreed to engage in further cooperation to address common threats and fight against external interference and threat. The smaller Central Asian states sought the support of China and Russia to counter the pressure placed by Western countries on their domestic issues such as minority rights and democracy, and their objection to the United States' TMD plan showed support for the Chinese position. Thus, the meetings of national defence ministers served both security-related and political functions.

The SCO's first meeting of national defence ministers was held in Moscow on 15 May 2002. Ministers from all of the member states except Uzbekistan participated in the meeting to negotiate the implementation of the agreement signed by the SCO leaders at the SCO summit in the areas of international and regional security, anti-terrorism and military cooperation. The ministers agreed to hold regular meetings of national defence ministers and chiefs of staff. They also agreed to establish a committee of national defence senior officials who would coordinate security and defence cooperation and a joint expert team comprising the national defence ministries of the SCO member states to explore engagement in joint anti-terrorism exercises.[3] This first meeting was important because it provided a direction for the major pillars of the SCO security cooperation that centred on military exercises. At the meeting of national defence ministers held in Beijing in April 2006, the ministers agreed that new threats and challenges were becoming increasingly acute and could only be addressed through regional and international cooperation. The ministers held that the SCO should serve as an effective instrument in ensuring regional security. They emphasised the importance of enhancing exchanges and cooperation between the national defence departments of the member states. As the Astana Declaration had been implemented on 5 July 2005, the ministers decided to strengthen the regular meeting mechanism to incorporate ministers of national defence and representatives of chiefs of staff. They agreed that it was necessary to define the main directions of future cooperation, organise various forms of exchange such as seminars and exchange views related to matters of common concern over regional security.[4] Over the years, the meetings of national defence ministers have become key mechanisms for the SCO member states to negotiate and cooperate on military and security matters.

In institutional terms, the RATS/RCTS stands out as the sole permanent SCO security agency. SCO leaders signed the agreement to establish the RATS at the St Petersburg summit in June 2002. After some internal mediation over the seat, the agency formally materialised in 2004 and is now hosted in Tashkent, Uzbekistan. The RATS is the only permanent institution involved in the SCO's security cooperation, serving essential roles in action coordination, information and intelligence sharing and policy initiation and preparation. Since its inception, the RATS has prepared a number of legal documents, including the Plan on the SCO's Cooperation on Countering down Terrorism, Separatism, and Extremism; SCO Convention on Anti-terrorism; and Agreement on Procedures of Organising Joint Anti-terrorism Actions in the Territories of the SCO Member States. These documents have provided a detailed legal basis for the member states to engage in anti-terrorist security cooperation. The RATS plays a supportive role in the security coordination of major events, coordination with other international organisations and joint anti-terrorism military exercises. In this way, it has established working relations with most of the important regional and international anti-terrorist organisations. For example, to strengthen information sharing and experience exchange, the RATS ran a joint seminar with the Anti-terrorist Centre of the CIS on fighting international terrorism in 2011. In 2012, it organised a roundtable anti-terrorism discussion with member and observer states of the SCO. The RATS has taken steps to address the issue of cyber security and cope with the new challenges involved in using the Internet for terrorist activities. In 2012, it formulated the Common Measures on Preventing and Fighting Use or Threat of Use of the Internet by the 'three evils'. In terms of concrete measures, the RATS set up an expert working group with a focus on countering cyber terrorism to conduct detailed work on cyber security issues. It has also engaged in the surveillance of key targets. It coordinates the intelligence sharing of member states in relation to terrorist suspects.[5] It has also become involved in joint military exercises. In March 2006, the SCO held the 'East-Anti-terrorism 2006' joint military exercise in Uzbekistan, marking the first time that all of the SCO member states including Uzbekistan participated in a joint exercise. The exercise was initiated and prepared by the RATS. According to Mr Vuacheslavt Kasymov, then secretary general of the RATS, the exercise aimed to improve the SCO member states' cooperation in searching for and fighting against terrorists who undermined the political and social stability of the Central Asian states through large-scale sabotage activities of important infrastructure.[6] These legal and institutional preparations have paved the way for the SCO's activities in security and political cooperation.

Major activities

Under the framework of the SCO's security and political cooperation, various activities including summits, joint military exercises and operations are implemented for specific purposes. The SCO summit brings together the top leaders of the member states. This lends a high profile to the event, which receives wide attention from observers, the media and the general public. The primary function of the SCO summit is to provide a direction, strategies and guidelines for the development of the organisation. Due to its high status, SCO leaders have taken advantage of the summit to achieve several political objectives and decide the organisation's general directions and guidelines. These objectives are both internal and external in nature and include promoting the visibility and solidarity of the organisation and articulating a joint voice to the wider world. In this sense, the SCO summit is an essential element of the organisation's political cooperation. The leaders of the member states issued a joint declaration in Almaty in 1998 during the 'Shanghai Five' period, stating that all of the parties agreed that any form of national separatism, ethnic exclusion or religious extremism was unacceptable. They declared that all of the parties would take measures to counter international terrorism; organised crime; weapons, drug and narcotics trafficking; and other cross-boundary crime. They also declared that no party would permit any kind of activity in its own territory that aimed to undermine the state sovereignty, national security and social order of any of the other member states.[7] This declaration was meant to demonstrate the solidarity of the group rather than the real measures taken on the ground. However, it was necessary and important, as it spoke to the local people and the outside world about the member states' determination to fight against terrorism in the region.

Apart from the focus on intra-regional issues, member states have increasingly used the SCO summit as a means of demonstrating internal solidarity, a common position and mutual support for issues with wider external implications. Under the SCO name, the leaders have given joint support to member states on certain issues of mutual concern. For example, the SCO leaders have issued joint declarations and statements about their common positions on Afghanistan, the Palestinian–Israeli conflict, Iraq, nuclear weapons in North Korea and United Nations reform. The SCO summit may lend support to an issue of direct concern to member states provided they share a consensus. This was the case when the SCO summit issued a joint declaration explicitly stating its objection to the US plan to install the TMD in Asia-Pacific and its support for China's policy on Taiwan. In this case, China succeeded in persuading its SCO partners to make a joint statement about issues it was concerned about. The most provocative moment occurred when SCO leaders issued a joint statement on the US military base in Uzbekistan at the Astana summit in 2005. SCO partners used this gesture to demonstrate their solidarity when Uzbekistan faced heavy pressure from the West due to its violent treatment of protestors in the Andijan incident on 13 May 2005.

Military exercises are another key activity of the SCO's security and political cooperation. These exercises aim to achieve a number of symbolic and practical goals. As summarised by Xing and Sun (2007: 77), anti-terrorism experiences can be accumulated through various forms of joint military exercises in which different governmental departments participate in a coordinated manner. These exercises also help to improve the capabilities of the state to counter terrorism. This is particularly true of newly independent Central Asian states, which can learn from their partners and quickly improve their national defence capabilities. Finally, they help to promote political significance by strengthening member states' cooperation in political and security matters and demonstrating their common determination to fight terrorism.

Directed by the SCO summit, the SCO's first meeting of national defence ministers in 2002 decided that the SCO should conduct joint military exercises as part of its anti-terrorism effort. In this context, China and Kyrgyzstan held a bilateral military exercise in October 2002, marking the beginning of such activity in the SCO framework and the first time China conducted military exercises with a foreign country. In 2003, China, Kazakhstan, Kyrgyzstan, Russia and Tajikistan conducted the 'Lianhe' (or 'Cooperation') joint military exercise, the first multilateral military exercise conducted in the SCO. This also marked the first time China participated in a large-scale multilateral military exercise. It set an example for successive SCO joint multilateral military exercises. In terms of content, scope and level of participation, these exercises were quite substantial rather than 'merely cosmetic' (Du Mont, 2003). In 2005, China and Russia conducted the 'Peace Mission-2005' joint military exercise in Shandong, China. This marked the first bilateral military exercise between China and Russia and also the beginning of the 'Peace Mission' series of military exercises. In March 2006, the SCO conducted the 'East-Anti-terrorism 2006'

Table 5.1 Military and security exercises in the SCO

	Date	Location	Code name	Participating countries	Nature	Notes
1	Oct. 10–11, 2002	Mountainous region of border area between China, Kyrgyzstan	Exercise-01	China, Kyrgyzstan	Organised by armed forces, with hundreds of troops from both sides	First joint military maneuver for the PLA with a foreign army and also the first bilateral anti-terrorism exercise conducted within the framework of SCO
2	Aug. 6–12, 2003	Ucharal and Ili in Kazakhstan and Xinjiang Uygur Autonomous Region in China	Coalition-2003	China, Kazakhstan, Kyrgyzstan, Russia and Tajikistan	Organised by armed forces, with altogether 1,000 troops in the exercise	First time for China in a multilateral joint military manoeuvre
3	Aug.18–25, 2005	Vladivostok in Russia and Shandong Peninsula in China	Peace Mission 2005	China and Russia	Organised by armed forces, with 10,000 troops from both sides	First joint military exercise bilaterally between China and Russia
4	Aug.24–26, 2006	Almaty in Kazakhstan and Xinjiang in China	Tianshan 1 (2006)	China and Kazakhstan	Organised by law enforcement and security departments	

	Date	Location	Code name	Participating countries	Nature	Notes
5	Sept. 22–23, 2006	Kulyab, Tajikistan	Coordination-2006	China and Tajikistan	Organised by armed forces, with more than 300 Tajikistan troops and 150 Chinese troops	First joint military exercise between China and Tajikistan
6	Aug. 9–17, 2007	Chelyabinsk in Russia's Ural Mountains and Urumqi, capital of China's Xinjiang Uygur Autonomous Region	Peace Mission 2007	China, Kazakhstan, Kyrgyzstan, Russia, Tajikistan and Uzbekistan	Organised by armed forces, with more than 4,000 troops from six countries	First joint anti-terrorism military exercise, participated by all the current six member states of the SCO
7	Jul. 22–26, 2009	Khabarovsk, Russia, and the Taonan tactical training base of the PLA in China's Jilin Province	Peace Mission 2009	China and Russia	Organised by armed forces, with 1,300 army and air force personnel from each side[a]	
8	Sept. 9–25, 2010	Kazakhstan's Ma tybulak training area	Peace Mission 2010	China, Russia, Kazakhstan, Kyrgyzstan and Tajikistan	Organised by armed forces; more than 5000 troops participated[b]	
9	May 6, 2011	Kashi, China	Tianshan-II (2011)	China, Kyrgyzstan and Tajikistan	Organised by security forces	

Table 5.1 (Continued)

	Date	Location	Code name	Participating countries	Nature	Notes
10	Jun.14–16, 2012	Northern Tajikistan	Peace Mission 2012	China, Russia, Kazakhstan, Kyrgyzstan, and Tajikistan	Organised by armed forces	
11	Jul. 27–Aug. 15, 2013	Chelyabinsk, Russia	Peace Mission 2013	China and Russia	Organised by armed forces, with 646 participants from China and 600 participants from Russia	
12	Aug. 24-29, 2014	Lhurihe training base in Inner Mongolia, China	Peace Mission 2014	China, Russia, Kazakhstan, Kyrgyzstan and Tajikistan	Organised by armed forces, with over 7000 personnel	SCO's largest joint military exercises to date.[c]
13	Apr. 21 to 25, 2015[d]	Shamsi Gorge, Kyrgyzstan	Peace Mission 2015	China, Russia, Kyrgyzstan, Kazakhstan, and Tajikistan	Organised by armed forces	

[d]http://en.sco-russia.ru/news/20150415/1013342851.html, accessed 16 October, 2015.

joint military exercise in Uzbekistan, coordinated by the newly operating RATS/ RCTS. This marked the first time all of the SCO member states including Uzbekistan participated in a joint exercise. In August 2006, China and Kazakhstan conducted the 'Tianshan One' anti-terrorist law enforcement (public security forces) exercise in Kazakhstan and China. In September 2006, China and Tajikistan conducted the 'Xiezuo (or "Collaboration") 2006' anti-terrorist military exercise in Tajikistan. This marked the first time China sent its complete military unit abroad for a military exercise.

The SCO joint military exercise was formally legalised at the meeting of the national defence ministers held in Bishkek, Kyrgyzstan in June 2007 when the ministers signed the SCO Member States' Agreement on Organizing Joint Military Exercises.[8] In August 2007, all of the SCO member states participated in the 'Peace Mission-2007' joint military exercise in Russia. Heads of state and defence ministers from all of the SCO member states observed the event, making it the most high-profile event in SCO history. It was also at that summit that the heads of state decided that joint military exercises should be held regularly. In 2009, China and Russia conducted the bilateral 'Peace Mission-2009' military exercise in China. In 2010, the 'Peace Mission-2010' multilateral military exercise was held in Kazakhstan. In May 2011, China, Kyrgyzstan and Tajikistan conducted the 'Tianshan Two' anti-terrorist legal enforcement exercise. In June 2012, 'Peace Mission-2012' was held in Tajikistan and all of the SCO member states except Uzbekistan participated in the event. In July and August 2013, China and Russia, the two countries conducted the regular 'Peace Mission-2013' anti-terrorism joint military exercise in Chelyabinsk, Russia. According to Chinese analysts, as joint military exercises in the SCO framework have become regularised and institutionalised, China has accumulated a significant amount of mutual trust and built confidence and joint capabilities with Russia and its Central Asian partners. This has resulted in a deepened cooperation of military technology between the SCO member states (Li and Wang, 2014: 197–202). This is particularly reflected in the intensified Sino-Russo bilateral military cooperation within and then beyond the SCO. In recent years, China and Russia have expanded the scope of their joint military exercises by launching the 'Haishang Lianhe' ('Maritime Cooperation'). The first of its kind was held in Qingdao, China in April 2012. More recently, in July 2013, China and Russia conducted the second 'Haishang Lianhe-2013' maritime joint military exercise in Vladivostok, Russia. The 2014 maritime joint exercise was held in the East China Sea and was witnessed by the leaders of the two states.[9] In a newsworthy move, the two states decided to conduct the 'Haishang Lianhe-2015' joint maritime exercise in the Mediterranean Sea in May 2015. Although the Chinese Navy officers emphasised that the manoeuvre was neither related to any regional situation nor targeted at any third party, analysts believed that this step was taken at a time when both states were under increasing strategic pressure from the US.[10]

Apart from the military, a wide range of national departments have become involved in SCO security, specialising in various areas. The national law enforcement departments of the member states are major participants in addressing organised crime. Concrete cooperation from the law enforcement departments of the SCO member states began during the 'Shanghai Five' period. This cooperation centred on the mechanism known as the 'Bishkek Team'. In December 1999, officials from the public security and enforcement departments of China, Russia, Kyrgyzstan, Kazakhstan and Tajikistan gathered for a meeting in Bishkek, Kyrgyzstan. The meeting produced several achievements, including the signing of an MOU on cooperation and mutual assistance; agreement on establishing the 'Bishkek Team'; and a coordination arrangement made by public security department officials of the five states, who agreed to hold regular annual meetings.[11] In April 2000, the officials of the 'Bishkek Team' held a meeting, issued a joint proposal for the leaders of the 'Shanghai Five' member states and formulated team regulations.[12]

The Afghanistan issue has become one of the few targets of the SCO's external action. Almost all of the SCO member states have substantial links with Afghanistan, be they geographical, historical, ethnic, social or religious. The domestic chaos and conflicts of Afghanistan have direct negative consequences for the SCO countries in terms of religious extremism, transnational terrorism, organised cross-border crime and particularly illicit drug trafficking. The US-led war in Afghanistan in 2001 added another concern for some SCO countries that were generally worried about the penetration of American and Western forces and thereby the great competition over power in the region. The Afghanistan issue has reached an impasse and no easy solution is expected. However, help from the international community is deemed necessary (Chan, 2008). Given the daunting challenges presented by the issue, the SCO member states have paid consistent attention and where possible taken measures to address it. Apart from rhetorical efforts and assistance programmes (Sun, 2009: 65–67), the SCO members have tried to incorporate Afghanistan more directly into the SCO framework since the organisation's early years. At the Tashkent summit in June 2004, Mr Hamid Karzai, who was then Afghani president, was invited as a special guest of the host state. Since then, it has become regular practice for the president of Afghanistan to attend the SCO summit along with representatives of the SCO observer states. At the same summit, an agreement was made to establish the SCO-Afghanistan Contact Group, which serves as a main mechanism for consultation and cooperation between the SCO and Afghanistan.[13] At the initiative of the SCO, a special international conference on the issue of Afghanistan was convened in Moscow in March 2009. Although the SCO-Afghanistan Action Plan is modest, the SCO has demonstrated its motivation to exercise its stabilising influence, if necessary, to cooperate with the US and NATO (Kahn, 2009: 14–15). However, to counter the US and Western influence, the SCO has stressed its respect for Afghanistan's autonomy, sovereignty and territorial integrity; its support for self-governing national unity; and the leading role of the United Nations in international efforts to solve the Afghanistan issue. The SCO has continued its efforts to incorporate Afghanistan, which was accepted as an observer state of the organisation in June 2012. Afghanistan has quite a large chance of being upgraded to an official member of the SCO. Given the official withdrawal of the US and NATO in 2014, the security situation in Afghanistan is now increasingly complicated. Evidence shows that multiple Central Asian militants have joined with Islamic State to challenge the secular Central Asian regimes. A new front line is forming against Islamic militancy involving all the SCO member states and other neighbouring states (Rashid 2015). The SCO has an opportunity to play a more active role in the Afghanistan issue. However, this would be a daunting task for the member states, given the nature of the issue.

China's role

Given the SCO's security and political cooperation, China's international leadership is helping the country achieve certain goals, including defining its direction and scope, uniting its partners and promoting its own national interests. The SCO, which can be traced back to the 'Shanghai Five', is starting from scratch. This requires the member states to formulate a general direction, scope, guidelines and rules of cooperation. In this process, the member states may diverge out of their respective interests and motivations. The main initiator is tasked with uniting the member states in the process. Finally, rational logic determines that a state's decision to invest resources in a project is made out of the expectation of potential returns. Throughout the whole process, China has been keen to play various types of international leadership, including structural, entrepreneurial and intellectual roles. In practice, these different types of leadership have been exercised in an integrated manner.

Defining the direction and scope of its security and political cooperation is China's major leadership goal. As China is new at leading multilateral diplomacy, it faces the challenge of promoting the SCO in its chosen direction. Nevertheless, Chinese policymakers understand that agenda setting is particularly crucial for a newly created organisation. Evidence has shown that China strives to put quite a few issues on the SCO agenda. In fact, the creation of the SCO itself resulted from the Chinese initiative to upgrade the original confidence-building forum of the 'Shanghai Five' into a formalised regional organisation. After solving the border issue in the early 1990s, China promoted the formalisation of a regional organisation that could manage partners' interests in security cooperation, economic development and cultural exchange (Kerr, 2010: 129). China's entrepreneurial leadership has also been exercised to push forward joint military exercises. This started with China's bilateral exercise involving Kyrgyzstan in October 2002. Since then, China has participated in most of the bilateral and multilateral joint exercises conducted each year. As a populariser, China stresses that transnational terrorism is a common challenge to the stability of every SCO partner and the region as a whole. It actively promotes joint military exercises through the SCO process, an unusual move if one considers the non-alliance principle long held by the Chinese government. Of course, its support of joint anti-terrorism exercises does not mean that China has changed its non-alliance policy. In fact, all of the SCO's members deny the possibility that they are forming an alliance. Rather, China's support for joint military exercises was offered more out of the country's wish to demonstrate the joint determination of the SCO members to combat terrorism and exhibit the strength of the SCO to the outside world. In the same vein, China has worked as a leader throughout most of the SCO's major efforts and institutionalisation, including through the organisation's secretariat in Beijing and the RATS in Tashkent.

SCO leaders have expressed their determination to commit to security and political cooperation on occasions such as the SCO summits. Accordingly, the SCO has approved a number of important documents related to security and political cooperation. However, officials from the member states continue to face big challenges in substantiating general guidelines and principles and carrying out more concrete measures. China plays a pivotal role in breaking through the implementation deadlock to find a way out. As a preliminary step of implementation, China initiates and hosts big-scale forums to provide means of exchange, reach a consensus and define steps and priorities. The Chinese Ministry of Public Security hosted an anti-terrorism seminar in Hainan, China in November 2005. Under the auspices of the RATS, officials and related representatives from the six member states participated in the event, at which they analysed the regional situation of anti-terrorism and exchanged national experiences and measures.[14] In the same month, a forum focusing on national defence and security was held at National Defense University in China. Military officers of the SCO member states and observer states participated in discussions on matters of relevance and importance.[15] China has also tried to expand its security and political cooperation by involving a wide variety of member state governmental agencies. For example, in October 2002, the Supreme People's Prosecutor General of China took the initiative to launch the coordinating mechanism of the national procuratorates of the SCO member states (Xing and Sun, 2007: 76). This marked the beginning of the regular meetings of this national function of the SCO member states.

These examples of security and political cooperation touch on politically sensitive areas and may arouse the suspicion of other countries about exclusive security alliances. As such, China takes a cautious approach in promoting the SCO's security cooperation process. It has reiterated that security cooperation within the SCO is not a traditional military alliance targeted at any other third state. Rather, it is characterised by several important elements that generally render suspicion and criticism unnecessary. According to Sun (2013: 124–125), the SCO is basically inward looking and its security cooperation focuses on coping with intra-regional security threats and challenges. It is non-military, as it does not intend to solve disputes by military means. Furthermore, it is an open organisation with transparent procedures and does not exclude cooperation with other states and organisations. However, practice in more recent years tends to suggest that the SCO has the potential to become more of a quasi-alliance, more outward looking when China and Russia find it useful.

Uniting partners in the process of cooperation is essential for the continuing operation and ultimate existence of the organisation itself. It is true that China enjoys a structural power advantage vis-à-vis the Central Asian SCO members and to a lesser extent Russia. The end of the Cold War, collapse of the USSR and improvements in Sino-Russian relations have made it possible for China to exercise its structural power in Central Asia. For security and political cooperation to proceed as planned, China must convince its partners of the necessity of the initiative. The other member states initially exhibited reserved attitudes towards the progress of the SCO process. For example, members had different views of the creation of a joint military exercise mechanism. Kazakhstan showed enthusiasm, as did Kyrgyzstan and Tajikistan to lesser extents. Russia was rather reluctant and suspicious of China's intentions in the beginning. Uzbekistan was simply absent (Du Mont, 2003). The mainstream Russian view is that the SCO is essentially a Chinese project. Russians would prefer that a group like the CSTO, in which Russia is the clear hegemonic leader and from which China is excluded, act as the main multilateral organisation with security responsibilities in Central Asia (Kuchins, 2007: 325). Shortly after 9/11, China took the opportunity to increase the urgency of the issue. Chinese Premier Zhu Rongji called the SCO's first heads of state meeting in Almaty, Kazakhstan in 2001 to speed up the SCO institutionalisation process.[16] This is just another example showing that the skills of negotiation and entrepreneurial leadership include the ability to seize opportunities.

It was more important for China to convince its partners about the direction of cooperation in times of big challenges. This was particularly the case in the SCO, given the more or less equal power status between China and Russia. After the US-led war in Afghanistan in 2001, China could not understand why Russia initially adopted an undiscriminating and accommodating attitude towards the American presence in Central Asia. Although the US War on Terror generally complemented the Chinese interest in coping with regional terrorism over the short term, Chinese leadership was worried that the US would take the opportunity to find permanent footing in Central Asia. China tried to raise this issue with Russia because it believed that the latter would find the permanent American military presence unacceptable. It tried hard to convince Russian leaders at the beginning. It is believed that China and Russia took the initiative during the SCO process to oust the American influence when later developments surfaced in the former Soviet sphere, particularly those made after the so-called 'Colour Revolution', which was suspected to feature American involvement or at least rhetorical/moral support. The Astana Declaration was issued in this context in 2005, requiring the US to withdraw from its military bases in Uzbekistan. In November that year, 'the US flaw was lowered' and 'the keys to the base were returned' (Rumer, 2006). The world audience saw this as a setback for the US government. Given the weakness of the Central Asian states, this action would not have been taken without the endorsement of China and Russia. The perception of strategic pressure from the US made Russia more determined to support the SCO as a balancing instrument against the American influence in Central Asia. Indeed, countervailing against the American influence in Central Asia bound Russia and China together in the SCO.

China has also used intellectual leadership skills to unite its SCO partners in security and political cooperation. The concept of a 'new outlook on security' advocated China's intellectual conceptualisation of security threats and solutions in the region and beyond. In general, security is considered as comprehensive in scope, common in nature and cooperative in approach (Yu, 2008: 6–11). The notion of comprehensive security makes it easy to argue that both traditional and non-traditional security issues are real threats to national, societal and human security. Furthermore, threats to security are commonly shared by different states and societies, which are becoming increasingly interdependent. Finally, approaches to various security issues rely on the cooperation of different actors. China has well applied this new conceptualisation of security to the SCO context. It serves several purposes, including defining various and mostly non-traditional security threats and challenges in the region, arguing the cross-boundary nature of these threats and challenges and advocating joint action on the part of the states in the region.

China's intellectual leadership efforts continue. At the SCO summit in Beijing in June 2012, then Chinese President Hu Jingtao proposed the concept of a 'destiny community', urging that the SCO partners should strive to construct a community with a common destiny in the SCO space. The new Chinese President Xi Jingping reiterated this concept at the SCO summit in Bishkek in September 2013, emphasising the importance of constructing the SCO region into a destiny community so that the member states could rely on it as a strategic goal for their stability and development. China's strategic plan for constructing the SCO into a community of common interest and destiny is an intellectual conceptualisation. A community of common destiny emphasises the basis of common challenges and objectives that bind states together to achieve a joint solution (Xu, 2014: 128–130). It argues that what China pursues is different from a traditional alliance strategy. In contrast, a community of common interest stresses burden sharing and mutual benefit to achieve a win-win situation.

Promoting its national interests is the primary objective of China's participation in and leadership of the SCO's cooperation, particularly in the areas of security and politics. Regional stability is one of China's primary concerns (Sheives, 2006). Facing suspicion from smaller neighbours at its northwest frontier, China has exhibited its resolve to create a stable borderland by attempting to settle its border demarcation issues with Russia, Kazakhstan, Kyrgyzstan and Tajikistan within a relatively short period. To cope with the ever-serious problem of religiously and ethnically based terrorism in Xingjiang, China has strived to promote the issue of anti-terrorism on the SCO agenda. Indeed, fighting the 'three evils' has become the paramount objective of the SCO. China's efforts have paid off. At the first meeting of national defence ministers held during the 'Shanghai Five' process in March 2000, the ministers expressed in a joint communiqué their support for the One China policy and objected to including Taiwan in the TMD system.[17] The ministerial meeting prepared the keynote for the summit meeting later that year. At the Dushanbe summit of the 'Shanghai Five' in July 2000, leaders of the member states urged in a joint statement that the Anti-ballistic Ban Treaty signed in 1972 be honoured without any condition, as it was key to maintaining strategic stability and a basis for further decreasing strategic offensive weaponry. Furthermore, all of the parties agreed that installing the TMD system in Asia-Pacific would undermine regional stability and security and supported China in its objection to any state's plan to include Taiwan in the TMD system.[18]

In its effort to promote various norms such as the 'Shanghai spirit', 'comprehensive security/new outlook on security', 'harmonious world' and 'destiny community', China has advocated certain values in defending its own national interests, including frontier security, ethnic unity and regime stability. The presence of similar types of authoritarian regimes has eased the process for China. The ideas of the 'Shanghai spirit' and 'new outlook on security' lend the impression that China and its SCO partners are wary of possible interference and that the US is probably the only power with the capability to intervene in regional affairs. This is why even an American analyst suggested that the 'Shanghai Five', the predecessor of the SCO, might have been intended to countervail American influence in the region (Gill, 2001). The 'Colour Revolutions' or revolts in some former Soviet republics and particularly Uzbekistan and Kyrgyzstan raised the concerns of Chinese leaders. They believed that these so-called revolutions were supported by the US and other Western countries as part of their efforts to promote democracy (Pan and Hu, 2006: 55–56). This may pose a threat to the stability of regimes in the states involved and thus to China's interests in Central Asia and even the stability of its own regime. More immediately, a regime change in Central Asia may produce pro-American governments in the region and therefore undermine the solidarity and even existence of the SCO.

Indeed, China and Russia (as 'critical states') have spared no effort to promote values like the 'Shanghai spirit' in the SCO process while emphasising 'stability' and 'diversity' (Ambrosio, 2008). There is a high level of consensus between all of the SCO members on this issue. Leaders of the Central Asian SCO states share similar perceptions of the American intentions behind the 'Colour Revolutions'. In fact, they have been more determined to countervail American and Western democracy promotion efforts in their countries. Therefore, China's soft balancing through norm promotion tends to be less problematic (Song, 2013: 674–676). Within the SCO, China has been relatively successful at adopting relevant discourses to bind together other members of the organisation, rebut criticism from the US and other Western governments and defend its positions. Promoting certain norms can be a major instrument for soft-balancing purposes as long as the norms are shared by the members of the international institution.

Progress and problems

The SCO is not easily neglected within and beyond the region, as originally predicted in the West. On the contrary, its visibility and influence is steadily increasing. It has established itself as a joint project for mutual support/consumption and to a lesser extent collective action. SCO leaders and officials have emphasised that the SCO does not aim to be a political and security-related organizational alliance targeting any other third state. However, it has been widely observed that the SCO is a group that specialises mainly in security and political cooperation. Its paramount function may be its coordination of member states' policies related to anti-terrorism, organised crime and other related non-traditional security matters. It has exhibited observable tendencies to form political and security alliances in traditional security spheres.

However, the SCO is not exempt from various problems. Its security and political cooperation is primarily based on common concerns and interests and an effort to address commonly perceived threats and challenges. In addition, members of the organisation and particularly China have tried to promote common values and enhance mutual trust to consolidate the organisation's security and political cooperation on a more normative basis. Noticeable progress has been made, as suggested by the evident legal and institutional setups, operations and activities. However, the process is largely top-down and driven by political leaders and governmentally associated elites. Although dominant SCO norms and values are more often shared by the leaderships of member governments, it is not clear whether these values permeate the various stratifications of the member states' societies. In other words, the SCO's security and political cooperation is subject to interest convergence and divergence depending on the specific context. This trait differentiates it from a typical security community such as the European Union, whose common values underpin its basic principles and rules. Due to this difference, the SCO's security and political cooperation is more volatile and unstable. Although its scope and institutions have been established, their effectiveness is not well founded.

The duality of China and Russia's leading roles in the SCO presents a thorny issue. China is a major driving force of security and political cooperation in the SCO and must cope with the varying degrees of its SCO partners' motivations and capabilities. In other words, power and interest are the two defining variables affecting the trajectory of the SCO's cooperation. This usually occurs when the member states and particularly China and Russia share similar positions. The success of the joint military exercise is a good example. China originally tried hard to persuade its SCO partners and especially the Central Asian states to participate in the joint military exercise. Faced with increasing strategic pressure from the West, Russia took a more active approach to pursuing collective action at various forums, with the SCO providing an important venue. At the 2006 ministerial meeting, Sergei Ivanov, who was then the Russian defence minister, proposed that the member states develop a military cooperation plan in the SCO and explore the possibility of cooperating with other international organisations with a focus on Central Asia. The SCO's plans for a shared use of military force by its member states were discussed during the session, and Ivanov revealed these plans to the press. According to Ivanov, the SCO states were prepared to use force together 'to fight back against new threats and challenges, especially international terrorism, in particular its large-scale acts organized with the help of IT and modern high-tech weapons'.[19] It was believed that Russia intended to use the SCO as a counterweight to NATO expansion in the region. At the Beijing summit in June 2011, the Council of Heads of State approved the SCO Mid-term Development Strategic Plan, which was the first of its kind in SCO history (Wang, 2013: 205). However, Russian policymakers later deemed the mid-term plan too brief and claimed that a more detailed 2025 strategic plan was under preparation.[20] This evidence only confirms the presence of leadership competition in the SCO.

Furthermore, various member states may differ on the SCO's security and political cooperation in terms of interest pursuit, priorities and expectations. Russia as a big power tends to use forums such as the SCO to exercise its international influence. In comparison, some Central Asian states may wish to keep a low profile to avoid a backlash from Western countries. However, these Central Asian states value their participation in the SCO for its role in maintaining their national security and regional stability (Li, 2009: 86). The SCO member states may diverge on some concrete measures of security and political cooperation. Although the Central Asian states are somewhat similar in terms of foreign strategy, their differences on more concrete issues are noteworthy (Chang, 2001). On matters of military security cooperation, Uzbekistan refuses to participate in the meetings of national defence ministers and joint military exercises for fear that its relations with the US and NATO would be undermined. This attitude changed for a period when relations between Uzbekistan and the US soured following Western criticism of the Karimov regime's policy on ethnic minorities. In fact, the SCO made an effort to win the steady participation of Uzbekistan in the group. The RATS was originally scheduled to be hosted in Bishkek, Kyrgyzstan as a follow-up to the 'Bishkek Team' established during the 'Shanghai Five' period. However, the SCO's permanent agency was finally seated in Tashkent, Uzbekistan.

The SCO's unity has also been tested due to one member state's individual foreign policy. On 8 August 2008, the opening day of the Beijing Olympic Games, Russia invaded Abkhazian and the South Ossetia regions, over which Russia and Georgia were engaged in an acute territorial dispute. The move embarrassed China and drew widespread criticism from the Western governments. Later in the same month, the SCO leaders issued a joint communiqué at the Dushanbe summit, stating that they showed 'support for Russia's active efforts in promoting peace and cooperation in that region'. Furthermore, they decried the 'use of armed force to resolve problems' and called for 'respect of the basic tenets of international law'. This was generally interpreted as a failure on Russia's part to persuade its SCO partners to endorse its military actions in Georgia (e.g., Katz, 2008: 184). However, a more nuanced reading argues that Russia's SCO partners including China stood with Russia and criticised the irresponsible Georgian policy on its minority-dominated regions. Russian leaders could have easily vetoed the wording, as the SCO rulemaking was based on consensus (Tkacik Jr., 2008). Ambiguous terms like these illustrate the typically sophisticated situation in the SCO.

In Central Asia, the coexistence of several multilateral security mechanisms has further curtailed the influence of the SCO (Allison, 2004). In particular, Central Asian countries are members of the CIS's CSTO and also have coordinating relations with the West. Russia and all of the Central Asian states including Turkmenistan are official members of the Organization for Security and Cooperation in Europe (OSCE) and North Atlantic Treaty Organization's (NATO) Partnership for Peace Programme. Russia retains the strategic intention of focusing on the CSTO as the main security mechanism in Central Asia when possible. More notably, Uzbekistan's adoption of a tantalising approach to the SCO and its swinging attitudes between the CSTO and GUAM are good illustrations of how a member state conducts its strategic calculations according to changing circumstances.[21] In practice, this means that China must defend and promote the SCO in competition with other multilateral groups for influence in the region.

Perhaps a positive aspect of the solidarity of the SCO is the current trend of strategic association between China and Russia. Russia and China have faced strategic pressure from the US over the issues of Russia's policy on Crimea and Eastern Ukraine and China's policy on South China Sea and disputes with Japan. It can be well predicted that China and Russia will unite more firmly in their security cooperation at various venues. Central Asia has become a major unifying element in Sino-Russian relations (Weitz, 2006: 162). The SCO is a natural and excellent choice for such a venue.

Notes

1 Much of the information related to the cross-border organised crime, disputes and demography of the Central Asian countries was drawn from the World Factbook published by the Central Intelligence Agency (CIA), accessed online at https://www.cia.gov/library/publications/the-world-factbook in May 2015.
2 The ministers of national defence of the 'Shanghai Five' member states signed a joint communiqué. See http://www.people.com.cn/GB/channel2/16/20000331/26509.html, accessed online on 4 May 2015.
3 The SCO National Defense Ministers' Meeting was officially held, http://ru.china-embassy.org/chn/eyxx/qthd/t67155.htm, accessed online on 3 May 2015.
4 The SCO National Defense Ministerial Meeting signed a joint communiqué, http://paper.people.com.cn/rmrb/html/2006-04/27/content_5398988.htm, accessed online on 3 May 2015.

5 Special Interview: The SCO's RATS will play ever important role, http://theory. people.com.cn/n/2014/0910/c40531-25634583.html, accessed online on 1 May 2015.
6 The SCO held a joint anti-terrorism exercise in Uzbekistan, http://news.xinhuanet. com/mil/2006-03/11/content_4288349.htm, accessed online on 3 May 2015.
7 Almaty Declaration, http://202.84.17.73/world/zzbd/shanghai5guo/bg/background5. htm, accessed online on 29 March 2015.
8 http://news.xinhuanet.com/ziliao/2009-06/08/content_11507552_4.htm, accessed 4 May 2015.
9 News Background: China and Russia's joint maritime military exercise, http://news. xinhuanet.com/world/2015-05/08/c_1115227559.htm, accessed 5 September 2015.
10 Nine warships participating in China Russia Joint Military Exercise in the Mediterranean for 10 days, http://news.qq.com/a/20150509/013846.htm, accessed 9 May 2015.
11 Chronicle of China Russia Relations in 1999, http://www.china.com.cn/chinese/ zhuanti/239546.htm, accessed 29 March 2015.
12 Officials of Legal Enforcement of the member states of the 'Shanghai Five' process met in Moscow, http://www.people.com.cn/GB/channel1/10/20000422/46250.html, accessed 29 March 2015.
13 The Contact Group was officially established in November 2005, composed of member states' representatives, permanent officials at the SCO Secretariat and officials of the Afghanistan Embassy in Beijing.
14 The SCO member states held a seminar on anti-terrorism, http://www.mps.gov.cn/ n16/n1237/n1342/119976.html, accessed 4 May 2015.
15 The SCO forum on national defense concluded, http://news.xinhuanet.com/world/ 2005-11/16/content_3790658.htm, accessed 4 May 2015.
16 The SCO member states convened the first heads of government meeting, http:// www.people.com.cn/GB/shizheng/16/20010914/561051.html, accessed 20 May 2015.
17 Ministers of national defense of the 'Shanghai Five' member states signed a joint communiqué, http://www.people.com.cn/GB/channel2/16/20000331/26509.html, accessed 4 May 2015.
18 The 2000 Dushanbe Declaration by China, Tajikistan, Kazakhstan, Russia, and Kyrgyzstan, http://www.people.com.cn/GB/channel1/10/20000705/131545.html, accessed 29 March 2015.
19 The Shanghai Cooperation Organization acquires military character, http://www. kommersant.com/p670100/The_Shanghai_Cooperation_Organization_acquires_m ilitary_character, accessed 4 May 2015.
20 Perspectives on the three major achievements of the Dushanbe summit, http:// news.xinhuanet.com/2014-09/13/c_1112468459.htm, accessed 29 March 2015.
21 The GUAM Organization for Democracy and Economic Development is a regional organisation of four post-Soviet states: Georgia, Ukraine, Azerbaijan and Moldova.

References

Allison, Roy (2004) 'Regionalism, Regional Structures and Security Management in Central Asia', *International Affairs*, 80(3): 463–483.
Ambrosio, Thomas (2008) 'Catching the "Shanghai Spirit": How the Shanghai Cooperation Organization Promotes Authoritarian Norms in Central Asia', *Europe-Asia Studies*, 60(8): 1321–1344.
Berman, Ilan (2004) 'The New Battleground: Central Asia and the Caucasus', *The Washington Quarterly*, 28(1): 59–69.
Chan, Samuel (2008) 'Breaking the Impasse in Afghanistan: Problems with Neighbors, Brothers, and Guest', *China and Eurasian Quarterly*, 6(4): 103–128.

Chang, Qing (2001) 'Zhongya Guojia: Guoji Zhanlue, Waijiao Zhengce yu Guojia Anquan' ['Central Asian States: International Strategy, Foreign Policy and State Security'], *Dongou Zhongya Yanjiu* [East European and Central Asian Studies], 3: 48–54.

Chouvy, Pierre-Arnaud (2006) 'Afghanistan's Opium Production in Perspective', *China and Eurasian Quarterly*, 2(1): 21–24.

Du Mont, Malia K. (2003) 'Cooperation 2003: Style, Substance, and Some Surprises', *China and Eurasia Forum Monthly*, September 2003.

Gill, Bates (2001) 'Shanghai Five: An Attempt to Counter U.S. Influence in Asia?' *Newsweek Korea*, 4 May 2001, http://www.brookings.edu/opinions/2001/0504china_gill.aspx, accessed 15 July 2010.

Hao, Yufan and Weihua Liu (2012) 'Xinjiang: Increasing Pain in the Heart of China's Borderland', *Journal of Contemporary China*, 21(74): 205–225.

Kahn, Simbal (2009) 'Stabilization of Afghanistan: U.S.-NATO Regional Strategy and the Role of the SCO', *China and Eurasia Forum Quarterly*, 7(3): 11–15.

Katz, Mark N. (2008) 'Russia and the Shanghai Cooperation Organization: Moscow's Lonely Road from Bishkek to Dushanbe', *Asian Perspective*, 32(3): 183–187.

Kerr, David (2008) 'China, Xinjiang, and the Transnational Security of Central Asia', *Critical Asian Studies*, 40(1): 113–142.

Kerr, David (2010) 'Central Asia and Russian Perspectives on China's Strategic Emergence', *International Affairs*, 86(1): 128–129.

Kuchins, Andrew (2007) 'Russia and China: The Ambivalent Embrace', *Current History*, 106(702): 321–327.

Li, Shuyin (2009) 'Shanghai Hezuo Zuzhi de Anquan Hezuo' ['Security Cooperation of the Shanghai Cooperation Organization']. In Xing Guangcheng (Ed.), *Shanghai Hezuo Zuzhi Fazhan Baogao 2009* [2009 Annual Report on the Shanghai Cooperation Organization]. Beijing: Shehui Kexue Wenxian Chubanshe, pp. 273–288.

Li, Shuyin and Wang, Jichang (2014) 'Shanghai Hezuo Zuzhi Junshi Hezuo Zongshu' ['Review of Military Cooperation of the Shanghai Cooperation Organization'], in Li Jingfeng, Wu Hongwei and Li Wei (Eds.), *Shanghai Hezuo Zuzhi Fazhan Baogao 2014* [2014 Annual Report on the Shanghai Cooperation Organization]. Beijing: Shehui Kexue Wenxian Chubanshe, pp. 193–204.

Menon, Raja (2003) 'The New Great Game in Central Asia', *Survival*, 45(2): 187–204.

Nourzhanov, Kirill (2009) 'Changing Security Threat Perceptions in Central Asia', *Australian Journal of International Affairs*, 63(1): 85–104.

Pan, Zhiping and Hongping Hu (2006) 'Zhongya Jiang Hequhecong: Yanse Gemin Haishi Fangkong' ['Central Asia, Where to Go: Color Revolution or Anti-terrorism'], *Eluosi Zhongya Dongou Yanjiu* [Journal of Eurasian Studies], 2:51–56.

Rashid, Ahmed (2015) 'Jihad's New Frontier', *International Herald Tribune*, 12 June 2015.

Rumer, Eugene (2006) 'The U.S. Interests and Role in Central Asia after K2', *The Washington Quarterly*, 29(3): 141–154.

Sheives, Kevin (2006) 'China Turns West: Beijing's Contemporary Strategy Towards Central Asia', *Pacific Affairs*, 79(2): 205–224.

Shi, Lan (2013) 'Zhongguo yu Zhongya Guojia de Anquan Hezuo' ['Security Cooperation between China and Central Asian Countries']. In Feng Shalei and Wang Haiyan (Eds.), *Shanghai Hezuo Zuzhi Fazhan Baogao 2013* [Annual Report on Development of SCO 2013]. Shanghai: Shanghai People's Press, pp. 361–374.

Song, Weiqing (2013) 'Feeling Safe, Being Strong: China's Strategy of Soft Balancing through the Shanghai Cooperation Organization', *International Politics*, 50(5): 664–685.

Sun, Zhuangzhi (2009) 'Shanghai Hezuo Zhuzhi yu Afuhan Wenti' ['The Shanghai Cooperation Organization and the Issue of Afghanistan']. In Xing Guangcheng (Ed.), *Shanghai Hezuo Zuzhi Fazhan Baogao 2009* [2009 Annual Report on the Shanghai Cooperation Organization]. Beijing: Shehui Kexue Wenxian Chubanshe, pp. 65–75.

Sun, Zhuangzhi (2013) 'Shanghai Hezuo Zuzhi Anquan Hezuo de Jiben Tezheng yu Youxian Fangxiang' ['The Main Characteristics and Priorities of Security Cooperation of Shanghai Cooperation Organization']. In Li Jingfeng, Wu Hongwei and Li Wei (Eds.), *Shanghai Hezuo Zuzhi Fazhan Baogao 2013* [2013 Annual Report on the Shanghai Cooperation Organization]. Beijing: Shehui Kexue Wenxian Chubanshe, pp. 122–133.

TkacikJr., John J. (2008) Olympic Invasion: China, the Shanghai Cooperation Organization and Russia's Aggression, Webmemo #2048, the Heritage Foundation. http://www. heritage.org/research/reports/2008/09/olympic-invasion-china-the-shanghai-cooperatio n-organization-and-russias-aggression, accessed 17 May 2015.

Tsepkalo, Valery V. (1998) 'The Remaking of Eurasia', *Foreign Affairs*, 77(2): 107–126.

Wang, Cong (2013) 'The SCO Security Cooperation'. In Jingfeng Li, Hongwei Wu and Wei Li (Eds.), *Shanghai Hezuo Zuzhi Fazhan Baogao (2013)* [Annual Report on the Shanghai Cooperation Organization (2013)]. Beijing: Social Sciences Academic Press, pp. 204–211.

Weitz, Richard (2006) 'Averting a New Great Game in Central Asia', *The Washington Quarterly*, 29(3),: 155–167.

Xu, Wenhong (2014) 'Shanghai Hezuo Zuzhi yinggai Chengwei "Liyi Gongtongti" he "Mingyun Gongtongti"' ['Shanghai Cooperation Organization to Become an Interest Community and a Destiny Community']. In Li Jingfeng, Wu Hongwei and Li Wei (Eds.), *Shanghai Hezuo Zuzhi Fazhan Baogao 2014* [2014 Annual Report on the Shanghai Cooperation Organization]. Beijing: Shehui Kexue Wenxian Chubanshe, pp. 127–144.

Xing, Guangcheng and Zhuangzhi Sun (2007) *Shanghai Hezuo Zuzhi Yanjiu* [Studies on Shanghai Cooperation Organization]. Changchun, China: Changchun Press.

Yang, Shu (2005) *Zhuanxing zhong de Zhongya he Zhongguo* [The Central Asia in Transformation and China]. Beijing: Peking University Press.

Yemelianova, Galina M. (2007) 'The Rise of Muslims in Islam Eurasia: Internal Determinants and Potential Consequences', *China and Eurasia Forum Quarterly*, 5 (2): 73–91.

Yu, Jianhua (2008) *Shanghai Hezuo Zuzhi Feichuangtong Anquan Yanjiu* [Studies on Non-Traditional Security Issues in Shanghai Cooperation Organization]. Shanghai: Shanghai Academy of Social Sciences Press.

6 Economic and functional cooperation

This chapter examines another major aspect of the cooperation amongst the member states of the SCO; namely, economic and related functional areas including trade, investment, energy, transportation, telecommunications, technology and agriculture. Encouraged by progress in institutional settings and security cooperation, some SCO member states, particularly China, have made efforts to advance economic cooperation within the SCO framework. This chapter describes the development of the member states' cooperation in these areas, with reference to the major variables of interest and power discussed in the analytical framework as defined in Chapter Two. This chapter argues that because of the divergent interests of the SCO member states, the organisation is taking a difficult track, despite some moderate progress. Therefore, the member states that are more motivated to obtain economic and functional cooperation, such as China, must resort to bilateral options to advance cooperation.

The background

All of the SCO countries are currently defined by international standards as developing or less developed countries. The World Bank classifies its member states on the basis of per capita Gross National Income.[1] By this classification, Russia is the only high-income member country (USD 13,850 in 2013), followed by Kazakhstan (USD 11,550) and China (USD 6560) as upper-middle-income countries, then Kyrgyzstan (USD 1210) and Uzbekistan (USD 1880) as lower-middle-income countries and finally Tajikistan as a lower-income country (USD 990). The International Monetary Fund (IMF) adopts analytical criteria in its classification, with a focus upon a country's aggregate gross domestic product and population, its main sources of export earnings and its financial position as a net creditor or debtor. By this definition, all of the SCO member states are classified as developing economies. China, Russia and Kazakhstan are defined as emerging markets and developing economies, whilst Kyrgyzstan, Uzbekistan and Tajikistan are defined as low-income developing economies (IMF, 2015: 151–152).

In terms of social and economic development, each of the SCO member states, including the Central Asian countries, China and Russia, is special in several respects. First, the SCO member states have similar economic backgrounds in which a transition was made from a strictly centrally planned economy to a market-based economy, although with varying approaches, scales and degrees of success. The former Soviet republics in Central Asia adopted different approaches in transforming their economic structures (Yang, 2005: 123–148). Nevertheless, all of the Central Asian countries had generally emerged from the economic and social chaos after their unexpected independence and completed their economic transition by the end of the 1990s. After difficult, sometimes controversial, implementation of political, economic and social reforms, most of the Central Asian countries have enjoyed economic growth. Russia has experienced a similar political, social and economic transformation on a much larger scale with much larger repercussions. From the end of the 1990s, the Russian economy began to witness a high rate of growth as a result of soaring energy prices. Unlike the 'shock therapy' type of radical economic reform policy adopted by the Central Asian states and Russia, China has adopted a cautious approach of gradual and piecemeal economic reform and has had no major political reform since 1978. The country has thus avoided massive social upheaval and has achieved continued phenomenal economic growth for more than three decades.

In terms of their individual economic structures and development potentials, the SCO member states exhibit both convergent, but more divergent, characteristics and trends.[2] Of the new Central Asian nations, Kazakhstan has been the most successful in securing social stability, achieving economic growth and promoting its international status due to shrewd political leadership, selective economic reform and booming energy exports (Olcott, 2008). The state leadership is ambitious and optimistic about the country's future development and has set a goal of reaching the world's top 30 economies by 2050.[3] It is also notable that the government of Kazakhstan considers education a high priority. In 2011, it ranked first on UNESCO's 'Education for All Development Index' by achieving near-universal levels of primary education, adult literacy and gender parity.[4] In comparison, its Central Asian neighbours have not fared so well. Kyrgyzstan and Tajikistan, two smaller Central Asian nations, each have a large, poor population and poor social and economic conditions due to a lack of investment in infrastructure and social services, weak governance capacity and high levels of corruption. In Tajikistan, for example, the national poverty rate was still high at about 36 per cent in 2013, but this was a great improvement from the astonishing figures of 96 per cent in 1999 and 47 per cent in 2009. Because both countries lack important natural resources like oil and gas, their economies are heavily dependent upon agriculture. Kyrgyzstan relies upon agriculture for one-fourth of its gross domestic product and one-third of total employment and upon gold mining for 26 per cent of its tax revenues and 50 per cent of its export earnings. Similarly, Tajikistan relies upon agriculture for 20 per cent of its gross domestic product and 53 per cent of its overall employment and remittances from migrant workers, mostly in Russia, as a major source of external earnings. The country also suffers from insufficient heating and sanitation facilities and extensive electricity shortages, especially in winter. Uzbekistan is the most populous country in the region. Its economy is based upon the export of raw materials such as natural gas and minerals. However, its development suffers from deteriorating security conditions such as terrorism and increasing tensions with its neighbours over regional issues, especially the management and use of trans-boundary energy and water resources. The government is also unable to provide quality social services such as education and health-care. Since the 1990s, the migration of labour from the Central Asian states to Russia has been a notable economic and social phenomenon. Most of the Central Asian labour migrants hail from Tajikistan, Kyrgyzstan and Uzbekistan (Laruelle, 2007) and their remittances are a major source of external earnings for these countries. The phenomenon has had both positive and negative social repercussions in both Russia and the Central Asian countries.

Since the prices of oil and natural gas soared at the end of the 1990s, the Russian economy has witnessed robust growth. This growth has contributed positively to its national development, in terms of the state balance of payment, income per capita and living standards. However, Russia is not free from some inherent problems with its economy, such as its heavy reliance upon the expor-tation of energy and other raw materials, rampant nepotism and corruption and a staggering legal system. Even more seriously, Russia has begun to face great setbacks in recent years due to a combination of economic and geopolitical factors. Since its annexation of Crimea and its policy on the Eastern Ukrainian crisis in 2014, it has endured economic sanctions from the West. Tensions between Russia and the West continue to grow. To make things worse for Russia, oil prices plummeted at about the same time. Hit by these factors, the Russian economy experienced a turning point. According to a World Bank estimate, a negative growth outlook for Russia is most likely in 2015 and 2016; the economy is expected to contract by 3.8 per cent in 2015 and modestly decline by 0.3 per cent in 2016.

After decades of economic reform and high rates of growth, China has achieved remarkable development. It replaced Japan as the world's second largest economy in 2010 and the United States as the largest trading state in the world in 2013 and has been a top state for foreign reserves for the years after 2009. Over the years, China has lifted more than 500 million people out of poverty. That said, the country still faces great challenges with regard to its economy. Its economic reform is incomplete, with state-owned enterprises dominating major sectors and underdeveloped private enterprises. For example, the financial and energy sectors are monopolised by several state banks and are troubled by inefficiency, bad loans, corruption and rigidity. In the manu-facturing sectors in which China has comparative advantages, it has the task of enhancing technological innovation and moving towards the upper end of the supply chain. The number of people under the poverty line is still huge. The problems of social inequality, environmental degradation and demo-graphic challenges are pressing and render more difficult the government's strategy to increase domestic consumption as another stimulant of economic growth, along with trade and investment.

There have been developments and problems in the bilateral economic relationships between the SCO member nations. Since the establishment of diplomatic relations in the early 1990s, China has actively pursued business opportunities with its Central Asian neighbours. Energy, in the form of oil and natural gas, is most attractive to China, so China is interested economically in Kazakhstan, Turkmenistan and Uzbekistan, the region's three oil and natural gas producers. Kazakhstan also possesses 20 per cent of the world's reserves of uranium, the source of nuclear energy. The two smaller and poorer states, Kyrgyzstan and Tajikistan, find themselves with very little to offer in their economic relationships with China. The only potential area is their possible exportation of hydropower, due to their abundant hydroelectric resources. However, that again depends upon their ability to secure sufficient financing. In addition, China sees potential markets for its service industries and manufactured commodities, both industrial and consumer goods, in the Central Asian nations.

Until the end of the 1990s, however, China's trade and economic relationships with the countries in the region still accounted for very little of its overall foreign trade. The only accountable development is the bilateral economic relationship between China and Kazakhstan, which has become more substantial over the years. The trade and economic relationship between the two sides was characterised by more traditional types of business activities. Small business traders in both China and Central Asia are active and benefit from the cross-border trading of Chinese-made consumer goods in Central Asian markets. Chinese small business owners have a sizable presence in various Central Asian countries, mostly in Kazakhstan, but also in Kyrgyzstan and Tajikistan (Olimova, 2009; Zhaparov, 2009) The wholesale markets and bazaars that are found in most Central Asian countries play a large role in the trading of Chinese consumer goods in the region (Ibraimov, 2009: 49–50). The movement of people between China and Central Asia is also a new development. Chinese migration to Central Asia is usually fluid and temporary and usually involves commercial and labour migrants (Sadovskaya, 2007: 153–159). In China, particularly in Muslim-dominated Urumqi, the capital of Xinjiang, small business owners from Central Asia find themselves at home. An interesting element in this regard are the cross-border minorities who act as cultural and economic mediators between China and the Central Asian countries. This is particularly the case with the Dungan people and the Uyghurs in Central Asian countries, particularly in Kazakhstan and Kyrgyzstan and the Central Asian minorities in China, particularly the ethnic Kazakhs in China (Laruelle and Peyrouse, 2009).

After the turn of the twenty-first century, bilateral economic and trade relations began to take off. Rapid progress in economic and trade relations was largely triggered by the high degree of economic complementarity and by geographic proximity. China has established world-class manufacturing

Table 6.1 China's economic relations with its SCO partners (Unit: USD1 million)

Year / Country		2013	2012	2011	2010	2005	2001
China's export	Russia	49591.17	44055.96	38903.52	29612.07	13211.28	2711.16
	Kazakhstan	12545.12	11000.73	9566.53	9320.07	3896.75	327.72
	Kirghizia	5075.35	5073.37	4878.29	4127.51	867.15	76.64
	Tajikistan	1869.36	1747.87	1996.78	1376.5	143.74	5.31
	Uzbekistan	2613.36	1783.34	1359.24	1181.02	230.06	50.68
China's import	Russia	39667.83	44155.04	40369.87	25921.04	15889.94	7959.38
	Kazakhstan	16050.84	14680.84	15394.7	11128.45	2909.36	960.65
	Kirghizia	62.35	88.95	98.16	72.12	105.05	42.22
	Tajikistan	88.75	108.83	72.23	56.06	14.2	5.45
	Uzbekistan	1938.09	1091.85	807.37	1302.24	450.5	7.62
China's FDI inflow	Russia	22.08	29.92	31.02	34.97	81.99	29.76
	Kazakhstan	3.63	5.55	11.27	1.55	2.33	0.33
	Tajikistan	Not available	0.11	Not available	0.07	0.21	Not available
	Uzbekistan	0.05	1.55	4.57	Not available	0.01	0.71
China's FDI outflow	Russia	1022.25	784.62	715.81	567.72	Not available	Not available

Sources: Annual data from National Bureau of Statistics of the People's Republic of China; http://data.stats.gov.cn/easyquery.htm?cn=C01, accessed 12 October 2015.

Notes: There is little data on China's outward FDI with its Central Asian SCO partners because Chinese investment in the four countries is so small, accounting for nearly 0 per cent of overall China outward FDI.

capabilities in both industrial and consumer goods but is in desperate need of energy. The Central Asian countries are generally rich in energy resources but are not self-sufficient in the provision of manufactured products. By the end of the 2000s, the pattern of bilateral trade was firmly established. The Central Asian countries export raw materials, particularly oil and natural gas, which account for more than 90 per cent of their overall trade with China. In return, China exports manufactured products, including more than 50 per cent of its industrial products and more than 30 per cent of its consumer products, to Central Asian markets (Ibraimov, 2009: 48–49). Trade turnover between the two parties has tripled every few years. Trade between China and Kazakhstan accounts for more than 80 per cent of China's total trade with all Central Asian countries. In comparison, development of investment is far behind. Although China's Foreign Direct Investment (FDI) has been on a steady increase, its outflow FDI to the SCO partner countries in Central Asia is almost negligible.

Further rhetoric and attempts have been made regarding the possibility of region-wide economic cooperation. This issue, however, faces several strategic choices. First, there is debate regarding intraregional cooperation within Central Asia and extraregional cooperation with outside parties. After their independence, Central Asian countries attempted regional economic cooperation amongst themselves. On 30 April 1994, Kazakhstan, Kyrgyzstan and Uzbekistan signed the Central Asian Economic Space Agreement, marking the beginning of multilateral economic agreement in the region. In 1998, the economic cooperation of these three Central Asian states was renamed the Central Asian Economic Community after Tajikistan was added as a member. Despite some modest progress, this economic organisation faced some deep-rooted obstacles on its way towards full-fledged multilateral regional cooperation. This intraregional initiative ended when the Central Asian Economic Community was absorbed into the Russia-dominated Eurasian Economic Community (EAEC) in 2006 (Qin, 2002). However, the idea never dies. As the most successful state in the region, Kazakhstan has become increasingly ambitious in taking the lead in regional cooperation. Nursultan Nazarbayev, the Kazakh president, proposed the formation of a Central Asian Union in 2005 (Zhang, 2008).

Regarding extraregional cooperation with states outside the region, another choice exists between greater alignment with Russia or with China. The Central Asian countries and Russia have strong economic ties for historical reasons. Until the beginning of the twenty-first century, all of the former Soviet republics in Central Asia, with the exception of Uzbekistan, retained close economic relations with Russia. To some extent, most Central Asian countries are in Russia's grip, due to the Soviet legacies of their economic planning structure and current Russian political influence. Because they find the current situation undesirable, the Central Asian states have strived for diversity in their external economic cooperation (Joint Research Team, 2004: 4). In this regard, China is their best possible alternative. Trade relationships are generally complementary between China and the other five SCO member nations, whereas the latter share much similarity in their economic structures (Liu, 2009: 94–96). The Chinese economy is based more upon labour-intensive sectors and increasingly upon technological and capital-intensive sectors due to upgrades in its manufacturing capabilities and its accumulation of financial resources. This gives China the capability and incentive to develop economic relationships with the Central Asian countries and with Russia to supply energy resources and markets for manufactured products and investment. Chinese analysts believe that the two factors of energy reserves and geographical proximity provide a solid basis for economic cooperation amongst the SCO member states (Sun, 2009: 121–122).

Extraregional cooperation involving both China and Russia still has obstacles. Most important of all, Russia never finds it easy to give up Central Asia as part of its traditional sphere of influence. It fears that greater economic cooperation between China and Central Asia would only help to boost Chinese expansion in the region given its growing economic might. In addition, the economies of Russia and the Central Asian SCO members are traditionally driven by energy and natural resources, which means that they compete for export markets. Furthermore, the Central Asian countries have problems amongst themselves. The thorny issue of water resources in Central Asia is one such example.[5] The dispute has direct negative effects upon the agricultural and energy sectors of the Central Asian countries and negative implications for regional cooperation in general. Finally, the region's abundant reserves of oil and gas have become a new battlefield for a number of outside players, triggering pipeline politics, social and political instability and conflicts amongst and within the countries in the region.[6]

Operation and activities

Although the SCO has established itself primarily as an organisation of regional security, cooperation in economic and other related functional areas has been increasingly incorporated. Currently, economic and functional cooperation has been defined as one of the SCO's two major pillars, along with security cooperation. Or to quote Chinese policymakers and analysts, it is better described in an analogous manner as 'one of the two wheels of the same cart'.[7]

Actually, economic and functional cooperation amongst the SCO members predated the organisation; some initiatives were already raised and discussed, mostly at the top level of state leadership, in the 'Shanghai Five' period. At the Almaty summit in 1998, the state leaders of the 'Shanghai Five' agreed that economic cooperation could be undertaken in the process, on the basis of equality and mutual benefit. Furthermore, some basic principles were suggested: to follow international practices in terms of trade and to encourage cooperation at the sub-state regional level and between large-scale enterprises and companies. Priority was also given to infrastructure projects such as oil and gas pipelines and to various transportation and power transmission projects.[8] At the Bishkek Summit in 1999, Mr Akaev, then-president of Kyrgyzstan, suggested the rejuvenation of 'Silk Road' diplomacy to promote sustainable development of the regional economy.[9] His initiative was nominally supported by the other leaders in the joint declaration. At the Dushanbe Summit in 2000, the leaders further expressed their goals for economic cooperation within the 'Shanghai Five' framework, including improving the investment and trade environments of the member countries to pave the way for the solution of possible economic disputes and to ensure the smooth operation of business activities. More specifically, the 'Shanghai Five' members rhetorically supported China's call for participation in its plan for the grand development of China's western region, and all agreed upon the great potential in cooperation in the energy sector.[10] It is clear that China and some Central Asian countries are motivated to carry on economic and functional cooperation alongside joint endeavours in security and political matters. However, the time was not mature, and it was therefore a largely vocal expression of interest at that stage.

This expression continued after the SCO was created in 2001. Without any concrete objectives or plans, the SCO member states agreed to include in the SCO Founding Charter one of the visions on strengthening economic cooperation.[11] This suggests that although the SCO was established as a regional organisation of security cooperation, some, if not all, of its member states have interest in and intend to develop regional economic cooperation within the same framework. China is seen as the major force behind this vision. After the SCO's inception, discussion of economic and functional cooperation has been more systematically undertaken and has led to further progress on economic cooperation apart from a mere expression of interest. Particularly between 2001 and 2006, the SCO achieved progress in economic and functional cooperation, along the major dimensions of legal and institutional arrangement, guiding principles and strategies and substantive programmes and activities.

Regarding the institutional dimension, the Council of Heads of Government has been designated as a major SCO organ that is responsible for defining the strategies, visions and priorities of the SCO's multilateral cooperation in substantive areas, particularly in the economic sphere. It was Kazakhstan's initiative to establish a regular meeting mechanism for the Council of Heads of Government (Prime Ministers) and for the joint expert working groups to be in charge of economic and functional cooperation in the SCO.[12] Article 6 of the SCO Charter stipulates that the Council of Heads of Government shall consider and decide upon major issues related to, especially, the economic spheres of interaction within the organisation. The prime ministers of the SCO member states held the first Council meeting in Almaty, Kazakhstan, in September 2001, marking the beginning of the regular annual meeting of the Council of Heads of Government (Chen, 2009: 37). Below the level of the meeting of the Council of Heads of Government, ministerial meetings of relevant portfolios, most importantly, trade and economic affairs and transportation, constitute another major element of the institutional arrangement of the SCO's economic and functional cooperation. In May 2002, the first meeting of economic and trade ministers began in Shanghai (Liu 2009: 89). The ministers signed a memorandum of understanding to provide the rules and procedures of the ministerial meeting and the senior officials committee. In November 2002, the first meeting of transportation ministers was held in Bishkek (Gao, 2009: 107). As a follow-up to the second ministerial meeting of economic and trade affairs in November 2003, the member states established the senior officials committee and five working groups for SCO economic cooperation.[13]

To encourage active participation in the societies, particularly by the business sectors of the SCO member states, the national governments have taken the initiative to establish several formally non-governmental entities that were largely organised by the national governments themselves. These entities include the SCO Business Council and the Shanghai Forum, which aim to promote dialogue, exchange and cooperation directly between businesses and academics, and the Inter-Bank Consortium, which is expected to facilitate investment and funding amongst the SCO countries. After the first meeting of the Board of the SCO Business Council in Moscow in October 2005, the inaugural annual session of the SCO Business Council was officially convened in Shanghai in June 2006, marking the establishment of the Business Council. The Representatives of the National Councils agreed upon basic documents regulating the operation of this nominally non-governmental entity of the SCO framework. It was also decided that the Secretariat of the Business Council would be located in Moscow.[14] Over the years, the Business Council has covered a wide range of issues, including energy, transportation, finance and investment, education and environmental protection and has made suggestions to the SCO leadership, usually through its annual report. The SCO Forum, also known as the Forum of Industrialists and Entrepreneurs of the SCO member states, was initiated by Mr Zhang Deguang, a veteran Chinese diplomat and the first secretary general of the SCO. The Forum is intended to provide intellectual and knowledge support to the SCO by bringing together experts and scholars from the SCO member states for exchange upon key issues regarding the development of the SCO and its member states. A number of think-tanks are selected to represent their respective states in the Forum. The first meeting of the Shanghai Forum was held in parallel with the annual session of the Business Council in Shanghai in June 2006.[15] At the initiative of the Chinese government, the SCO Council of Heads of Governments decided to establish the SCO Interbank Consortium (IBC) and signed the Agreement on Interbank Cooperation (Consortium) within the SCO framework in October 2005. According to its founding charter, the IBC aims to provide an institutional mechanism of funding and banking services for investment projects supported by the national governments and to facilitate business connections between the banking sectors of the SCO member states. The IBC is composed of constituent banks designated by the SCO member states and was officially established in Moscow in November 2005.[16]

In addition to legal and institutional development, another dimension of the SCO's economic and functional cooperation is to define main strategies, principles and approaches to carry out substantive activities and programmes. As the major organ in this sphere, the SCO Council of Heads of Government takes the lead in this regard. Since the first meeting in September 2001, the prime ministers of the SCO member states have convened council meetings on an annual basis. Following the general direction and guidelines defined by the SCO Council of Heads of State, the prime ministers make major decisions on economic and other related functional multilateral cooperation. At the first meeting in Almaty, Kazakhstan, in September 2001, the SCO prime ministers agreed to begin multilateral economic and trade cooperation by signing the SCO's intergovernmental memorandum of understanding on the main goals and directions of regional economic cooperation and by facilitating trade and investment. It is noteworthy that Chinese Premier Zhu Rongji proposed the four principles of the SCO's economic and functional cooperation, including equality and mutual benefits, rules of market economies, a gradual step-by-step approach and the combination of multilateral and bilateral mechanisms.[17] In general, these principles reflect the strong motivation of member states like China to undertake economic cooperation within the SCO, whilst their flexibility shows that realistic considerations are taken well into account. At the second Council of Heads of Government meeting in Beijing, in September 2003, the prime ministers signed the 'General Guidelines of Multilateral Economic and Trade Cooperation of the SCO Member States'. A three-step strategy of economic cooperation was agreed upon by the national prime ministers, starting with the facilitation of trade and investment, followed by further economic and technological cooperation and finally the free movement of goods, capital, services and technology in the long term.[18] At the third meeting of the Council of Heads of Government in Bishkek in September 2004, the prime ministers approved an action plan as a follow-up to the General Guidelines. The leaders also stressed that cooperation in economic and related functional areas is based upon voluntary participation by the member states.

The first years of the SCO's economic cooperation prepared the basic and essential settings of the legal and institutional basis, principles and strategies. However, this development was not followed by more real progress in concrete activities and programmes in various sectors. What has taken place is more discussion in specific areas, implementation of sporadic projects and more effective cooperation on a bilateral basis.

Although lofty goals in trade and economic cooperation are stated in various documents, the SCO member states have made only modest progress in matters related to trade and the facilitation of investment. The SCO member states signed an agreement on cooperation and mutual assistance in customs affairs in March 2007.[19] The agreement aims to standardise and facilitate customs clearance for the trade of goods amongst the member states. A similar agreement was reached regarding cooperation in some technical standards, regarding measurement regulation, quality control and inspection and accreditation and certification. Some initial work has been done in the promotion of e-commerce, investment, the telecommunications industry, technology and human resources. However, most of the work has involved discussion and some symbolic or exploratory projects. Only in energy cooperation have there been more substantial activities, but these have been achieved on a bilateral basis under the guise of the SCO's multilateral framework. Energy cooperation projects by the SCO's member states are characterised by state-driven initiatives, run by monopolistic state-owned energy companies and focusing on oil and gas trade, pipeline construction and energy exploration. It follows a one-way route from Russia through Central Asia to China. Nevertheless, it has been mutually beneficial between the parties in securing a stable market and a supply of energy resources for the geographic neighbours. In addition, in the transportation sector, several highway construction projects have been implemented in Kyrgyzstan, Uzbekistan and Tajikistan, largely with China's financial support (Liu, 2011: 39–41). Overall, the evidence shows that economic and trade cooperation in the SCO follows a trajectory of cheap talk, but little work.

China's role

If China is considered to be a major driving force of the SCO project, this is especially the case in promoting cooperation in economic and functional affairs. Indeed, China has been passionate about promoting economic and functional cooperation throughout the SCO process for both economic and political considerations. The economic motivations are more straightforward. Given the geographic proximity and economic complementarity, China has advantages in strengthening its economic relationships with the Central Asian countries and enhancing its economic power in the region. China has defined a number of key areas for economic cooperation with the Central Asian countries. The energy sector is the major area in the current stage. The development of transportation infrastructure is a priority for further economic cooperation. Trade and communications technology are large potential sectors for Chinese businesses. In addition, cooperation in agricultural sectors could be an area for China's development policy regarding the Central Asian countries (Chen, 2004: 51–52). At the same time, its political motivations are hardly negligible. Official Chinese analyses suggest that China should play a leading role in the SCO's economic cooperation for the consolidation of the organisation itself (Joint Research Team, 2004: 13). Therefore, encouraging the enhancement of China's economic involvement in the region is an essential political choice as well as being in China's economic interests. It is understandable that China would take more concrete measures to invest substantially in the economic cooperation of the SCO as an exercise of its economic statecraft for political purposes.

It is true that China vigorously sells its aspiration for multilateral economic cooperation within the SCO, with only a few echoes from its fellow members. Regardless of its success, however, there is no doubt that China plays the pivotal role in promoting economic and functional cooperation within the SCO. In this regard, its major contributions are to define the direction and scope of economic and functional cooperation, to provide incentives for the operation of economic and functional cooperation, and to pursue flexible approaches whenever possible. In its pursuit of these objectives, China uses various types of international leadership, whether structural, entrepreneurial, or intellectual.

To encourage the SCO's expansion into economic and functional cooperation, China must take the lead in defining the scope, direction, principles and strategies as a basis for implementation of concrete measures. Ultimately, China has an ambitious plan to construct a free-trade area within the scope of the SCO (Jia, 2007). However, China is realistic. Because this plan is impossible in the foreseeable future, it has proposed more modest goals and plans. The legal basis of the economic cooperation; namely, the four principles and the three-step strategies, have been formulated at Chinese proposal. At the first meeting of the Council of Heads of Government, then-Chinese Premier Zhu Rongji proposed four key principles or points, with an emphasis on launching the process of trade and facilitation of investment and formulating guidelines for the SCO's economic and trade cooperation. Zhu urged the SCO's member states to enhance economic cooperation amongst themselves. He further argued that all of the states must put their priorities upon the development of their national economy in the era of economic globalisation. Economic complementarity and geographical proximity would render the aggregate market potentials enormous given the overall size, population and natural resources of the member states. The traditional links between the SCO countries would be helpful in the development of economic relations. That said, Zhu also admitted that not all of the six member states of the SCO have well-established market economy status, with less improvement in the trade and investment environment. As a result, economic cooperation within the SCO should be actively pursued with long-term goals, whilst concrete steps should be steadily and realistically taken.[20] This gradual approach was further elaborated in the three-step strategy enshrined in the SCO member states' agreement regarding the guidelines of multilateral economic and trade cooperation in 2003.

Furthermore, China has also taken several specific initiatives, for example, the SCO Inter-bank Consortium and the Shanghai Forum. At the Chinese initiative, the SCO Inter-Bank Consortium was established to provide the financial means for cooperation between the SCO member states. After the SCO Heads of Government Meeting signed the Cooperation Agreement on the Banking Consortium of the SCO in October 2005, the SCO Banking Consortium was officially inaugurated in Moscow in November 2005.. The Consortium is composed of national development banks designated by their respective SCO member states. The China Development Bank is the major member of the SCO Banking Consortium which has provided massive funding to the SCO. After the global financial crisis, the SCO member states took financial cooperation more seriously. A regular meeting mechanism was set up, and joint meetings of national financial ministers and governors of national central banks were held in 2009 and 2012. This new mechanism is replacing more traditional practices such as fiscal donations in interstate financial cooperation (Guo, 2014: 237). It is predicted that the new mechanism would be conducive to China's 'go global' strategy because Chinese enterprises could take advantage of the financial tools and ultimately aid in the expansion of China's influence in the SCO region. China's international leadership has been exercised in this dimension of defining principles and major initiatives. Most noteworthy is its intellectual leadership in initiating several of the most important principles and strategies and in its entrepreneurial leadership, an ability to grasp the opportunity and project its proposals.

In a suasion game, China must find ways to provide incentives for economic and functional cooperation. The attitudes of the SCO member nations have varied regarding economic cooperation within the SCO framework. The Central Asian states are generally interested because they perceive the potential benefits of the SCO framework, which in practical terms means more cooperation with China. China would provide a valuable alternative in their external economic relations. In particular, Kazakhstan and Uzbekistan, two countries with rich energy resources, are more positive in this regard. Tajikistan and Kyrgyzstan do not have this advantage, but China is also expected to be a major source of investment in their infrastructure and in the development of their rich hydropower potential. China has become an important supplier of more affordable consumer and industrial products for the Central Asian markets. China also provides an inspirational model of development for these countries. The Central Asian governments find it appealing that China has achieved economic development in recent decades while the Chinese Communist Party has firmly retained its power and secured social stability. Kazakhstan has adopted a quite similar strategy of national development, with an emphasis upon political control, state-dominated economic development and education as a priority.

That said, the Central Asian countries may also have reservations regarding the enhancement of their economic relationship with China. Mostly they are afraid of possible uncontrollable penetration of cheap Chinese consumer products into their markets and Chinese labour migration. The weaker and more fragile economies of the Central Asian countries do not have the capacity to compete with their economic giant neighbour. This suspicion is generally shared by Russia. Furthermore, Russia has a strategic consideration in economic cooperation with China within the SCO framework. Russia's reluctance mainly derives from its concern about retaining its traditional advantage in the Central Asian economies. It predicts that enhancing economic cooperation amongst the SCO member nations would simply give China an opportunity to expand its economic and overall influence into Russia's traditional sphere of influence. For this reason, Russia has its own multilateral initiative regarding economic cooperation with the other former Soviet republics, including the Central Asian states. As a result, unlike the security and political domains, China does not find much empathy and support from its Russian partner in undertaking economic cooperation in the SCO. On several occasions, China has even found Russia to be a major obstacle to furthering economic cooperation in the SCO.

China must therefore face competition with other multilateral groups in its efforts regarding economic cooperation in the SCO. Although China has a great advantage over Russia in terms of its aggregated economic clout, it faces many difficulties in competing with Russia in Russia's traditional backyard. The Soviet legacy has given Russia a historical and structural presence in the region that is also reflected in the economic field. The Central Asian countries, for example, rely upon the Russian pipeline network for exportation of their energy resources. Russia is also the main target of Central Asian labour emigration and a major source of foreign remittances. Amongst the former Soviet republics, the Central Asian countries still have the most substantial economic and social links with Russia. In October 2000, Kazakhstan, Kyrgyzstan and Tajikistan joined Russia and Belarus in forming the EAEC. The EAEC then absorbed the already-existing Central Asian Economic Community in January 2006 under a Russian proposal. The Russia-dominated EAEC has become the multilateral arrangement by which Russia retains and strengthens its links in the region. The EAEC has become China's primary obstacle to the development of economic cooperation within the SCO. The Central Asian states actually attempt to implement multi-vector diplomacy in external economic relationships, but with different orientations. Kazakhstan and Kyrgyzstan joined Russia, Belarus and Armenia in the Eurasian Economic Union (EEU) in 2010. At the same time, Uzbekistan joined the GUAM Organisation for Democracy and Economic Development to attain more economic cooperation with another group of former Soviet states. It is true that the Central Asian countries attach great importance to the development of economic relations with China, but they cannot afford to neglect Russia. Meanwhile, they have also welcomed countries such as India, Iran, Turkey, Japan and the United States in developing bilateral economic relations.

China needs to attract its Central Asian neighbours in this multilateral contestation. Of the two options usually available to a hegemon in international negotiations, China chooses persuasion over coercion. The coercion approach is unfeasible because of competition with other players such as Russia and the United States. China can persuade the Central Asian states into multilateral cooperation only by offering side payments (also known as 'arm twisting' and 'bribery'). Therefore, China has begun to play this game of payment in the SCO. At the SCO summit in Tashkent, Uzbekistan, in June 2004, then-Chinese president Hu Jintao stated in his speech that the Chinese government would provide USD 900 million in preferential buyer's credit to the other SCO members to see more concrete results in economic cooperation. The China Import and Export Bank is the sole bank authorised by the Chinese government to provide government concessional loans and preferential buyer's credit within the SCO framework. By June 2006, the Bank had fulfilled the Chinese promise by signing preferential buyer's credit agreements with Kazakhstan, Kyrgyzstan and Tajikistan (Guo, 2014: 239). China continues to provide preferential loans to the other SCO members. In 2007, the Chinese government provided USD 1.2 billion of preferential buyer's credit. In 2009, then-Chinese president Hu Jintao announced at the SCO summit that China would provide USD 10 billion in government concessional loans and preferential buyer's credit to support its fellow SCO members in the improvement of basic infrastructure such as transportation, power and communications. A decision on another USD 10 billion in government concessional loans was announced by Hu at the 2012 SCO summit to provide funding for further economic cooperation in the SCO (Guo, 2014: 239–240). Government concessional loans and preferential buyer's credits are a concrete measure of financial cooperation in the SCO that relies upon China for funding. The funds from these two categories are used to support key projects and infrastructure projects in the SCO member states. In fact, China has become a major source of developmental funding in Central Asia, alongside the World Bank and the Asian Development Bank (Guo, 2014: 239). It is evident that China has used its international leadership, particularly the structural and entrepreneurial types, to attract its fellow SCO members in promoting economic and related cooperation.

In its efforts regarding economic cooperation with the Central Asian states, China has been sufficiently flexible to find its way out of deadlock. In this regard, the most noteworthy approach is the combination of bilateral and multilateral mechanisms of economic and functional cooperation within the SCO. It is true that real economic cooperation is dominated by the energy sector. The energy issue has been defined as a security in China's conceptualisation of comprehensive security. China must currently rely greatly upon the sea lanes for its energy imports from countries as distant as the Middle East, Africa and Latin America for half of its overall oil and natural gas consumption. Therefore, China considers Central Asia and Russia to be important and safer alternatives to securing its huge energy demands because of their rich energy reserves and geographic proximity. The SCO members have reached a growing number of bilateral and multilateral agreements on concrete projects in the energy sector. Energy cooperation in the SCO is characterised by a number of bilateral arrangements in parallel, including China and Russia,

Table 6.2 China's energy cooperation with its SCO partners: the import and export of oil and gas between China and its SCO partners (Unit: USD)

		2014	*2010*	*2005*	*2001*
China's oil import	**Kazakhstan**	4222821654	5552401247	517260192	96862877
	Russia	24982370394	8882171741	4958784927	327106404
China's oil export	**Kazakhstan**	159579	7470	No data available	41130
	Russia	7791204	81477091	55880348	40035330
China's gas import	**Kazakhstan**	136817336	998043	4224012	No data available
	Russia	87101632	196027296	71	89460
	Uzbekistan	799284762	No data available	No data available	No data available
China's gas export	**Kazakhstan**	44000	70996	No data available	No data available
	Russia	30440285	27877522	10550879	7402840
	Uzbekistan	159810	No data available	No data available	No data available

Sources: United Nations Commodity Trade Statistics Database, http://comtrade.un.org/db/defa ult.aspx, accessed 12 October 2015.

Notes: 1. The import commodity to China is under the category of petroleum oils, oils from bituminous minerals, crude.
2. The export commodity from China is under the category of petroleum coke, bitumen & other oil industry residues.

China and the Central Asian countries and Russia and the Central Asian countries (Sun, 2014: 226–234). It is also featured by a one-way flow of oil and gas into China from its SCO partners, Russia, Kazakhstan, more recently Uzbekistan, and the gas-rich neutral state of Turkmenistan.

China and the Central Asian countries are particularly bound together by their high degree of complementarity. China is much in need of energy, whilst the Central Asian countries have energy reserves and production far beyond their own consumption. The landlocked geography makes China a highly valued target market for Kazakhstan and other energy-exporting countries in the region in their strategies for diversification. In this regard, the bilateral cooperation between China and Kazakhstan stands out as the most successful development in China's economic venture into Central Asia. Since 1997, the Chinese National Petroleum Corporation (CNPC), a major Chinese state-owned energy company, has entered Central Asia, particularly, Kazakhstan, in an active search for business opportunities. In May 2004, an agreement to construct the Atasu-Alashankou oil pipeline from the western part of Kazakhstan to Xinjiang province of China was signed during Nazarbayev's visit to China (Saurbek, 2008: 87–89), and the pipeline was put into operation in June 2006, marking the first time that China imported oil via a pipeline. A further agreement was reached to expand the pipeline for greater oil exports from Kazakhstan to China.[21] There is also great potential for the two nations to cooperate in nuclear energy projects because China has the equipment and technology and Kazakhstan is rich in the raw materials needed for nuclear energy. In fact, it is the world's largest producer of uranium, an important nuclear material.

China has also succeeded in reaching multilateral agreements in energy cooperation by overcoming some great obstacles. To satisfy its thirst for energy, China has sought opportunities around the world, including Central Asia. One great success was its deal with Turkmenistan, a gas-rich country, in 2006. However, there is no direct geographic link between the two countries, so a transit route through Uzbekistan and Kazakhstan was secured (Sir and Horak, 2008: 84–86). This achievement illustrates China's efforts to overcome some difficult obstacles. First, Turkmenistan's energy diversification strategy could undermine the longstanding Russian control of Turkmenistan's energy exports. Second, negotiation with several states at the same time to establish consensus on the route of the pipeline entailed enormous effort. The Central Asia–China natural gas pipeline connects Turkmenistan, Uzbekistan and Kazakhstan via three parallel pipelines. Lines A and B have been in operation since 2008 and 2011, respectively, and Line C will be in operation by the end of 2015.[22] China has thus become a major consumer of the natural gas exports of these three Central Asian countries.

China has also tried to strengthen its economic ties with its Central Asian neighbours in other areas. In March 2006, the Chinese government approved the Sino-Kazakh Khorgos international border cooperation centre, specifying its role and status and related preferential policies. The project has been implemented by consensus between China and Kazakhstan.[23] In the 1990s, when Chinese companies began to meet consumer demand in Central Asia, the Chinese government arranged special flights and other transportation facilities to establish and strengthen the business links between China and Central Asia and within Central Asia. China plays an active role in the construction and funding of transportation and electric power projects in Central Asia, particularly in Kyrgyzstan and Tajikistan (Ibraimov, 2009: 49–52).

Meanwhile, China has also devoted much effort to its economic cooperation with Russia, particularly in the energy sector. The two states reached an agreement after a decade-long period of difficult negotiations on several long-term contracts for China's importation of oil and natural gas from Russia, including the construction of long-range cross-border pipelines. In this process, China actually devoted a great deal of effort by various means, for example, the provision of preferential loans and direct investment in the exploration for oil and gas and in the construction of pipelines. The Russia–China oil pipeline has been in operation since January 2011 between Siberia and the northeastern Chinese city of Daqing. This pipeline can allow a rapid increase in the oil trade between the two countries.[24] Agreement on two pipe lines for natural gas have been reached after a decade long strenuous process of negotiations, linking the Altai region in Russia and Xinjiang in China via the west line and Russia's east Siberia and China's Daqing via the east line. The east line is under construction and is scheduled to be put into operation from 2018. It is expected that Russia will be China's main supplier of natural gas in a few years.[25] The two countries also engage in technological cooperation on nuclear power projects.

Progress and problems

Over the years, the SCO has achieved modest progress in economic and functional cooperation. The main achievements include regularisation of the multilateral framework, agreement upon several principles and strategies and implementation of a few concrete programmes and projects for economic and functional cooperation.

That said, the current status is far from satisfaction for those who are enthusiastic about economic and functional cooperation within the SCO. A number of structural problems exist that obstruct more substantial economic cooperation. Economic cooperation in the SCO takes place amongst a group of developing and least developed countries that differ considerably in their economic structures, development strategies and marketisation. China's emergence as an economic power has 'differential effects' upon its neighbouring countries (Eichengreen, 2006). Its more advanced neighbours benefit from the rapidly growing Chinese market for their capital goods, components and technology. Countries that are rich in natural resources like Russia and Kazakhstan are also beneficiaries of the booming Chinese economy. However, most of China's neighbouring countries in the region have less developed economies. Very often, these countries find that they must compete with their giant neighbour for foreign investment and export markets.

Furthermore, the national economies of the SCO member states are largely state-dominated, with less developed market-based models. Because they lack salient private business sectors, economic cooperation within the SCO suffers from insufficient bottom-up dynamism. The existence of cross-border small businesses is helpful but does not account for much. Relative to the Central Asian economies, China is indeed an economic giant. However, several obstacles inhibit Chinese businesses' success in Central Asia. The current economic and trade relationships between China and the Central Asian countries are largely driven by interstate deals, small business dealers and cross-border traders. There is little normal commercial business in the sense that the organised businesses of established Chinese enterprises are insignificant in the Central Asian markets (Spechler, 2009). Apart from official bureaucratic and other non-trade barriers, problems faced by China in its business dealings in Central Asia include most seriously the rampant corruption in the Central Asian governments and illegal trading, including smuggling, run by organised crime groups and networks in the region, which is often associated with government officials (Ibraimov, 2009: 56–59).

The SCO member states also differ in their priorities and strategies regarding multilateral economic cooperation. China believes that economic cooperation should begin with trade and investment liberalisation before stepping up to substantive economic and technological cooperation, whereas most Central Asian states generally are not content with the agreements reached. They look forward to more investment for the construction of their infrastructure and developmental aid but are reluctant to engage in direct economic competition with countries like China on an equal footing. Therefore, they believe that their needs are not directly fulfilled if the SCO focuses upon trade and investment liberalisation alone. Furthermore, Russia believes that the SCO should focus upon security cooperation rather than economic cooperation (Xing and Sun, 2007: 119). This divergence has resulted in policy ambiguity and indecisiveness. The SCO's three-step strategy for economic cooperation states that the final goal is to achieve the free movement of goods, capital, services and technology when the time is appropriate. Nevertheless, the term 'free trade area' has been intentionally avoided. The member states could not agree upon the ultimate goal of a free trade area, which is a usual goal and practice of regional economic cooperation. It is also worthwhile to note that the free movement of people was not included as an objective. According to Chinese analysts, some SCO members are concerned that possible Chinese labour migration would undermine their domestic employment markets.[26]

Due to these general differences, cooperation is difficult to implement in specific areas. Each SCO member has different interests in the energy sector. China is interested in importing oil and natural gas from the other member states and securing a cross-border energy transit system. Russia maintains its control of the Central Asian countries' energy sectors by transmitting their exports through its own pipeline systems. Kazakhstan and Uzbekistan are interested in strengthening their capacities in the exploration and exportation of their energy resources, in the renovation of their equipment and in development of their petrochemical industries. Kyrgyzstan and Tajikistan are concerned about the construction of hydropower stations and a power grid network and exploration of their water resources (Xing and Sun, 2007: 115). The oil and gas pipeline networks in the region were built during the Soviet era and were designed for exportation to Europe through the other Russian territories. This situation has lingering effects upon the Central Asian countries, which find it difficult to reduce their reliance upon Russia for exportation of their energy (Saurbek, 2008: 82–83). Several issues in the energy sector demand multilateral coordination and cooperation, including oil and gas, uranium and water resources. Unfortunately, the SCO cannot make itself an effective platform for the management of these issues at this time (Matusov, 2007: 87–91). At the SCO Council of Heads of Government in June 2006, then-Russian Prime Minister Vladimir Putin proposed the establishment of the SCO Energy Club. This proposal was raised again by Putin in October 2009 and by Dmitry Medvedev in his capacity as prime minister in December 2012. However, it is not clear when the idea of the SCO Energy Club could be realised due to a lack of consensus amongst the member states on its objectives and rules. The SCO does not play any role in water resources, along with other organisations such as the World Bank, the Asian Development Bank and the United Nations, although the latter's efforts are not so successful (Libert et al., 2008: 18–19). Another major problem of the economic and functional cooperation in the SCO lies in insufficient funding. It is estimated that at least USD 10 billion is needed to implement the projects in the SCO Implementation Plan of Multilateral Economic and Trade Cooperation Guidelines (Xing and Sun, 2007: 118). Various problems in the financial sector inhibit further cooperation, including the insufficiency of funding, the lack of well-established financial systems in the SCO member states, particularly in Central Asia, economic differences between the member states and divergent political motivations (Guo, 2014: 244–246). The Chinese government has been keen on establishing the SCO Development Bank and Development Fund following the models of the World Bank and the IMF. Since Wen Jiabao, then Chinese Premier, proposed the establishment of the SCO Development Bank and Development Fund at the Council of Heads of Government meeting in October 2010, the Chinese government has raised the proposal on various occasions. However, the Chinese proposal has been resisted by Russia, which is mainly concerned about the increasing role of China in the SCO and its possible competition with the multilateral entities dominated by Russia.[27]

To make things even worse, the SCO faces direct competition with other multilateral organisations that include some of its own members. In the energy sector, cooperation between Russia and the Central Asian countries is much more substantial because of its long history. Most of their current energy cooperation is conducted either within the multilateral EAEC or on a bilateral basis. Russia has played the role of broker between the Central Asian oil and gas producers and the consumer states in Europe. Russia has spared no effort in retaining this role by connecting the Central Asian states to its oil and gas pipeline networks. Due to Russia's position, therefore, it is extremely difficult to implement multilateral energy cooperation in the SCO, as China has proposed. Pipeline politics have resulted in competition between China and Russia in the Central Asian energy sector. From the Chinese perspective, the Russia-dominated EAEC has become the greatest obstacle to economic cooperation within the SCO. China was particularly concerned when the Eurasian Customs Union was established in January 2010 and even more so when it was combined with the EAEC to form the newly upgraded EEU in January 2015. Kazakhstan and Kyrgyzstan currently participate in the EEU with Armenia, Russia and Belarus.[28] Tajikistan will also join soon. The EEU aspires to become a European Union type organisation. The situation has become a nightmare for China and the SCO. Although the Russia-led organisation has many difficulties to overcome, its success would essentially exclude Chinese involvement in Central Asian economic integration.

As a result of the divergences and competition, bilateralism prevails over multilateralism in the economic and functional cooperation within the SCO. Several concrete cooperation projects are described as bilateral agreements under multilateral guises. For example, China's preferential loans are actually negotiated and signed separately with the individual SCO members, not officially stated multilateral agreements (Matusov, 2007: 86–87). In this regard, the strong economic relationship between China and Kazakhstan has overshadowed economic cooperation with the other SCO members. With the operation of the oil and natural gas pipeline between the two countries, Kazakhstan has become China's most important supplier of energy resources. Kazakhstan also remains the best potential transit route for China's trade with Central Asia and beyond. This presents great incentives for China to cooperate and invest in infrastructure projects such as railways, highways and telecommunications in Kazakhstan. In return, China has become Kazakhstan's largest trade partner. The leadership of Kazakhstan also values China as a significant opportunity for the state's strategy of multi-vector diplomacy. The bilateral relationship has improved rapidly. In 2005, the two states established a 'strategic partnership', the only one of its kind in China's relations with Central Asian countries. This relationship is mutually beneficial for the two partners but may also suggest the stalemate of multilateral cooperation within the SCO.

That said, economic and functional cooperation in the SCO still has potential, given the high degree of complementarity between the economic situations of its member states and the ever-growing economic capabilities of countries like China and Kazakhstan. In fact, the SCO is still appealing to its member states, including Russia (Zhou and Wang, 2006). A Russian official hinted at the possibility that China would create a free-trade zone with the EEU.[29] However, several obstacles should be tackled before economic cooperation can be more smoothly carried forward. Security situations in the region are still complicated. The issue of Afghanistan has brought challenges to the Central Asian countries, most of which have a great deal of work to do in securing domestic stability. The states should also reach a consensus regarding the benefits of multilateral economic cooperation within the SCO. If these problems could be solved, the SCO's economic and functional cooperation would no longer rest solely with China. China has become more assertive in its foreign strategy; for example, it launched the ambitious 'New Silk Road Economic Belt', which could bring more opportunities and incentives for the other SCO members. At the same time, Russia's influence in the region has continuously declined due to the fluctuation of energy prices and its mistaken foreign policy. If successful, economic cooperation within the SCO could also have wide implications for its neighbouring countries (Norling and Swanström, 2007). Countries such as India, Pakistan and Iran could benefit substantially from engagement with the SCO in the development of particular areas of trade, infrastructure and energy. Given the prospects of upcoming expansion, the inclusion of new member states would bring greater stimulus for the SCO to take serious steps towards economic and functional cooperation.

Notes

1 Income Classifications, http://data.worldbank.org/country, accessed 18 June 2015. As of 1 July 2014, low-income economies are defined as those with a per capita gross national income (GNI), calculated using the *World Bank Atlas* method, of $1045 or less in 2013; middle-income economies are those with a per capita GNI between $1045 and $12,746; and high-income economies are those with a per capita GNI of $12,746 or more. Lower–middle-income and upper–middle-income economies are separated at a per capita GNI of $4125.
2 Information on the economic development of individual SCO member states is largely drawn from the World Bank and IMF websites, accessed online in June 2015.
3 President Nazarbayev's speech at the annual state of the nation in December 2012, http://www.akorda.kz/en/page/page_poslanie-prezidenta-respubliki-kazakhsta n-lidera-natsii-nursultana-nazarbaeva-narodu-kazakhstana, accessed 22 June 2015.
4 Take Note of Kazakhstan, Foreign Policy Journal, http://www.foreignpolicyjourna l.com/2012/11/21/take-note-of-kazakhstan, accessed 29 June 2015.
5 The Amu Darya and Syr Darya are the two major rivers in the region. In the Soviet era, management of the water systems in the region was largely undertaken by the Soviet Central Government, which managed them with Afghanistan and Iran, two other countries that share the rivers. Kyrgyzstan and Tajikistan, two upstream states, were compensated for electricity supply for their conservation of water resources for irrigation of the agricultural sectors of the downstream countries such as Uzbekistan, Turkmenistan and Kazakhstan. After their independence, this issue has remained unresolved, causing trouble in the relationships between the new Central Asian states (Libert et al., 2008).
6 'The Devil's Tears', *The Economist*, 20 November 2003.
7 Xi's attendance at SCO summit, Asian visits to boost neighbourhood diplomacy, China Daily, http://www.chinadaily.com.cn/world/2014xisco/2014-09/11/content_ 18580273.htm, accessed 29 June 2015.
8 Articles 6 & 7, The Almaty Declaration, http://news.sina.com.cn/c/ 2006-05-31/095210022508.shtml, accessed 30 March 2015.

9 Shanghai Five 1999 Bishkek Declaration, http://www.mfa.gov.cn/chn//gxh/zlb/sm gg/t5406.htm, accessed 29 March 2015.

10 Article 14, Heads of State of China, Tajikistan, Russia, Kazakhstan and Kyrgyzstan signed Dushanbe Declaration, http://www.people.cn/GB/paper39/951/132019.html, accessed 30 March 2015.

11 Clause One of the SCO Charter states that 'the Member States are encouraged to implement effective regional cooperation on politics, economy and trade, national defense, legal enforcement, environmental protection, culture, science and technology, education, energy, transportation, finance and other areas of mutual interest. On basis equal partnership, the member states of the SCO should take joint action to improve overall development of regional economy, society and culture, improve living standards of the peoples of the member states, and coordinate respective positions in participation in global economy.'

12 See note 6.

13 The five working groups are headed by the individual member states, including the e-commerce group headed by China, the customs affairs group by Russia, the technological standards and quality evaluation group by Kazakhstan, the investment promotion group by Tajikistan and the border transit development group by Uzbekistan. In 2005, two more groups were established: the energy affairs group headed by Russia and the information technology and telecommunications group headed by Kyrgyzstan. The Economic Cooperation of the SCO, http://www.sco-ec.gov.cn/crweb/scoc/info/Article.jsp?a_no=83446&col_no=290, accessed 19 June 2015.

14 History of the SCO Business Council, http://bc-sco.org/?level=2&lng=en, accessed 20 June 2015.

15 Shanghai Cooperation Organization Forum, http://www.mgimo.ru/sco-en, accessed 20 June 2015.

16 http://www.sectsco.org/EN123/bankunite.asp, accessed 20 June 2015. Due to its domestic problems, Kyrgyzstan could not participate in the first years of the IBC activities. In June 2006, the Settlement and Savings Company of the Kyrgyz Republic was authorised by the Kyrgyz government to be its national representative in the IBC.

17 The details of the four principles are as follows: (1) To uphold the principle of equality and mutual benefits, which is a basic norm of international economic cooperation and also a major part of the 'Shanghai Spirit'. (2) To abide by the rules of a market economy, which is key to following international practice in the SCO's economic cooperation. At that point, only Kyrgyzstan was a WTO member. (3) To take a gradualist approach, with a focus on outcomes. The economic cooperation of the SCO should start in less complicated areas and make steady progress in enhancing the process of trade and investment facilitation. For example, the member states can take measures to reduce tariff barriers and transaction costs, promote investment projects and establish and improve mechanisms for the implementation and supervision of various agreements. (4) To carry out multilateral and bilateral cooperation in an integrated manner. While implementing multilateral trade and economic and technological cooperation, the member states should consolidate and further develop projects and mechanisms in the existing bilateral cooperation. The Prime Ministers of the SCO convened the first meeting, http://www.people.com.cn/GB/shizheng/16/20010914/561051.html, accessed 20 June 2015.

18 The Process of SCO Economic Cooperation, http://www.sco-ec.gov.cn/crweb/scoc/info/Article.jsp?a_no=83446&col_no=290, accessed 27 April 2015.

19 SCO PMs vow to strengthen co-op in customs, agriculture, http://news.xinhuanet.com/english/2007-11/03/content_7002311.htm, accessed 26 June 2015.

20 Zhu Rongji proposed four principles for economic cooperation of the six states, http://www.chinanews.com/2001-09-14/26/122493.html, accessed 30 March 2015.

21 Deal signed to expand Sino-Kazakh oil pipeline, http://www.chinadaily.com.cn/china/2013-04/07/content_16379084.htm, accessed 26 June 2015.

22 Flow of natural gas from Central Asia, http://www.cnpc.com.cn/en/Flowofnatura lgasfromCentralAsia/FlowofnaturalgasfromCentralAsia2.shtml, accessed 26 June 2015.
23 The Centre is located on the border between the two states, with a total area of 5.28 sq km, and is used for various business activities such as trade negotiations, commodity exhibition and sale, warehousing and storage, transportation, hotel hospitality, shopping and financing. For a brief introduction to the Sino-Kazakh Khorgos international border cooperation centre, see http://leaders.people.com.cn/ n/2013/0220/c355955-20540135.html, accessed 4 June 2006.
24 Russia-China oil pipeline opens, http://www.bbc.com/news/world-asia-pacific-12103865, accessed 26 June 2015.
25 China and Russia Gas Deal, http://www.chinanews.com/ny/z/html/zhongetianra nqitanpan.shtml, accessed 26 June 2015.
26 The Process of SCO Economic Cooperation, http://www.sco-ec.gov.cn/crweb/scoc/ info/Article.jsp?a_no=83446&col_no=290, accessed 27 April 2015.
27 By Opposing SCO Development Bank, Is Russia Biggest Loser? http://www.eura sianet.org/node/72701, accessed 29 June 2015.
28 Introducing the Eurasian Economic Union: Where three is a crowd, http://www. economist.com/blogs/banyan/2014/05/introducing-eurasian-economic-union, accessed 29 June 2015.
29 China and Russia-led Eurasian Economic Union may set up free trade zone, http:// rt.com/business/230567-china-eurasian-economic-union, accessed 29 June 2015.

References

Chen, Yurong (2004) 'Zhongguo yu Zhongya Diqu Jingji Hezuo' ['China and Economic Cooperation in Central Asia'], *Guoji Wenti Yanjiu* [Studies of International Affairs], 2004(4): 50–56.

Chen, Yurong (2009) 'Shanghai Hezuo Zuzhi Chengyuanguo Zhengfu Shounao Lishihui' ['The Council of Heads of Government of the Shanghai Cooperation Organization']. In Xing Guangcheng (Ed.), *Shanghai Hezuo Zuzhi Fazhan Baogao 2009* [2009 Annual Report on the Shanghai Cooperation Organization]. Beijing: Shehui Kexue Wenxian Chubanshe, pp. 35–44.

Eichengreen, Barry (2006) 'China, Asia, and the World Economy: The Implications of an Emerging Asian Core and Periphery', *China & World Economy*, 14(3): 1–18.

Gao, Meizhen (2009) 'Shanghai Hezuo Zuzhi de Jiaotong Hezuo' ['Transportation Cooperation in the Shanghai Cooperation Organization']. In Xing Guangcheng (Ed.), *Shanghai Hezuo Zuzhi Fazhan Baogao 2009* [2009 Annual Report on the Shanghai Cooperation Organization]. Beijing: Shehui Kexue Wenxian Chubanshe, pp. 106–119.

Guo, Xiaoqiong (2014) 'Shanghai Hezuo Zuzhi Jinrong Hezuo' ['Financial Cooperation of the Shanghai Cooperation Organization']. In Li Jingfeng, Wu Hongwei and Li Wei (Eds.), *Shanghai Hezuo Zuzhi Fazhan Baogao 2014* [2014 Annual Report on the Shanghai Cooperation Organization]. Beijing: Shehui Kexue Wenxian Chubanshe, pp. 235–247.

Ibraimov, Sadykzhan (2009) 'China-Central Asia Trade Relations: Economic and Social Patterns', *China and Eurasian Forum Quarterly*, 7(1): 47–59.

International Monetary Fund (2015) 'World Economic Outlook 2015: Uneven Growth, Short- and Long-term Factors', World Economic and Financial Surveys, Washington, DC: International Monetary Fund.

Jia, Lizhen (2007) 'Goujian Shanghai Hezuo Zuzhi Ziyou Maoyiqu de Zhanlue Sikao' [Strategic Thinking on Constructing Free Trade Area of the Shanghai Cooperation Organization], *Eluosi, Dongou, and Zhongya Yanjiu* [Studies of Russia, Eastern Europe and Central Asia], 1: 75–80.

Joint Research Team, Europe Bureau and Institute of International Trade & Economic Cooperation, Chinese Ministry of Commerce (2004) 'Shanghai Hezuo Zuzhi Quyu Jingji Hezuo Yanjiu' [Studies on Regional Economic Cooperation of the Shanghai Cooperation Organization], *Eluosi, Dongou, and Zhongya Yanjiu* [Studies of Russia, Eastern Europe and Central Asia], 1: 2–13.

Laruelle, Marlène (2007) 'Central Asian Labor Migrants in Russia: The "Disporization" of the Central Asian States?' *China and Central Asian Forum Quarterly*, 5(3): 101–119.

Laruelle, Marlène and Sébastien Peyrouse (2009) 'Cross-Border Minorities as Cultural and Economic Mediators between China and Central Asia', *China and Eurasian Forum Quarterly*, 7(1): 93–119.

Libert, Bo, Erkin Orolbaev and Yuri Steklov (2008) 'Water and Energy Crisis in Central Asia', *China and Central Asian Forum Quarterly*, 6(3): 9–20.

Liu, Huaqin (2009) 'Shanghai Hezuo Zuzhi de Quyu Jingji Hezuo' ['Regional Economic Cooperation in the Shanghai Cooperation Organization']. In Xing Guangcheng (Ed.), *Shanghai Hezuo Zuzhi Fazhan Baogao 2009* [2009 Annual Report on the Shanghai Cooperation Organization]. Beijing: Shehui Kexue Wenxian Chubanshe, pp. 89–105.

Liu, Huaqin (2011) 'Shanghai Hezuo Zuzhi de Quyu Jingji Hezuo' ['Regional Economic Cooperation in the Shanghai Cooperation Organization']. In Enyuan Wu and Hongwei Wu (Eds.), *Shanghai Hezuo Zuzhi Fazhan Baogao 2011* [2011 Annual Report on the Shanghai Cooperation Organization]. Beijing: Shehui Kexue Wenxian Chubanshe, pp. 36–52.

Matusov, Artyom (2007) 'Energy Cooperation in the SCO: Club or Gathering?' *China and Central Asian Forum Quarterly*, 5(3): 83–99.

Norling, Nicklas and Niklas Swanström (2007) 'The Shanghai Cooperation Organization, Trade, and the Roles of Iran, India, and Pakistan', *Central Asian Survey*, 26(3): 429–444.

Olcott, Martha Brill (2008) 'Kazakhstan: Will "BRIC" Be Spelled with a K?' *China and Central Asian Forum Quarterly*, 6(2): 41–53.

Olimova, Saodat (2009) 'The Multifaceted Chinese Presence in Tajikistan', *China and Central Asian Forum Quarterly*, 7(1): 61–78.

Qin, Fangmin (2002) 'Zhongya Jingji Yitihua Fazhan Pingxi' ['Review of Central Asian Economic Integration'], *Dongou Zhongya Yanjiu* [Studies of Eastern Europe and Central Asia], 1: 77–81.

Sadovskaya, Elena Y. (2007) 'Chinese Migration to Kazakhstan: a Silk Road for Cooperation or a Thorny Road of Prejudice', *China and Central Asian Forum Quarterly*, 5(4): 147–170.

Saurbek, Zhanibek (2008) 'Kazakh-Chinese Energy Relations: Economic Pragmatism or Political Cooperation', *China and Central Asian Forum Quarterly*, 6(1): 79–94.

Sir, Jan and Slavomir Horak (2008) 'China as an Emerging Superpower in Central Asia: the View from Ashkhabad', *China and Central Asian Forum Quarterly*, 6(2): 75–88.

Spechler, Martin C. (2009) 'Why Does China Have No Business in Central Asia?' *China and Central Asian Forum Quarterly*, 7(2): 3–15.

Sun, Yongxiang (2009) 'Shanghai Hezuo Zuzhi de Nengyuan Hezuo' ['Energy Cooperation in the Shanghai Cooperation Organization']. In Xing Guangcheng

(Ed.), *Shanghai Hezuo Zuzhi Fazhan Baogao 2009* [2009 Annual Report on the Shanghai Cooperation Organization]. Beijing: Shehui Kexue Wenxian Chubanshe, pp. 120–133.

Sun, Yongxiang (2014) 'Shanghai Hezuo Zuzhi de Nengyuan Hezuo' ['Energy Cooperation in the Shanghai Cooperation Organization']. In Li Jingfeng, Wu Hongwei and Li Wei (Eds.), *Shanghai Hezuo Zuzhi Fazhan Baogao 2014* [2014 Annual Report on the Shanghai Cooperation Organization]. Beijing: Shehui Kexue Wenxian Chubanshe, pp. 226–239.

Xing, Guangcheng and Zhuangzhi Sun (2007) *Shanghai Hezuo Zuzhi Yanjiu* [Studies on Shanghai Cooperation Organization]. Changchun, China: Changchun Press.

Yang, Shu (2005) *Zhuanxin de Zhongya he Zhongguo* [The Central Asia Transformation and China]. Beijing: Peking University Press.

Zhang, Ning (2008) 'Qianxi Nazarbayev's "Zhongya Guojia Lianmen" de Zhuzhang' ['A Brief Study of Nazarbayev's Proposal on "Central Asian Union"'], *Eluosi, Dongou, and Zhongya Yanjiu* [Studies of Russia, Eastern Europe and Central Asia], 4: 21–26.

Zhaparov, Amantur (2009) 'The Issue of Chinese Migrants in Kyrgyzstan', *China and Central Asian Forum Quarterly*, 7(1): 79–92.

Zhou, Yanli and Bingyin Wang (2006) 'Tuijing Shanghai Hezuo Zuzhi Fazhan: Eluosi Shishi Quyu Jingji Yitihua de Zhongyao Zhanlue Xuanze' ['Promoting the Development of Shanghai Cooperation Organization: An Important Strategic Choice of Russia's Regional Economic Cooperation'], *Eluosi, Dongou, and Zhongya Yanjiu* [Studies of Russia, Eastern Europe and Central Asia], 3: 68–72.

7 Cultural and educational cooperation

This chapter covers the cooperation of the Shanghai Cooperation Organisation (SCO) in the fields collectively known as *Renwen* (the Chinese term for the humanities). The humanities represent an interesting but often neglected area of the member states' cooperation. In this chapter, the major components of the SCO's humanities cooperation are described, and the motivations of individual member states are analysed using the framework defined in Chapter Two. Culture, education and related issues are relatively new and undeveloped areas of focus for the SCO. However, China and, to some extent, other members of the SCO have become increasingly motivated to increase their 'soft' power by pursuing cultural and educational advancement through channels such as public diplomacy. In recent years, the SCO has made some progress in its humanities cooperation. However, this cooperation is significantly impeded by member states' lack of resources and motivation, as well as cultural and religious differences across the SCO. Of the many SCO member states, China has the greatest motivation and capacity to contribute to the SCO's humanities cooperation.

The background

The primary objective of the SCO is to secure regional stability in Central Asia. Therefore, security cooperation is prioritised in the organisation's agenda. Nevertheless, its cooperation extends beyond security to other functional areas such as economics and energy. More recently, the member states have sought to increase their soft power by cooperating in areas collectively defined as Renwen (the humanities), namely culture, education, science and technology, healthcare and medicine and sports. Culture and education are the pillars of the SCO's humanities cooperation.[1]

The member states' cooperation in the fields of culture and education may be regarded as a natural consequence of the expansion of SCO cooperation from security and other political spheres to economics, energy and other functional matters. United by the common goal of preventing cross-border terrorism and organised crime, the SCO's member states decided to institutionalise their informal coordination mechanisms to produce a permanent regional joint initiative specialising in non-traditional security cooperation. Having established this framework, most of the member states welcomed the opportunity to expand their institutional cooperation to economic and other functional areas. They were also motivated by the need to improve relationships between the citizens of different member states. In addition, each member of the SCO sought to publicise its national culture and image. Certain member states, such as China and Russia, were particularly keen to increase their soft power by promoting various cultural and educational activities.

Since its coinage by Joseph Nye, Jr. some 25 years ago, the term 'soft power' has received increasing currency among both policymakers and the general public, due to its conceptual and practical usefulness. Nye argues that soft or co-optive power is just as important as 'hard' command power, for the following reasons:

> If a state can make its power seem legitimate in the eyes of others, it will encounter less resistance to its wishes. If its culture and ideology are attractive, others will more willingly follow. If it can establish international norms consistent with its society, it is less likely to have to change. If it can support institutions that make other states wish to channel or limit their activities in ways the dominant state prefers, it may be spared the costly exercise of coercive or hard power.
>
> (Nye, 1990: 167)

Power is conventionally defined as the result of exercising one's influence through coercion and/or inducement. In other words, power is usually conceived in materialistic terms. The concept of soft power breaks away from this traditional understanding of material power. Some researchers have cast doubt on the very existence of soft power, while others have challenged its validity as an analytical framework. However, according to the originator of the term, 'soft power is an important reality' (Nye, 2008: 96). Throughout history, various actors, from individuals to states, have successfully used their attractiveness, reputation and/or moral authority to influence others. For example, the tremendous soft power wielded by the United States is evident from the widespread fondness for American culture, acceptance of American ideology and norms and emulation of American political and economic institutions in both the West and the East.

The useful and innovative concept of soft power has gradually received wide acceptance from academics and policymakers, who are increasingly interested in developing tools to analyse and measure states' soft power. For example, five indices have been used to rank the soft power exerted by the major modern states worldwide:[2] government, culture, diplomacy, education and business/innovation (McClory, 2013: 7–8).[3] This measurement tool is largely derived from Nye's categorisation of the three major sources of a state's soft power: attractive cultural activities, both high and popular; favourable political values and ideology; and a legitimate and welcoming foreign policy. Culture and education are major sources of soft power, as well as evidence of that power. The majority of the top 40 nations in the soft-power ranking are developed states in the West. The highest positions are always occupied by major Western nations such as France, Germany, the United Kingdom and the United States. In 2012, China was ranked 22nd, close to the middle of the cohort. It was surpassed only by major Western states in Europe and elsewhere, and by two developing states: Brazil and Turkey. China's performance is particularly strong in the culture and education indices (in which it ranked sixth and fifth, respectively, in 2012), due to its cultivation of international tourism, the achievements of its athletes in international sporting events and the success of its educational exchange programmes. Russia was ranked 28th in the overall soft-power index; slightly lower than China. Russia's performance is less impressive than that of China, as its scores for the five indices are roughly equal.

Interest in nations' soft power is growing among policymakers as well as scholars and analysts. Despite some scepticism, many state governments around the world are attaching increasing importance to the accumulation and exertion of soft power. Modern politics are no longer based solely on traditional military and economic power, but on the competition to secure credibility; that is, to determine 'whose story wins' (Nye, 2008: 100). A range of state governments have begun to invest in various strategies to enhance their countries' soft power. As public diplomacy is a major means of promoting and exercising soft power, many states now compete to win the 'hearts and minds' of citizens in other countries.

The United States has traditionally led the world in investment in public diplomacy. However, other countries and organisations are catching up. China and Russia, two major international powers, are particularly interested in building their soft power. In 2009, the Chinese government announced its intention to spend almost $7 billion in just one year on globally expanding China's media activities to improve its international image. In 2010, the Russian government allocated only slightly less – $1.4 billion – to international propaganda (Dale et al., 2012: 1). The Chinese government is aware of the importance of a positive national image and the utility of public diplomacy. Indeed, its ideological approach to international propaganda has been replaced with more conventional public diplomacy (Chang and Fen, 2014). Despite several major obstacles, the efforts made by the Chinese government to implement public diplomacy have had impressive outcomes in recent years. Similarly, albeit on a lesser scale, Russia's investment in soft-power accumulation has increased under the Putin leadership. Its main aim is to achieve the stability and security required for Russia's economic development, particularly in the territories of the former Soviet Republics (Tsygankov, 2006).

Although China and Russia are the two major competitors for global soft power, the much smaller Central Asian SCO member states are by no means absent from the competition. The governments of Kazakhstan, Uzbekistan and Kyrgyzstan have been seeking to make the world more aware of their countries since their independence in the early 1990s. Despite differences in communication modes, these three governments have begun to pursue nation-branding public diplomacy in a manner similar to that of China and Russia, focusing on international business and the global political community. Their activities increasingly meet international standards for national-image promotion (Marat, 2009: 1123–1124). Due to its increase in power, Kazakhstan has new political, economic and cultural incentives to create a national brand (Bogoviyeva and Dostiyarova, 2010). In recent years, the country has been able to enhance its soft power through public diplomacy. In general, the public diplomacy practised by Kazakhstan, Uzbekistan and Kyrgyzstan is highly politically driven and strictly controlled by the countries' respective governments, particularly those of Kazakhstan and Uzbekistan.

Following China's initiative, the SCO member states have begun to accumulate and exercise soft power primarily through humanities cooperation. However, cooperation in soft areas such as culture is not as straightforward as it may appear. The SCO members show greater diversity in culture and education than in many other spheres. This diversity is exacerbated by the insulation of China from Central Asia for the last two centuries, and the bitter rivalry between China and Soviet Russia during the Cold War. China and the Soviet Union criticised and demonised each other throughout the Cold War era, creating long-lasting mutual suspicion and widening the gap between their cultures. Anxiety about the 'China threat' persists in Russia and some Central Asian states (Zhang, 2009: 136). At a deeper level, the six countries belong to three of the major civilisational patterns identified by Samuel Huntington (1993). China and Russia are the pillar states of the Confucian and Slavic-Orthodox civilisations, respectively, and the Central Asian SCO members are all Islamic states. Therefore, these countries have strikingly different languages, histories, religions, customs, institutions and self-perceived identities. Religious differences create the greatest divisions between countries that belong to different civilisations (Murdon, 2008: 423–426). Cultural and educational cooperation is an important means of improving mutual understanding between citizens of different countries by intensifying person-to-person exchange. However, such cooperation is severely impeded by the ingrained differences between the SCO's member states.

A number of international-cooperation regimes emphasising cultural exchange are already in place in the geographical region constituted roughly by the SCO territories. As noted by a Chinese analyst, the cultural ties between Russia and the Central Asian states date back to Soviet history and beyond. In addition, the cultural influence of the United States, the European Union and other Western countries is clearly evident in the region, with important implications for professional and everyday lives in Central Asia. In particular, Western values such as human rights, democracy and liberalism have influenced the region's youth (Zhang, 2009: 136). As a result, the success of the SCO's humanities cooperation depends on its effectiveness in withstanding rival regimes as well as overcoming the deeper obstacles created by internal divisions.

The Chinese government regards humanities cooperation as an important complement to security and economic cooperation, and thus an important component of bilateral and multilateral cooperation between the SCO's member states. As a result, the Chinese government is highly motivated to support the SCO's humanities cooperation, with two main objectives (Xing and Sun, 2007: 125–126). The first is to secure internal cohesion. Chinese policymakers regard cultural and related cooperation as an effective means of enhancing the mutual understanding of citizens in different SCO member states, and thus increasing organisational solidarity. Second, the Chinese government antici-pates that the SCO's humanities cooperation will help to resist the penetration of Western values and ideologies into the region. If so, a 'Confucian-Islamic connection' (Huntington, 1993: 45–47) is likely to emerge in opposition to Western interests, values and power.

Operation and activities

Although the SCO's humanities cooperation covers a range of sectors, culture and education are the two main spheres of cooperation. Indeed, the various sectors that make up the SCO's Renwen cooperation can be defined collectively as culture in its broadest sense. Joseph Nye, Jr. (2008: 96) argues that the term 'culture' refers to all of the practices that create meaning for a society. Culture has many manifestations, but a general distinction can be made between high culture and popular culture. The former comprises areas that appeal primarily to elites, such as literature, art and education, while the latter offers mass entertainment. The governments of the SCO member states cooperate more frequently on matters of high culture than popular culture.

The SCO's humanities cooperation takes place through three main channels: rhetorical, institutional and operational. Rhetorical cooperation is enacted by national leaders during summits, official visits and similar events, and takes the form of declarations, communiqués, speeches, etc. Institutional or policy-based cooperation is carried out by national policymakers, namely government ministers and senior officials, who negotiate terms of cooperation agreements and formulate implementation plans, usually during meetings with other ministers and experts. SCO staff members, usually from the Secretariat, may play some role in this process. Operational humanities cooperation entails the substantive activities carried out during the implementation stage by various actors in the SCO countries.

Contrary to widespread belief, the idea of cooperating on cultural and related matters was mooted as early as the establishment of the SCO. In the Joint Communique of the inaugural SCO summit in June 2001, China's representatives proposed that a Cultural Ministerial Meeting be held. This proposal received support from other SCO members (Xing and Sun, 2007: 126). The proposed humanities cooperation was also incorporated into the SCO Charter at the St Petersburg Summit in June 2002, as follows: 'cooperation in environmental protection, culture, science and technology, education should be implemented as an integral part of the overall SCO cooperation'. Although the focus of the Heads of Government Meeting in September 2003 was multilateral economic and trade cooperation, the leaders of the member states acknowledged the importance of enhancing cultural cooperation between the SCO member states.[4] This position was reiterated at the Heads of Government Meeting in 2004, during which the premiers of the SCO governments agreed that the SCO should cooperate on culture, education, public health and sport to strengthen the relationships between the countries' respective citizens.[5] On 16 August 2007, at the Bishkek Summit, the SCO leaders signed the SCO Cultural Cooperation Agreement, which provided the legal basis for and upgraded the status of the organisation's cultural cooperation. Four main areas of cultural cooperation were defined in the agreement: arts activities, personnel and information exchange, arts research and opposition to culture-related crime. At the eighth Heads of Government Meeting in Beijing in October 2009, the humanities were officially designated as a main theme of the SCO's cooperation, along with economics.

The SCO's educational cooperation began noticeably later, for various reasons. Most importantly, China's educational system differs considerably from those of Russia and the SCO's Central Asian members, most of which follow the Russian educational model as a legacy of Soviet rule. These two educational systems show particular differences in the structure of their degree and diploma programmes. Educational quality also varies across the member states. On 16 June 2006, the national governments of the SCO member states signed an Agreement on Educational Cooperation. This agreement was regarded as a major outcome of the 2006 summit, and provided the main foundation for educational cooperation within the SCO framework. The following two major educational responsibilities were outlined in the agreement. First, the SCO states were required to cooperate to enhance educational exchange by merging their educational systems, encouraging student and researcher exchange and information sharing, promoting direct ties between educational institutions and organisations in different member states, and organising multilateral educational activities such as academic conferences, seminars and roundtable discussions. Second, the SCO states agreed to encourage mutual recognition by sharing information on the official certification and evaluation procedures of their respective governmental agencies, and securing mutual governmental recognition for degrees and diplomas (Yang, 2009: 142). This agreement was prepared and completed by a group of senior officials from the national educational ministries of the SCO members in a meeting later institutionalised as the Educational Expert Meeting.

The SCO's institutional and policy-based humanities cooperation is headed by ministerial meetings in the relevant sectors and supported by a meeting of senior officials. Cultural exchange is prioritised in the SCO's humanities agenda. Two institutionalised mechanisms for cultural exchange have been established: the SCO Cultural Ministerial Meeting and the SCO Cultural and Art Festival (Xing and Sun, 2007: 130). The ministerial meetings on culture provide a regular platform for consultation and negotiation on the directions, principles and methods of cultural cooperation. The first Cultural Ministerial Meeting was held as early as 2002, just one year after the inception of the SCO. After the meeting, a declaration was issued on the importance of respecting cultural, ethnic and national diversity during the process of globalisation. According to the declaration, civilizations should co-exist peacefully, pursue equal exchange, learn from each other and develop jointly.[6] It was decided at the first ministerial meeting that the cultural ministers would meet every other year in different member states, on a rotating basis. However, the second ministerial meeting was not held in 2004 as originally scheduled, due to unresolved financing and logistics problems (Xing and Sun, 2007: 131). The second meeting was delayed until 2005, by which time the problems had been solved. The SCO's Cultural Ministerial Meetings have since been held every year. The Cultural Ministerial Meeting was supported by the Cultural Expert Meeting, involving an executive body of senior officials from the member states' cultural ministries. At the first meeting, the ministers decided that the SCO Cultural and Art Festival would be the most high-profile form of cultural exchange between the SCO member states. The festival was to be held annually in different member states on a rotating basis.

At the second Cultural Ministerial Meeting in Astana, Kazakhstan in July 2005, the cultural ministers agreed on a plan for the SCO's multilateral cultural cooperation in 2005–2006. This first annual plan outlined a number of channels for cultural exchange between SCO members, such as cultural exhibitions, performances, art festivals and other connections between the cultural organisations of different SCO member states (Xing and Sun, 2007: 132). It has since become customary for national ministers to approve the SCO's annual or multi-year cooperation plans, which are prepared during the senior officials' meeting, at the Cultural Ministerial Meeting.

The first Educational Ministerial Meeting was held as late as 18 October 2006. This meeting in Beijing marked the beginning of the SCO's multilateral educational cooperation. The Educational Ministerial Meeting has since been regularised as a biennial event. Each meeting is supported by a meeting of SCO educational experts responsible for making concrete and operational arrangements. Uzbekistan has not participated in these meetings since the second Educational Ministerial Meeting in Astana from 22 to 24 October 2008. The reasons for Uzbekistan's lack of participation are unclear.[7] The progress made by the SCO in educational cooperation owes much to the efforts made by the SCO Secretariat to secure substantive educational cooperation in such forms as mutual recognition of degrees and joint curriculum and degree programmes (Xing and Sun, 2007: 134–135). For the first time in the history of the SCO, officials belonging to the permanent institution have begun to exercise their influence.

At the operational level, the SCO Cultural and Art Festival is an important government-led instrument promoting cultural exchange between the SCO's member states. The cultural cooperation of the SCO is driven predominantly by the governments of its member states, which reach agreement on general principles, implement plans and allocate funding to various cultural activities. The first SCO Cultural and Art Festival was held at the Astana Summit in July 2005. It has since become customary to hold the festival at the same time and in the same host state as the SCO summit. Other regularised cultural activities include an exhibition of design and fine art held during the SCO's Cultural Ministerial Meeting; an SCO film festival hosted by Kyrgyzstan; a cultural-exchange forum hosted by Russia; folk art and international theatre festivals held in Tajikistan; and an exhibition of children's paintings organised by the Chinese government (Zhang, 2009: 139–140). High culture is disproportionately emphasised in the SCO's cultural agenda; very few popular-culture events are organised. Interestingly, however, President Vladimir Putin of Russia proposed at the 2009 SCO summit that a popular song competition be organised in the manner of the age-old Eurovision Song Contest.[8]

The main themes of the SCO's educational cooperation are the mutual recognition of degrees and diplomas and the SCO University. As hurdles to mutual recognition are difficult to overcome multilaterally, the member states usually conduct more formal educational cooperation bilaterally. For example, China has made individual bilateral agreements with Russia, Kazakhstan, Kyrgyzstan and Tajikistan on educational activities such as the mutual provision of government scholarships, the exchange of faculty members and researchers and the mutual recognition of degrees and diplomas. The SCO members have approved an annual implementation plan for their multilateral educational activities, with five major objectives: to improve the legal and institutional bases for cooperation by establishing an educational information exchange centre and a university rectors' forum, and producing a list of universities selected for inter-university exchange; to improve educational-service provision; to improve educational-quality assurance; to make provision for the mutual recognition of degrees and diplomas; and to organise concrete educational activities (Yang, 2009: 143–144).

The SCO University represents a major part of the SCO's educational cooperation. At the SCO's summit in Bishkek, Kyrgyzstan on 16 August 2007, the Russian president Putin proposed that the SCO establish a university with branches in all of the member states. The university was originally intended to grant its own degrees, with curriculums and programmes standardised across its various branches. However, this plan has yet to be fully realised, due to numerous practical obstacles such as variation in educational standards and systems. To overcome these obstacles, the SCO members decided to establish a network of universities selected by the member states. In October 2008, the educational ministries of the SCO member governments signed a letter of intent to establish an SCO university network, and in April 2010, the participating universities in China, Russia, Kazakhstan, Kyrgyzstan and Tajikistan signed a memorandum of understanding as an initial stage in their participation in the project (Xu, 2012: 149). In 2009, at another meeting of the member states' educational ministries, all of the SCO members except Uzbekistan agreed on five major priorities and nominated institutions for educational cooperation. The areas of priority were selected primarily for practical reasons.[9] As the first step in the creation of the SCO's university network, the member states have initiated inter-university cooperation in the form of student-exchange programmes and joint degrees.

In parallel with the SCO's multilateral cooperation, China has actively pursued bilateral cultural cooperation with its partners. In 2009, for example, China and Russia signed a bilateral agreement to reciprocally establish cultural centres. In addition, the states agreed to organise a number of cultural activities in both countries to encourage language learning, youth exchange and media and cultural exchange (Yu, 2010: 96–97). China has also cooperated bilaterally on culture with the other four Central Asian SCO members. In most cases, China has cooperated more actively than its partners (Zhang, 2009: 140–141). In terms of educational cooperation, the East China Normal University in Shanghai has been responsible for organising the SCO Summer School Programme since 2009. The programme is part of China's public diplomacy within the SCO framework, and involves university students from Russia, Belarus and all of the Central Asian SCO member states apart from Uzbekistan. The main aim of the programme is to familiarise students from other nations with Chinese culture.[10] However, China's most impressive act of educational and cultural exchange is the global establishment of Confucius Institutes. This project plays a major role in China's efforts to increase its soft power; in this case, by providing Chinese-language training and increasing awareness of Chinese culture worldwide (Paradise, 2009). China has established Confucius Institutes and classrooms in all of its SCO partners: four in Russia, two in Kazakhstan, 14 in Kyrgyzstan and one each in Uzbekistan and Tajikistan.[11] Some of these institutes, such as those in Russia, Kyrgyzstan and Kazakstan, were developed from existing Chinese-language centres in place before the first Confucius Institute was officially opened in Seoul, South Korea in November 2004.

Analysis of the above activities yields two main insights into the SCO's cultural and educational cooperation: first, it is heavily government-driven, with little input from civil society; and second, China differs from the other SCO members in its level of motivation and investment. The former characteristic is explained by the prevalence in the SCO of authoritarian regimes that levy strict control over their respective states. The latter is better explained by suasion game theory: as China has a greater incentive to further the SCO process, its contribution is broader and more substantial.

China's role

Due to its strong motivation and considerable capacity to pursue educational and cultural development, China drives the SCO's cooperation in these areas. The first goal of the Chinese government is to introduce China's cultural and educational values to citizens of Central Asia and Russia, and ultimately thereby to increase its soft power in these neighbouring countries. The government's second goal is to increase the internal cohesion of the SCO by establishing more solid cultural relationships between states. Third, it seeks to reinforce the external unity of the SCO against competing values and ideologies, mostly from the West. The success of China's plan will depend primarily on its existing and future soft-power resources, which can only be obtained through effective international leadership of multilateral organisations.

Soft power has been globally ranked using five indices corresponding to the major sources of states' soft power. However, each of these five dimensions can be argued to occupy a dialectical relationship with soft power. In other words, a state's existing soft-power resources and its capacity to accumulate additional soft power are mutually enhancing. A state's capacity to attract and persuade can be measured by easily observable indicators such as its high and popular culture, its political values and development model, and its foreign aid and development policies. However, the soft power of a state actor may also increase as a result of effective policy practice, such as the implementation of traditional and public diplomatic initiatives designed to raise awareness of the state's merits.

Analysing the cultural and educational cooperation of the SCO casts light on the interaction between the sources of China's soft power and its multilateral cooperation activities. First, China has used its own resources to propel the SCO's humanities cooperation in areas such as diplomacy, government, culture, education and business. China has accumulated significant soft power over the last few decades, largely due to its successful economic development. Ramo (2004) coined the now widely used term 'Beijing Consensus' to describe this success. He argues that China has invented a new development approach driven by the desire for 'equitable, peaceful high-quality growth', defined by a 'lively defense of national borders and interests' and characterised by 'stable, if repressive, politics and high-speed economic growth'. This model is applicable not only to China but to a range of countries in the developing world seeking to emulate China's formidable economic growth. The Beijing Consensus has had a 'gigantic effect outside of China' in showing other nations around the world how to effectively pursue development and fit into the international order while retaining their independence and protecting their lifestyle and political preferences (Ramo, 2004: 3–4). Ramo's 'China Model' also explains China's success in accumulating soft power, at least in some parts of the world. Economic success has given China the resources and ambition necessary to exercise its soft power beyond state borders. As almost all of the SCO member states are ruled by more or less authoritarian governments, the leaders of China's partner states are particularly interested in emulating the success of the Chinese government in securing steady economic growth while retaining tight control of its country. The SCO has become the ideal setting for China to practise various types of organisational leadership, drawing on its own soft-power resources to support the SCO's cultural and educational cooperation.

Structural leadership is usually defined in terms of the traditional understanding of power as hard and coercive. However, this definition is less appropriate in the context of cooperation in soft areas such as culture and education. In these areas, structural leadership is more likely to entail payment or inducement using material resources such as financial and human support. However, most of the SCO's Central Asian member states lack financial resources and have little interest in prioritising cultural and educational cooperation. Therefore, the progress of multilateral cooperation in these areas is progressing far more slowly than expected by the Chinese government, which is eager to pursue a soft-power campaign within the framework of the SCO.

China's structural leadership is more fully reflected in its promotion of the SCO's cultural and educational cooperation. After the SCO members first agreed to cooperate on culture, China's former president Hu Jintao stressed repeatedly in his talks at SCO summits the importance of humanities cooperation as the third major area of SCO cooperation, alongside security and economic cooperation. This emphasis on humanities cooperation came in response to specific socioeconomic conditions. At the ninth SCO summit on 16 June 2009, during the global financial crisis, President Hu urged the SCO members to strengthen their humanities cooperation – covering culture, education, public health and tourism – to increase their solidarity and strength (Yu, 2010: 101). Mr Hu is not the only Chinese leader to have advocated consistently for increased humanities cooperation. At the SCO's Heads of Government Meeting in September 2006, the former Chinese premier Wen Jiabao urged the SCO members to upgrade their humanities cooperation. More specifically, Premier Wen argued that the educational agreement reached at the SCO's 2006 summit should be implemented as rapidly as possible via student and scholar exchange, joint educational programmes and the mutual recognition of degrees and diplomas. He also advised the SCO members to strengthen their cultural exchange and cooperation through various channels, and to improve the institutional mechanisms of the Cultural Ministerial Meeting and the SCO Cultural and Art Festival.[12]

China also manifests its structural leadership by drawing on its own abundant financial resources to contribute unilaterally to cultural and educational cooperation in the form of various cultural- and student-exchange programmes. At the Astana Summit on 5 July 2005, the former Chinese president Hu Jingtao offered to enhance the SCO's cooperative provision of human-resources training. Accordingly, China funded the training of 1,500 professionals from other SCO member states in management and other areas. At the Dushanbe summit in August 2007, President Hu announced the China Scholarship project, which was designed to enable individuals from other SCO countries to study in China (Yang, 2009: 145). Outside the SCO framework, China has cooperated bilaterally with its SCO partners on various cultural and educational issues. For example, the Chinese government has established language centres and later the Confucius Institutes to raise awareness of the Chinese language and culture in the SCO territories and beyond. The Chinese government provides scholarships to encourage students from the SCO countries and elsewhere to enrol in Chinese universities. It also cultivates artistic and cultural exchange between China and its SCO partners.

Another example of China's unilateral contribution to Renwen cooperation is its support for academic and policy research on the SCO. This research was initially carried out by several government-sponsored think-tanks specialising in foreign affairs in Beijing and Shanghai. Subsequently, several academic institutions in Shanghai began to contribute to research on the SCO, probably inspired by the name of the organisation. The Joint Institute of SCO Studies was established by the East China Normal University in Shanghai and the China Development Bank (CDB) in June 2009. Although the CDB's collaboration with the university to establish a think-tank was at first sight surprising, the institute is simply another example of the SCO's state-driven model of development. The CDB plays a pre-established role in national development by providing long-term financing to support infrastructure projects and projects in other sectors fundamental to the running of the state. In addition, the CDB has been appointed by the Chinese government as China's representative in the SCO Banking Consortium. Indeed, the CDB's governor Chen Yuan, who urged the SCO to pursue financial cooperation, was the first chairman of the SCO Banking Consortium.[13] The China Institute for SCO International Exchange and Judicial Cooperation (CISCO) was inaugurated in May 2014 by the Shanghai University of Political Science and Law. The establishment of CISCO was announced by the Chinese president Xi Jinping in his talk at the 13th SCO Summit on 13 September 2013. According to Mr Xi, the institute was established to train judicial specialists from other SCO member states. More concretely, Mr Xi announced China's intention to offer 30,000 government scholarships to individuals from the SCO member states in the following 10 years.[14] The SCO's Public Diplomacy Institute was established by Shanghai University in March 2011. Supported by the Chinese Ministry of Foreign Affairs, the institute was expected to become an influential think-tank specialising in research, exchange and training in public diplomacy within the SCO framework.[15] All of these university-based think-tanks are to some extent supported by the government, and play some notable roles in China's diplomacy, particularly its public diplomacy.

In terms of entrepreneurial leadership, China has a pivotal role in driving the SCO's cultural and educational cooperation, usually by setting agendas and pushing for agreement. At the SCO's inaugural summit in Shanghai, China on 15 June 2001, China's representative proposed that a meeting of cultural ministries be held on a regular basis (Xing and Sun, 2007: 126). At the first Cultural Ministerial Meeting in April 2002, Sun Jiazheng, then China's Cultural Minister, emphasised the importance of respect for the cultural diversity of the SCO member states. Sun also linked cultural cooperation with the SCO's main security and economic objectives, urging the SCO members to enhance their cultural and religious cooperation to create a solid foundation of mutual understanding and common values.[16] At the 2006 Heads of Government Meeting, the Chinese premier Wen Jiabao argued that humanities cooperation, covering culture, education, science, healthcare, tourism and sports, should become another major area of the SCO's cooperation.[17]

Public diplomacy is the most common means by which states exercise and enhance their soft power, as it directly involves the general public of the target countries. China's entrepreneurial leadership of the SCO's cultural and educational cooperation is also exercised in its public-diplomacy initiatives within the SCO framework. The Chinese government has several goals in practising public diplomacy and exerting China's soft power: to maintain peace and stability on the country's borders, to represent the country to other nations as a benign and constructive international actor, to provide a model for other developing nations and to obtain resources needed for furthering Chinese economic development (Kurlantzick, 2007: 130). China's foreign policy has traditionally addressed only high-level politics and inter-governmental relations. However, the government has recently realised the importance of public diplomacy, and thus considerably increased its investment in this area. Despite some limitations, it has made noticeable progress (Wang, 2008). The same is true of the SCO's public diplomacy.

Driving the SCO's humanities cooperation has enabled China to fully exert its intellectual leadership, which is exercised through its establishment of organisational norms and values. The SCO is less legalistic and more normative than international organisations in the West; its members share common values and attitudes (Aris, 2009: 479). Although the primary role of organisational norms and values is to increase an organisation's solidarity, they may also be used as weapons against perceived threats. China is responsible for inventing and promoting key concepts and ideas as institutional norms shared by its SCO partners. The best example is provided by China's relentless efforts to advocate 'Shanghai Spirit' in the SCO's cultural and educational cooperation. According to this model, exemplary inter-state relations are based on principles of 'mutual trust, mutual benefi[t], equality, cooperation, respect for civilizational diversity, and [...] co-prosperity'.[18] Respect for civilisational diversity, which entails recognition of and respect for historical, cultural, social and developmental differences, is the criterion most relevant to the SCO's humanities cooperation. World peace can only be realised by 'agreeing to disagree', rather than attempting to impose one's own ideology and system on other states (Pan, 2003: 35–36). This argument appeals to China's SCO partners. First, the acknowledgement of diversity helps to harmonise the relationships between the members of the SCO, as it alleviates the anxiety of Central Asian members about ideological imposition from China and Russia. Second, and equally importantly, China's valorisation of diversity enables the SCO's members to collectively defend the organisation against Western criticism and intervention on the grounds of the region's human-rights failings and lack of democratic principles (Ambrosio, 2008). These motivations amply explain the consistent emphasis in the SCO's cultural and educational activities on civilisational diversity and the peaceful co-existence of different cultures.

China's international leadership activities in the SCO suggest that the country's soft power derives from all three potential sources: its culture, its political values and its foreign policy. Its traditional tolerance of cultural diversity, its emphasis on socio-political stability and its foreign policy of non-interference have been welcomed by its SCO partners and the wider developing world. In terms of public diplomacy, there is evidence that most of China's international propagandistic activities have been replaced with public-diplomacy initiatives designed to promote national interests by presenting the country favourably or raising awareness of its values. This conceptual change has worked in China's favour by removing the ideological burden that characterised the country's international image in the first decades of the Cold War (Chang and Fen, 2014: 457). Despite some hurdles, such as anti-Chinese sentiment, China's efforts in the SCO region have paid off. The Chinese government has successfully drawn on China's immense economic power to increase its public influence and appeal in Central Asia. As explained by a respondent in Kyrgyzstan, more people are now learning Chinese, and information about Chinese culture has become more widespread. 'Chinese firms are opening up here, and there are jobs for people who understand the country and speak the language.'[19]

However, China continues to wield far less soft power than the major Western countries, and its approach to public diplomacy must be refined. There are certain intrinsic limitations to China's pursuit of soft power (Gill and Huang, 2006; Wang, 2008). China has two main methods of obtaining soft power: inter-governmental diplomacy and public diplomacy. Engaging in traditional inter-state diplomacy is much easier for China than implementing public diplomacy. In addition, China has won many followers through common interest rather than common values. As a result, China has been described as trying to 'buy friends' – i.e., cultivating influential figures in developing countries – to displace Western influences and values (Dale et al., 2012: 5). China's public diplomacy is still at a preliminary stage, although it has made notable investment and progress in its public-diplomacy initiatives in recent years.

Progress and problems

According to the official documents published by the SCO, the member states' humanities cooperation covers a range of areas, such as culture, education, technology, health and sport. Cooperation in these areas enables the SCO's member states not only to deploy their soft-power resources but to enhance their soft-power capacity and status. As the two focal areas of the SCO's humanities cooperation, culture and education are the main sources of the states' soft power. These two areas are related to three other sources of soft power, namely government, diplomacy and, more indirectly, business/ innovation. The SCO's cultural and educational cooperation is driven by governmental diplomacy and supported predominantly by the political and economic activities of the member states' governments.

Recognising the importance of soft power, the governments of the SCO member states have begun to pursue national-branding and public-diplomacy activities. Policymakers in China are extremely interested in the utility of soft power, and have drawn enthusiastically on China's soft-power resources to support its foreign policies. Power resources such as a successful development model, a peaceful-development image and an emphasis on national heritage have enabled the Chinese government to increase China's influence abroad, particularly in its neighbouring countries (Yong and Jong, 2008). Similarly, the Russian government has paid increasing attention to soft power and public diplomacy. Russia's public diplomacy is determined purely by pragmatic considerations and national interests. The government attempts primarily to present Russia to the world as an attractive country and a positive force in international relations. The government has sought to use Russia's soft-power potential and brand the country as a constructive force to gain entry to world politics. Its objectives and thus its methods differ according to the country or countries targeted. The main objective of the former Soviet Republic is to take control of weaker states. Russia's soft power is projected to nations in other parts of the world through activities such as sports, culture and education (Simons, 2014: 448). Following China and Russia, Central Asian countries such as Kazakhstan, Kyrgyzstan and Uzbekistan have made increasing investments in national branding to raise international awareness of their countries' merits. For example, the governments of Kazakhstan and Uzbekistan have branded their respective countries as crossroads of culture and civilisations (Marat, 2009: 1128)

Like national branding, public diplomacy is driven by international competition. China and Russia are currently competing aggressively with the United States to win the heart and minds of people around the world. In particular, they have launched expensive and sophisticated media campaigns to fill the ideological void in their traditional representation (Dale et al., 2012). As in this case, the SCO's cultural, educational and related cooperation is most successful when it unifies its member states against external interference. The SCO's member states announced their collective support for cultural and civilisational diversity in the Declaration on the SCO's Fifth Anniversary, as follows:

> Diversity of civilization and model of development must be respected and upheld. Differences in cultural traditions, political and social systems, values and model of development formed in the course of history should not be taken as pretexts to interfere in other countries' internal affairs. Model of social development should not be 'exported'. Differences in civilizations should be respected, and exchanges among civilizations

should be conducted on an equal basis to draw on each other's strengths and enhance harmonious development.[20]

In this declaration, China and Russia were represented as 'big brothers' of the Central Asian member states. Collectively, the SCO argued that the unique historical and cultural traditions of Central Asian nations deserve the respect and understanding of the international community, and that the governments of these countries should be supported in their efforts to safeguard national security and stability, maintain their countries' social and economic development and improve their citizens' livelihoods.

Compared with its cooperation in other spheres, the SCO's humanities cooperation is a recent phenomenon. Overall, the performance and outcomes of this cooperation have been mixed. There is still considerable room to improve the soft power of the SCO member states as a collective. For example, the main hurdle to the mutual recognition of degrees and diplomas is the variation in educational quality across the SCO member states. However, the low status of educational qualifications offered by the SCO member states is another major problem. For several years, the SCO member states have cooperated on education mainly with more developed Western countries. Russia and several other countries in Central Asia have taken part in a number of educational-cooperation programmes with European countries. The Chinese government has enthusiastically pursued educational cooperation with Western countries to enable China to catch up with global technological development. However, although the governments of the SCO member states are highly politically motivated to promote educational cooperation, universities and students have fewer incentives to cooperate. In particular, universities and students in China are often unwilling to pursue educational cooperation with other SCO countries due to various practical drawbacks, such as threats to educational standards, language and career opportunities (Yang, 2009: 150). The SCO's humanities cooperation is also weakened by a lack of consensus from its member states. For instance, Uzbekistan has not contributed to the SCO's educational activities since the first Educational Ministerial Meeting. Due to the relative ineffectiveness of their multilateral cooperation, the SCO members often resort to bilateral cooperation to secure feasible and effective solutions.

Although traditional inter-governmental diplomacy is usually more successful, it is difficult for the SCO countries to engage in mutual public diplomacy. While the members of the SCO are at least externally unified in response to common challenges, the SCO's goal of improving internal cohesion between member states has only partially been achieved. As China's Communist regime has long been associated with international propaganda, the goals of the government's activities beyond China's borders remain unclear (Chang and Fen, 2014: 457). Indeed, all of the SCO member states encounter similar suspicion about their motives when conducting public diplomatic activities such as media expansion, events organisation and cultural exchange and training, particularly in the West. The effectiveness of public diplomacy is also influenced by national foreign policy. For example, Russia's efforts to increase its soft power have been seriously undermined by its recent policies in Crimea and Eastern Ukraine. In addition, the success of public diplomacy between SCO members is limited by cultural differences, historical insulation and political suspicion.

The SCO's efforts to cooperate in the fields of culture and education are also limited by a lack of civil participation; approaches to cooperation in these areas are largely government-driven. This lack of active civil participation is primarily due to the prevalence of authoritarian regimes in the SCO countries. In both China and Russia, attempts to exercise and bolster soft power through public diplomacy and other means are made predominantly by the government, whose activities are widely perceived as propaganda efforts with doubtable credibility (Nye, 2013). In addition, countries in Central Asia wield insufficient hard power, as they lack the material resources required to conduct effective public diplomacy. In light of these failings, it is impossible to be optimistic about the SCO's humanities cooperation in the short term, despite its limited progress so far.

Notes

1 In the SCO's official documents, cooperation in this area is defined as 'humanities cooperation', covering the softer issues of culture, education, science and technology, healthcare and medicine and sports.

2 The media company Monocle produces an annual ranking of soft power in association with the Institute for Government, a UK think tank. The measurement process is based on the three sources of soft power – culture, political values and foreign policy – identified by Joseph Nye, Jr (2004: 8, 11).

3 The culture index comprises measures such as the annual number of tourists, the global reach of the national music industry and international sporting success. The government index is designed to measure states' public institutions, political values and major policy outcomes. The diplomacy index measures states' diplomatic resources and global footprint. The education index measures states' ability to attract foreign students and facilitate educational exchange. The business/innovation index measures the attractiveness of a national economic model in terms of its innovation, corruption and competiveness.

4 From the 2003 Joint Communique of the SCO Heads of Government (Premiers) Meeting, http://www.sectsco.org/CN11/show.asp?id=164 accessed 9 March 2015.

5 From the 2003 Joint Communique of the SCO Heads of Government (Premiers) Meeting, http://www.sectsco.org/CN11/show.asp?id=168 accessed 9 March 2015.

6 From the Joint Declaration of the SCO Cultural Ministers, http://www.zjwh.gov. cn/dtxx/2007-12-11/30694.htm accessed 10 March 2015.

7 One may try to trace the reason behind by recalling the news of the Uzbek government's recent decision to ban teaching of political science which is called by 'western pseudo science,' http://www.theguardian.com/world/2015/sep/05/uzbekistan-islam-karimov-bans-political-science, accessed 18 September 2015. It is possible that the Uzbek government imposes strict control of its educational system for fear of external influences even from its SCO partners.

8 Putin's proposal that the SCO member states hold a singing contest is available at http://gb.cri.cn/27824/2009/10/15/2585s2648325.htm, accessed 14 May 2015.
9 Five subject areas were selected: area studies, ecology, energy, information technology and nano-technology. Fifty-three participating universities were selected by the member states, comprising 10 from Kazakhstan, 7 from Kyrgyzstan, 10 from China, 16 from Russia and 10 from Tajikistan. However, this number increased to 62 (13 from Kazakhstan, 8 from Kyrgyzstan, 15 from China, 16 from Russia and 10 from Tajikistan) at the SCO's educational ministerial meeting in September 2010. The number of universities involved in the programme continued to grow. In 2012, there were 70 participating universities. The number of key subject areas has also increased to seven.
10 http://www.saias.ecnu.edu.cn/iv4762.htm, accessed 12 March 2015.
11 2012 Annual Report of the Confucius Institute Headquarters (Hanban), www.hanban.edu.cn/report/pdf/2012.pdf, accessed 16 March 2015.
12 Wen Jiabao's speech at the SCO Heads of Government Meeting, http://www.chinanews.com/other/news/2006/09-15/790908.shtml, accessed 9 March 2015.
13 Establishment of the SCO Banking Consortium, http://www.cdb.com.cn/web/NewsInfo.asp?NewsId=1187, accessed 11 March 2015.
14 Introduction to the China Institute for SCO International Exchange and Judicial Cooperation, http://cisco.shupl.edu.cn/html/english/AboutfhUs/ProfilefhandfhObjectives/1.html, accessed 11 March 2015.
15 Introduction to the Public Diplomacy Institute to the SCO, http://cms.shu.edu.cn/Default.aspx?tabid=20910, accessed 12 March 2015.
16 http://news.xinhuanet.com/newscenter/2002-04/12/content_356324.htm, accessed 23 March 2015.
17 http://www.gov.cn/gongbao/content/2006/content_443254.htm, accessed 23 March 2015.
18 The SCO Founding Declaration, http://www.sectsco.org/CN11/show.asp?id=100, accessed 19 May 2015.
19 'Kyrgyzstan: China Expanding Influence, One Student at a Time', http://www.eurasianet.org/node/64788, accessed 29 March 2015.
20 Declaration on the Fifth Anniversary of the Shanghai Cooperation Organisation, http://www.sectsco.org/EN123/show.asp?id=94, accessed 10 March 2015.

References

Ambrosio, Thomas (2008) 'Catching the "Shanghai Spirit": How the Shanghai Cooperation Organization Promotes Authoritarian Norms in Central Asia', *Europe-Asia Studies*, 60(8): 1321–1344.

Aris, Stephen (2009) 'The Shanghai Cooperation Organization: "Tackling the Three Evils"; A Regional Response to Non-traditional Security Challenges or an Anti-Western Bloc?' *Europe-Asia Studies*, 61(3): 457–482.

Bogoviyeva, Elmira and Dostiyarova, Alima (2010) Kazakhstan Nation Brand: Economic, Political, and Cultural Narratives, Institute for Cultural Diplomacy discussion paper, Berlin, www.culturaldiplomacy.org/...papers/Alima-Dostiyarova.pdf, accessed 28 February 2015.

Chang, Tsan-kuo and Lin Fen (2014) 'From Propaganda to Public Diplomacy: Assessing China's International Practice and its Image, 1950–2009', *Public Relations Review*, 40(3): 450–458.

Dale, Helle C., Ariel Cohen and Janice A. Smith (2012) Challenging America: How Russia, China, and Other Countries Use Public Diplomacy to Compete with the U.

S., Backgrounder No. 2698, the Heritage Foundation, http://www.heritage.org/resea rch/reports/2012/06/challenging-america-how-russia-china-and-other-countries-use-p ublic-diplomacy-to-compete-with-the-us, accessed 7 March 2015.

Gill, Bates and Yanzhong Huang (2006) 'Sources and Limits of Chinese "Soft Power"', *Survival*, 48(2): 17–36.

Huntington, Samuel (1993) 'The Clash of Civilizations', *Foreign Affairs*, 72(3): 22–49.

Kurlantzick, Joshua (2007) *Offensive Charm: How China's Soft Power Is Transforming the World*. New Haven and London: Yale University Press.

Marat, Erica (2009) 'Nation Branding in Central Asia: A New Campaign to Present Ideas about the State and Nation', *Europe-Asia Studies*, 61(7): 1123–1136.

McClory, Jonathan (2013) The New Persuaders III: A 2012 Global Ranking of Soft Power, London: Institute for Government, http://www.instituteforgovernment.org. uk/publications/new-persuaders-iii, accessed 3 May 2015.

Murdon, Simon (2008) 'Culture in World Affairs'. In John Baylis, Steve Smith and Patricia Owens (Eds.), *The Globalization of World Politics: An Introduction to International Relations*, 4th ed. Oxford: Oxford University Press, pp. 418–433.

Nye, Joseph, Jr. (1990) 'Soft Power', *Foreign Policy*, 60(80): 153–171.

Nye, Joseph, Jr. (2004) *Soft Power: The Means to Success in World Politics*, New York: Public Affairs.

Nye, Joseph, Jr. (2008) 'Soft Power: Public Diplomacy and Soft Power', *Annuals of American Academy of Political and Social Science*, 616(1): 94–109.

Nye, Joseph, Jr. (2013) 'What China and Russia Don't Get about Soft Power', http:// foreignpolicy.com/2013/04/29/what-china-and-russia-dont-get-about-soft-power, accessed 16 March 2015.

Pan, Guang (2003) 'Shanghai Hezuo Zuzhi he "Shanghai Jingshen"' ['Shanghai Cooperation Organization and "Shanghai Spirit"'], *Shehui Kexue* [Journal of Social Sciences], 12: 31–40.

Pan, Guang (2009) 'A New Diplomatic Model: A Chinese Perspective on the Shanghai Cooperation Organization', *The Washington Journal of Modern China*, 9(1): 55–72.

Paradise, James F. (2009) 'China and International Harmony: The Role of Confucius Institutes in Bolstering Beijing's Soft Power', *Asian Survey*, 49(4): 647–669.

Ramo, Joshua Cooper (2004) The Beijing Consensus, published by the Foreign Policy Centre, http://fpc.org.uk/publications/TheBeijingConsensus, accessed 6 March 2015.

Simons, Greg (2014) 'Russian Public Diplomacy in the 21st Century: Structure, Means, and Message', *Public Relations Review*, 40(3): 440–449.

Tsygankov, Andrei P. (2006) 'If not by Tanks, then by Banks? The Role of Soft Power in Putin's Foreign Policy', *Europe-Asia Studies*, 58(7): 1079–1099.

Wang, Yiwei (2008) 'Public Diplomacy and the Rise of Chinese Soft Power', *Annuals of American Academy of Political and Social Science*, 616(1): 257–273.

Xing, Guangchen and Zhuangshi Sun (2007) *Shanghai Hezuo Zuzhi Yanjiu* [Studies of Shanghai Cooperation Organization]. Changchu, China: Changchun Press.

Xu, Haiyan (2012) 'Shanghai Hezuo Zuzhi de Jiaoyu Hezuo' [Educational Cooperation of the SCO]. in Li Jingfeng and Wu Hongwei (Eds.), *Shanghai Hezuo Zuzhi Fazhang Baogao 2012* [Annual Report on the Shanghai Cooperation Organization 2012]. Beijing: Social Sciences Academic Press, pp. 148–160.

Yang, Shu (2009) 'Shanghai Hezuo Zuzhi de Jiaoyu Hezuo' [Educational Cooperation of the SCO]. In Xing Guangcheng and Wu Hongwei (Eds.), *Shanghai Hezuo Zuzhi Fazhang Baogao 2009* [Annual Report on the Shanghai Cooperation Organization 2009]. Beijing: Social Sciences Academic Press, pp. 142–150.

Yong, Nam Cho and Jong Ho Jeong (2008) 'China's Soft Power: Discussions, Resources, and Prospects', *Asian Survey*, 48(3): 453–472.

Yu, Shuyi (2010) '2009nian Shanghai hezuo zuzhi de wenhua hezuo' ['Cultural Cooperation of the SCO in 2009]. In Enyuan Wu and Hongwei Wu (Eds.), *Shanghai Hezuo Zuzhi Fazhang Baogao 2010* [Annual Report on the Shanghai Cooperation Organization, 2009]. Beijing: Social Sciences Academic Press, pp. 94–107.

Zhang, Ning (2009) 'Shanghai Hezuo Zuzhi zhong de Wenhua Hezuo' [Cultural Cooperation in Shanghai Cooperation Organization], in Xing Guangcheng and Wu Hongwei (Eds.), *Shanghai Hezuo Zuzhi Fazhang Baogao 2009* [Annual Report on the Shanghai Cooperation Organization, 2009]. Beijing: Social Sciences Academic Press, pp. 134–141.

Conclusion
The road ahead

Forms and substance of the SCO

In June 2011, the leaders of the SCO member states met in Astana, Kazakhstan, to celebrate the organisation's 10th anniversary. The Summit Declaration asserts that the organisation was created as a result of a 'strategically calculated historic step' and had become a 'generally recognised and influential multilateral association'. It boasts of a number of achievements made over the previous decade, the first being that it had 'successfully established and institutionalised effective mechanisms of interaction in various fields'. It also states that the SCO was pursuing a low profile due to 'pragmatic and important results in the field of common development'. The contradictory tone of the declaration suggests that although the SCO members had made modest achievements in various aspects of regional cooperation, they were well aware of the on-going problems and difficulties. To some extent, the SCO has achieved more form than substance; the form of a multilateral organisation has been well established, but the substance of international multilateralism requires much improvement.

The SCO partners had good reason to celebrate on the important occasion of the SCO's 10th anniversary as they had all benefited from this multilateral association to a greater or lesser extent. Most importantly, China and Russia had regularised their interactions in Central Asia in this more institutionalised setting. In addition, the Central Asian states are generally satisfied with their presence in an international grouping with the two major global powers. Political and security cooperation is the relatively developed field in the SCO process. In fact, it has served as the cornerstone of multilateral cooperation within the organisation. Convergence of member states' interests has contributed to a consensus for carrying out various activities and operations for collective problem-solving, symbolic displays of unity, and joint performance of domestic and mutual consumption for their visibility, recognition, and reputation respectively. The SCO member states have also managed to reach a number of multilateral agreements for economic and functional cooperation, such as preferential loans for construction of infrastructure and telecommunications in less developed Central Asian countries. In humanitarian or people-to-people cooperation, a number of regular activities have promoted the mutual under-standing of peoples of the different member states. In terms of concrete arrangements and final results progress has been uneven across the different areas.

Despite some progress, the problems and limitations of the SCO are not inconsiderable. Even in the more successful area of political and security cooperation, the SCO's solidarity is challenged when members cannot reach an agreement to support one member's assertive action, as was the case when Russia took military action against Georgia in 2008. The SCO's reputation can also be undermined when one of its members faces a serious domestic situation. For example, the organisation could do little when Kyrgyzstan plunged into domestic turmoil in 2010. In terms of economic and functional cooperation, the problem is more serious. Although members like China have made continued efforts to promote economic cooperation within the SCO, little progress has been achieved so far. The goal of trade and investment facilitation has only been partially achieved and a free trade area is far from the agenda. China has had to opt for a bilateral approach to economic cooperation with its Central Asian partners, mostly in the energy sector. Cultural, historical and political barriers inhibit humanitarian exchanges between the peoples of the various member states. Current cooperation is dominated by governments and produces very few real results on the ground. Moreover, Uzbekistan somehow does not fully participate in humanitarian cooperation.

The progress and problems of the SCO are largely determined by the motivations of the member states and sometimes influenced by major external powers, particularly the United States. The relationship between China and Russia is essential to the development of the organisation. The complicated configuration of interests and power relations among the SCO partners suggests that negotiations within the organisation will always be fraught with difficulty. However, China will surely continue to play a suasion game, given the huge stakes involved, including its international reputation and credibility as well as material interests. China's enthusiasm for the SCO is based on its many interests in the region. In general, China involves itself in Central Asia out of strong self-interest, and concern over the regional stability of its bor-derlands in the northwest, including the Xinjiang Uyghur Autonomous Region. The SCO platform allows China to better tackle the issue of separatist activities on its western front. Furthermore, China is interested in the energy resources and market potential in Central Asia and is making geopolitical calculations. A multilateral organisation in the region can confer the strength to cope with influences from great powers such as the United States, to a lesser extent Russia and, increasingly, India. Finally, China considers the SCO to offer a good opportunity to lead Central Asian regionalism from within the Eurasian heartland and free from the Western powers. This motivation corresponds with China's ambition to be a responsible great power rising peacefully from its neighbourhood.

Russia and the Central Asian states also understand very well the utility of the SCO. Over the years, Russia has been increasingly keen to use the SCO as a tool to demonstrate its international clout. It needs organisations like the SCO more than ever, given the increasing strategic pressures of the West after the Ukrainian crisis in 2013. Unlike the groups in which it dominates, such as the CIS, Collective Security Treaty Organization (CSTO) and Eurasian Economic Union (EAEU), Russia can have China as a strong partner within the SCO. Facing similar strategic pressures from the United States, Russia and China have a common position in terms of SCO political and security cooperation. However, Russia is wary of China's influence in Central Asia and has therefore taken a pick-and-choose attitude to the SCO, with an emphasis on political and security functions and a delaying approach to economic and functional cooperation. Central Asian states are generally pragmatic about cooperation with China and Russia. The SCO not only affords them some immediate material benefits, but also international prestige. Mostly, Central Asian states are interested in the organisation's useful role of collective unity, through which they can demonstrate their capabilities in countering terrorism and other organised crimes. It is also a useful platform from which they can answer Western criticism of some of their domestic policies. Additionally, they are interested in economic returns from cooperation with China. This is particularly the case for the energy producing states. For all these reasons, the difficult yet useful game of the SCO is destined to continue. Observers will have ample opportunity to witness the continued interplay of the actors' interests and power variables in various aspects of the organisation, including its internal formalisation process and external cooperation processes in the major areas of politics, security, economy, energy, culture and education.

The new momentum

The SCO held its 15th summit in Ufa, Russia, on 9 and 10 July, 2015, at a time when Russia's relations with the West were particularly acrimonious given the Ukrainian crisis. The SCO summit immediately followed the BRICS summit held in the same city, which brought together the emerging economies of Brazil, Russia, India, China and South Africa. Russia took the opportunity to make a show of hosting the two big events to counter Western attempts to isolate and marginalise it.[1] By addressing the leaders of the most important emerging powers in the world, President Vladimir Putin showed the Russian domestic audience and the outside world, particularly the United States and other Western countries, that his government still has a global reputation and influence.

Apart from being a symbolic stage show, this high-profile event was also productive. In contrast to the institutional stalemate of previous years, after two days the SCO leaders decided to take several big steps to further develop the organisation. Observers have paid special attention to three major measures achieved at this summit: strategic planning for the SCO for the next decade, the first enlargement of the organisation, and organisational bridging between China's Silk Road Economic Belt and the Russian-dominated EAEU.[2] The first measure is about deepening cooperation within the organisation and the second is about widening it by accepting new member states. The third is the more complicated issue of a compromise between China and Russia, which have reached agreement on using the SCO as a bridge for their respective institutional priorities of economic cooperation.

The SCO Development Strategy through 2025 is a strategic document, approved by the SCO leaders, which sets targets and tasks for the organisation's development in the next decade. The document presents the first large-scale and long-term strategy of its kind in the SCO's history, according to Dmitry Mezentsev, the SCO secretary general, who explained that the Development Strategy project is not an abstract list of things to do over the next 10 years, but a very detailed document that was initiated by the Russian team.[3] It provides guidelines and roadmaps for the SCO member states to follow in the three areas of SCO cooperation, including politics and security, trade and economy, and people-to-people exchanges. The 2015 SCO declaration highlights joint efforts by the member states to counter threats to regional and global security, and deepen economic and humanitarian cooperation, based on this strategic document. As Wang Jisi, a renowned Chinese analyst, points out, a strategic plan like this helps to consolidate the unity of the member states and observer states, and a mid-term roadmap can provide a clear agenda to follow, resulting in smoother cooperation and less negative interference (Wang, 2015). As the host of the 15th SCO summit, the Russian government devoted much energy to preparing for the event, with the Development Strategy as the core task. Russia's attitude reflects its awareness of the importance of the SCO in its effort to break out of isolation and regain its international reputation and influence. However, history suggests that although the SCO has a good record of producing nice-looking documents, it has much to do to prove its capabilities on the ground.

Perhaps the most eye-catching news of the 15th SCO summit was the decision on the first planned enlargement of the organisation since its founding in 2001. India and Pakistan are set to join the club, most probably at the 2016 summit in Tashkent, Uzbekistan. The declaration of the 2015 summit states that all members believe that enlargement of the SCO and deepening of relations with observer states and dialogue partners are important for the development of the organisation because this will help promote the SCO's potential. Along with the planned admission of the two South Asian states, the SCO has decided to upgrade Belarus to an observer state and accept Azerbaijan, Armenia, Cambodia and Nepal as new dialogue partners. The SCO has become the first major non-Western international organisation with a global security influence. Although it still has a long way to go before it is a well-functioning organisation, its appeal to several states in the developing world is already clear.

India and, especially, Pakistan have shown an interest in joining the SCO for some time. The issue of their membership has led to many internal debates and negotiations between SCO members, particularly China and Russia. On joining the SCO, India will expand its geopolitical influence and gain institutional access to Central Asia, where it is most interested in the region's rich energy resources. For Pakistan, the SCO may bring not only opportunities for multilateral cooperation in political, security and economic matters, but also increased international visibility and reputation. It is also predicted that Pakistan and India will gain a permanent multilateral forum to better manage their bilateral relations. Iran is another state enthusiastic to join the SCO, but its bid for membership has so far been problematic. Although China and Russia are interested in including Iran in the club, they do not want to take a confrontational position with the West, which is hostile to Iran's controversial nuclear weapons programme. Perhaps to express its disappointment, Iran only sent its vice foreign minister to attend the SCO summit in its capacity as an observer. However, it would not be surprising if Iran joins the SCO in the near future, as a comprehensive deal on Iran's nuclear programme has been reached, which has eliminated the main barrier for Iran's SCO membership.[4] It is clear that the SCO is becoming a pan-Asian international organisation. China has expressed its support for the upcoming enlargement. President Xi Jinping has said that the addition of new member states will bring new and fresh forces for SCO cooperation in various sectors. However, China may find it more difficult to take a leading role when big powers like India join the club. A trilateral game among China, India and Russia is likely in the SCO's near future.

Bridging the Silk Road Economic Belt with the EAEU was another major measure taken at the 2015 summit. This decision is a compromise between China and Russia on economic cooperation. For some time, China's attempt to promote economic cooperation in the SCO was resisted by Russia, which was wary of China's rising influence. More recently, China has adopted a more assertive approach to its overall foreign policy, largely based on its growing economic clout. The Silk Road Economic Belt is a part of China's ambitious grand strategy known as 'One Belt, One Road'. The Silk Road part of the strategy focuses on establishing and strengthening economic links with countries roughly along the ancient Silk Road, from Central Asia through the Caucasus and the Middle East and finally to Europe. Central Asia is thus a key link in China's overall Silk Road strategy. However, China is worried about its exclusion from the EAEU, a Russian-dominated economic grouping of some of the former Soviet republics, which tries to follow EU-type economic cooperation based on exclusive customs union.

Nevertheless, competition between China and Russia for Central Asian economic cooperation seems to have turned in China's favour, largely as a result of power shifts in the region. Although Russia has tried hard to retain its traditional geopolitical advantage with the former Soviet countries, it does not have enough clout to 'deliver the economic stimulus promised to its members'.[5] China has managed to secure an advantage by proposing its Silk Road project to its SCO partners. Its investment clout appeals to its SCO partners and also to non-SCO members of the EAEU. Kyrgyz President Almazbek Atambaev called on member states to expedite creation of a Development Bank within the organisation. China's longstanding plan for an SCO Development Bank has hitherto been delayed by Russian resistance. In 2015 China achieved a breakthrough; it was decided at the Ufa summit that member states will work on the details of setting up the SCO Development Bank and a Development Fund to promote trade and investment within the region.

The SCO leaders explicitly stated in the declaration at the Ufa summit that all the member states support China's call for the construction of the Silk Road Economic Belt and delegate their respective governments to work on the details. President Xi expressed the opinion that China's initiative on joint construction of the Silk Road Economic Belt has been successfully instigated, thanks to the positive response and support of its partners. China hopes that its Silk Road project will be matched by the development plans of other SCO member states, and integrated with planned projects and activities of the EAEU. In this context, the SCO would serve as the auspices under which China's Silk Road Economic Belt would merge with the Russian-dominated EAEU. Economic cooperation could thus be considerably stimulated, with China as the major investor and members of the SCO and the EAEU as the providers of infrastructure.

China's next steps

The SCO's reinvigoration reflects the Sino-Russian strategy of drawing closer over recent years. Both states are facing strategic pressures, particularly from the United States. The SCO has been re-emphasised as a useful instrument for strengthening their ties and under these circumstances, it is natural that decisions about significant developments in the SCO will be made. As Russia becomes more serious about SCO cooperation, the organisation gains momentum to formulate concrete plans and measures for the next decade. Despite some hesitation, China has reached agreement with Russia on enlarging the SCO. This may help China to stabilise its relations with India and strengthen the ties among the major emerging powers. New members could also help to trigger new developments in the organisation. To combine the Silk Road Project and EAEU within the same framework is in China's interest of expanding its economic influence. Moreover, it is an important strategic step to engage its SCO partners and other states in the former Soviet space, including Russia. It is not in China's interest to see Russia decline too fast at a time when it really needs allies.

The declaration of the 15th SCO summit emphasised that the member states attach great importance to the consolidation of the global governance systems formulated after the end of World War Two, in particular the United Nations. This rhetoric is the SCO members' expression of the principle of non-interference and their position on a multipolar world system. It is a gesture of mutual support under Western pressure. However, it does not mean that the SCO is becoming a formalised security alliance, as most SCO members do not have the intention of creating a NATO-type organisation. Uzbekistan's president Islam Karimov is representative in this regard, saying that it is necessary 'to rule out any kind of bloc mentality and not turn the SCO into a military and political alliance'.[6] Although some individual states may have an interest in moving the SCO towards a more traditional alliance, most members, including China, have ruled out the possibility of using the SCO for military action against any other state. It is more likely that the SCO will continue to serve as a venue of rhetorical support and mutual cooperation in the foreseeable future.

From the Chinese perspective, the SCO is significant for the strategic planning of its foreign policy. First, it plays a problem-solving role. The SCO has promoted confidence building and mutual trust between China and its SCO partners, starting from the border demarcation. It also serves as a good platform for China to cooperate closely with its partners on issues arising from the 'three evil forces' of terrorism, extremism and separatism and various other cross-border criminal activities. Additionally, the SCO provides an opportunity for economic cooperation that is directly conducive to China's 'Grand Western Development' programme, particularly given Central Asia's market potential and its potential for providing easily accessible energy resources. In terms of national unity, China perceives the SCO as a potentially effective means of consolidating its control of one of the peripheral regions of Xinjiang. In geopolitical terms, the SCO is an effective vehicle that can be used to secure a favourable neighbourhood and international environment for China's peaceful development. Last, but not least, the SCO has served as a helpful laboratory in which China has been able to practice international leadership.

The international system is moving towards a multipolar structure, given the relative decline of dominant American power and the rise of a number of emerging powers. International politics is becoming more volatile. As a major rising power, China is likely to play a more influential role. Power transition theory argues that a rising power will necessarily challenge the existing power. However, this theory misses an important part of contemporary international relations, namely, complex interdependence in the era of globalisation. Sino-American relations are especially complicated as the two powers compete in some areas but cooperate in many others. China understands this sophistication. Deviating from the predictions of power transition theory, China is trying not to confront the United States directly while seeking opportunities for cooperation with other states. Contested multilateralism (Morse and Keohane, 2014) is one option for its power expansion in this era of globalisation and interdependence. In existing multilateral institutions, China tries to increase its influence through adaptation and diversion. Usually, this is difficult due to power resistance and path dependence, as exemplified by its difficult experience in the reform of power structure within the World Bank and IMF.

China is more interested in creation and combination, particularly when it fails to change existing institutions or there is a strategic gap between reality and opportunity. The SCO is China's first major attempt at creating a multi-lateral institution. Throughout the process, China has practised its international leadership skills, gaining not only experience, but also confidence. Building on that confidence, China has become more ambitious in recent years. It has implemented an active 'Go Global' policy. In Central Asia, it now takes a consolidation approach to combine or bridge its own Silk Road Economic Belt and the SCO with other institutions including the EUEA, BRICS and the Conference on Interaction and Confidence Building Measures in Asia (CICA). Despite these advances, China's adventurous path will not be smooth, and the future is full of uncertainty as well as promises.

Notes

1 After BRICS, Putin hosts Shanghai Cooperation Organization summit in Ufa, http://www.rferl.org/content/russia-putin-shanghai-cooperation-organization-summ it-brics-ufa/27120442.html, accessed 13 July 2015.
2 Xi Jinping making efforts to the fulfilment of three major items at the SCO summit, http://www.chinanews.com/gn/2015/07-11/7398970.shtml, accessed 12 July 2015.
3 SCO to adopt development strategy through 2025, http://in.sputniknews.com/world/20150710/1015074033.html, accessed 13 July 2015.
4 Iran nuclear deal reached in Vienna, http://www.theguardian.com/world/2015/jul/14/iran-nuclear-deal-expected-to-be-announced-in-vienna, accessed 14 July 2015.
5 China and Russia lay Foundation for massive economic cooperation, http://foreignp olicy.com/2015/07/10/china-russia-sco-ufa-summit-putin-xi-jinping-eurasian-union-silk-road, accessed 14 July 2015.
6 After BRICS, Putin hosts Shanghai Cooperation Organization summit in Ufa, http://www.rferl.org/content/russia-putin-shanghai-cooperation-organization-summ it-brics-ufa/27120442.html, accessed 13 July 2015.

References

Morse, Julia C. and Robert O. Keohane (2014) 'Contested Multilateralism', *Review of International Organizations*, 9(4): 385–412.
Wang, Jisi, 'Go West: China's Rebalancing in Geopolitical Strategy', *Global Times*, 17 October 2012, http://opinion.huanqiu.com/opinion_world/2012-10/3193760.html, accessed 8 July 2015.

Appendix

Table A.1

Shanghai Five summits (1996–2000)	Date	Location	Participating countries	Agenda and outcomes	Notes
1	Apr. 26, 1996	Shanghai, China	Shanghai Five (China, Russia, Kazakhstan, Kyrgyzstan and Tajikistan)	Discuss security confidence-building measures in the border areas between them.[1]	
2	Apr. 24, 1997	Moscow, Russia	Shanghai Five	Concluded an agreement on mutual reduction of military forces in the border areas and agreed on non-use of force, not to threaten to use force against each other, and not to seek unilateral military superiority.	
3	Jul. 3, 1998	Almaty, Kazakhstan	Shanghai Five	Focused on promotion of peace and stability of the region and economic cooperation between the five member countries and agreed to fight against various forms of national separatist and religious extremist activities, terrorist operations, weapon smuggling, and drug trafficking.	China and Kazakhstan accelerated their border talks and concluded another border agreement on the basis of the previous one concluded in April 1994.
4	Aug. 24, 1999	Bishkek, Kyrgyzstan	Shanghai Five	Restated firm opposition to national separatism and religious extremism and announced that they would enhance cooperation in their efforts to combat international terrorism, drug trafficking and other transnational criminal activities.	In the wake of the summit, China and Kyrgyzstan concluded a supplementary border agreement in August on the basis of their 1996 border agreement.
5	Jul. 5, 2000	Dushanbe, Tajikistan	Shanghai Five	They agreed to hold annual foreign ministers' meetings and establish council of national coordinators to facilitate cooperation.	China and Tajikistan successfully concluded an agreement that permanently settles the remaining problems along their common borders.

	Date	Location	Participating countries	Agenda and outcomes	Notes
Shanghai Five summits (1996–2000)					
1	Jun. 14-15, 2001	Shanghai, China	Members of the former Shanghai Five and Uzbekistan	The summit signed the Declaration of Shanghai Cooperation Organisation. China and Russia signed the Treaty of Good-Neighbourliness and Friendly Cooperation.	
2	Jun. 7, 2002	St. Petersburg, Russia	All six members of SCO	The summit signed three documents, including the Charter of the SCO, an agreement on Regional Anti-terrorism Structure, and the presidents' declaration.	
3	May 29, 2003	Moscow, Russia	All six members of SCO	The summit reached consensus on the institutionalisation of the SCO and on some major international issues.	The summit also approved the appointment of then Chinese Ambassador to Russia Zhang Deguang as the SCO's first secretary general.
4	Jun. 17, 2004	Tashkent, Uzbekistan	All six members of SCO	The summit launched the Regional Anti-terrorist Structure of the SCO, and pledged in a joint declaration to cooperate in fighting terrorism and coping with new security threats and in strengthening their economic and trade ties.	Mongolia became the first country to receive observer status.
5	Jul. 5, 2005	Astana, Kazakhstan	All six members of SCO	The summit issued a declaration on strengthening cooperation within the organisation.	The leaders agreed to grant SCO observer status to India, Iran and Pakistan.
6	Jun. 15, 2006	Shanghai, China	All six members of SCO	The summit signed the Declaration on the Fifth Anniversary of SCO the Statement of Heads of Member States of SCO on International Information Security, approved a new version of the regulations of the SCO Secretariat and a cooperation programme of SCO members on combating terrorism, separatism, extremism from 2007 to 2009, adopted a series of resolutions concerning personnel arrangement and the structure.[2]	The summit agreed Mr. Bolat K. Nurgaliev from Kazakhstan will be the secretary general of the organisation from 2007 to 2009.

Table A.1 (Continued)

Shanghai Five summits (1996–2000)	Date	Location	Participating countries	Agenda and outcomes	Notes
7	Aug. 16, 2007	Bishkek, Kyrgyzstan	All six members of SCO	The summit signed the Treaty among the member states of SCO on good-neighbourly relations, friendship and cooperation and approved the Bishkek Declaration and approved the Action Plan.[3]	
8	Aug. 28, 2008	Dushanbe, Tajikistan	All six members of SCO	The meeting was chaired by President Rakhmon in Tajikistan. The summit signed the Agreement on the order of organisation and staging of joint counterterrorism exercises, the Agreement on cooperation among the governments of the member states of SCO and the Memorandum on partnership relations between the Interbank Association of the Shanghai Cooperation Organisation and the Eurasian Development Bank.[4]	
9	Jun. 16, 2009	Yekaterinburg, Russia	All six members of SCO	The meeting was chaired by President Medvedev in Russia. The summit signed the SCO Counter-Terrorism Convention which cements the legal base for counter-terrorism interaction in the SCO framework and its potential, cooperation in this field was taken to a new level and approved the SCO Regulations on Political Diplomatic Measures and Mechanisms of Response to Events Jeopardising Regional Peace, Security and Stability.[5]	It was the first time that leaders from observer states – Mongolia, India, Pakistan and Iran – were included in a restricted meeting of the SCO Heads of State Council. Belarus and Sri Lanka were granted dialogue partner status.
10	Jun. 11, 2010	Tashkent, Uzbekistan	All six members of SCO	The meeting was chaired by President I. A. Karimov in Uzbekistan. The Regulations on procedure for admitting new members to SCO and Rules of Procedure of SCO were approved.[6]	

	Date	Location	Participating countries	Agenda and outcomes	Notes
11	Jun. 15, 2011	Astana, Kazakhstan	All six members of SCO	The meeting was chaired by President N. Nazarbayev in Kazakhstan. The summit approved Counternarcotics Strategy of the SCO for 2011–2016 and its Action Plan.[7]	
12	Jun. 7, 2012	Beijing, China	All six members of SCO	The meeting was chaired by President Hu Jintao of China. The summit approved the Strategic Plan for the Medium-Term Development of the SCO and the revised version of the SCO Regulations on Political and Diplomatic Measures and Mechanism of Response to Events Jeopardizing Regional Peace, Security and Stability and the Programme of Cooperation in the Field of Combating Terrorism, Separatism and Extremism for 2013–2015.[8]	Afghanistan received observer status. Turkey was granted dialogue partner status. The summit also appointed Dmitry Fyodorovich Mezentsev of Russia as the secretary general for the duration of January 1, 2013 to December 31, 2015.[9]
13	Sept. 3, 2013	Bishkek, Kyrgyzstan	All six members of SCO	SCO leaders signed the Bishkek Declaration.	
14	Sept. 11–12, 2014	Dushanbe, Tajikistan	All six members of SCO	The SCO leaders signed the Dushanbe Declaration and two documents: the Order for Granting the Status of SCO Member State and Revised Model Memorandum of Commitments by the Applicant State for Obtaining SCO Member State Status.	Legal preparations made for enlargement of the SCO.

Table A.1 (Continued)

Shanghai Five summits (1996–2000)		Date	Location	Participating countries	Agenda and outcomes	Notes
	15	Jul. 9–10, 2015	Ufa, Russia	All six members of SCO	The summit signed the Ufa Declaration of the Shanghai Cooperation Organisation Heads of State. The SCO Development Strategy through to 2025 was also signed. They adopted a number of statements, including on cooperation on celebrating the 70th anniversary of victory in World War II, and a statement on the drug threat.[10]	Belarus gained observer status. With official approval of the SCO, India and Pakistan are expected to join as SCO full members by 2016.

Notes

1 http://www.comw.org/cmp/fulltext/0110jia.htm, accessed 17 and 18 October 2015.
2 http://www.sectsco.org/EN123/show.asp?id=95, accessed 17 and 18 October 2015.
3 http://www.sectsco.org/EN123/show.asp?id=93, accessed 17 and 18 October 2015.
4 http://www.sectsco.org/EN123/show.asp?id=91, accessed 17 and 18 October 2015.
5 http://www.sectsco.org/EN123/show.asp?id=88, accessed 17 and 18 October 2015.
6 http://www.sectsco.org/EN123/show.asp?id=223, accessed 17 and 18 October 2015.
7 http://www.sectsco.org/EN123/show.asp?id=293, accessed 17 and 18 October 2015.
8 http://www.sectsco.org/EN123/show.asp?id=443, accessed 17 and 18 October 2015.
9 http://www.sectsco.org/EN123/secretary.asp, accessed 17 and 18 October 2015.
10 http://en.kremlin.ru/events/president/news/49907, accessed 17 and 18 October 2015.

Index